TALES OF
TAHITIAN WATERS

SPECIAL INTRODUCTION

I am very pleased to announce this initial volume of an exciting new deluxe, leather-bound series of my father's great fishing stories now to be published by the Derrydale Press. This will be the first time these books have been reprinted in the U.S. other than as articles in magazines, for more than 30 years.

Of all the exotic places my father visited during his many travels in the South Seas, the one I think which drew him more irresistibly than did any other—as it had done to so many renowned authors before him: Stevenson, Melville, Maugham, to mention only a few—was Tahiti. During the 13 years after his first brief stop at Papeete on his way to New Zealand in 1926, he came back for extended journeys to fish, explore, and to marvel at the visual beauties and wonders of Tahiti and her surrounding islands at least eight more times. His last visit was in 1938 when he spent four months recovering from the crippling sun stroke which had struck him so severely a year earlier. He wanted desperately to fish then, but was too ill, so he left the "chores" to me and my young friends Gus and Lyle Bagnard and John Vitalich. Our adventures with giant tackle-busting marlin and tuna during those months would fill a book by themselves, but that is another story. . . .

Before the end of his third trip in 1930, Dad had already written enough for this great book. Later he was to go on to create his only modern, non-Western novel whose locale was also Tahiti. He had always been fascinated by what he saw there of the curious racial and ethnic melange of cultures with their casual sexual and social mores which were so radically different from the strict Victorian standards of his day, under which he had been reared. Although the Polynesians appeared to care little about their subjugation by their white rulers, Dad was outraged by what he saw as the same kind of prejudice inflicted on them that he felt had destroyed the American Indian and his culture at home. From this came *The Reef Girl*, which was so daring and sexually explicit in its conception that it was not published until 1978—nearly 40 years after his death.

TALES OF TAHITIAN WATERS, though similar in scope to his earlier fishing books, depicts the many triumphs and failures he endured in his quest for the mighty Pacific Blue Marlin (which he called the Giant Tahitian Striped Marlin), that roamed Tahiti's waters, and grew larger here than anywhere else in the world. Specimens have been seen, even recently, more than 30 feet in length, and in those early days the native fishermen feared these giants even more than the fierce sharks which abounded Tahiti's waters. Here Dad had earlier captured two other world record game fish, including a 464 lb. striped marlin, landed after 83 days of exhausting trolling without a single strike, under the blazing tropic sun. Then five weeks later came the crowning achievement of his illustrious fishing career—the capture of his 1040 lb. blue marlin, the first thousand pounder ever landed.

The vivid account of this grand battle—first to subdue the fish, and then to fight off the hordes of ravenous sharks which chewed off great chunks of one side and the tail after it had been gaffed—is only one of the many exciting tales in these great volumes. Also, this saga of the 83 days trolling, day after day without a strike, and the giant marlin eaten by sharks, is reputed to have been a partial inspiration for Earnest Hemingway's great Nobel Prize winning novel, *The Old Man and the Sea*. The book also recounts—as only Dad could describe—encounters with even greater deep sea monsters: 50 ft. sharks, under-billed swordfish, and other strange and previously unknown sea creatures found only in these hot, tropical waters, as well as describing in vivid detail the incredible natural beauty of one of the most fabulous and once-idyllic islands on the face of the earth.

Loren Grey
Woodland Hills, CA
October 24, 1990

The Zane Grey Outfit at Flower Point Camp, Vairao, Tahiti

Tales of
TAHITIAN WATERS

— by —

ZANE GREY

INTRODUCTION BY LOREN GREY
ILLUSTRATED WITH PHOTOGRAPHS TAKEN BY THE AUTHOR

THE DERRYDALE PRESS

LANHAM AND NEW YORK

THE DERRYDALE PRESS

Published in the United States of America
by The Derrydale Press
4720 Boston Way, Lanham, Maryland 20706

Distributed by NATIONAL BOOK NETWORK, INC.

Original Derrydale printing 1990
First paperback printing with french folds 1999

☉™ The paper used in this publication meets the minimum requirements of
American National Standard for Information Sciences—Permanence of
Paper for Printed Library Materials, ANSI/NISO Z39.48-1992.
Manufactured in the United States of America.

ILLUSTRATIONS

THE ZANE GREY OUTFIT AT FLOWER POINT CAMP, VAIRAO, TAHITI
Frontispiece

Facing page

THE *Fisherman* AT TAHITI	6
ZANE GREY WITH FIRST SWORDFISH CAUGHT IN TAHITIAN WATERS	7
ZANE GREY AND SON ROMER AT RANGIROA, IN THE PAUMOTUS	24
STRANGE GREEN FISH, UNCLASSIFIED, ABOUT 100 POUNDS IN WEIGHT, CAUGHT BY ZANE GREY	25
TROLLING OFF VAIRAO	40
THE COCOANUT CLIMBER	41
NATIVES DRAWING NET	72
IN THE TAHITIAN JUNGLE	73
A NATIVE MAIDEN	88
R. C. WITH HIS LARGEST TAHITIAN MARLIN, 357 POUNDS	89
CAPTAIN MITCHELL WITH SAILFISH CAUGHT ON FEATHER GIG, 109 POUNDS	136
WORLD-RECORD MARLIN OF THIS SPECIES, 464 POUNDS, CAUGHT BY ZANE GREY AT TAHITI	137
THE *Fisherman* AT RAIATEA	152
CAPTAIN MITCHELL'S 163-POUND WORLD-RECORD SAILFISH, CAUGHT AT RAIATEA	153
THE FISH DRIVE	168
THE FISH DRIVE	169
NOTE THE WAVE OF FISH ENTERING THE TRAP	169
THE BELLE OF THE DRIVE	184
WORLD-RECORD DOLPHIN, 63 POUNDS, ZANE GREY	185
BEAUTIFUL TAHITI	200
WAHOO, 62 AND 67 POUNDS	220
ZANE GREY'S SILVER MARLIN, 618 POUNDS. ANOTHER NEW SPECIES	221
MITCHELL'S LONG-FIN TUNA, 128 POUNDS. FIRST TO BE CAUGHT ON ROD	228
NATO-FISHING	229
WHITE WILD HORSES OF THE SEA	248
THE GREAT TAHITIAN MARLIN HOOKED AT LAST	252
HIS PLUNGE AFTER BEING GAFFED	253

Showing the Sharp, Almost Flattened, Small Head, Something New in Spearfish	260
Weighing the Monster. This Picture Shows Where the Sharks Tore Off Flesh	261
Giant Tahitian Striped Marlin, 1040 Pounds	282
Water Color of the Island—Tahiti	283
Water Color of the Ship	294

PART ONE
1928

CHAPTER ONE

WHEN the S. S. *Tahiti* entered the roadstead off Papeete on May 30, 1928, I espied my yacht *Fisherman* shining like a great white gull against the wonderful rich bright green of this tropic island. Sight of the *Fisherman* after some little lapse of time always thrilled me, but on this occasion I was not so excited as usual.

Perhaps I was a little homesick. Five months in New Zealand waters, during four of which we suffered very bad weather, had somewhat cooled my fishing ardor, and I would just as lief have remained on the *Tahiti* with my brother R. C., who was going home on her in time to catch the swordfish at Catalina.

Romer and his pal, Johnny, were just about broken-hearted at leaving the steamship. They had interested themselves in Australian young ladies who were en route to the United States, and therefore had more than homesickness to contend with. On shore, however, buying ice cream and Polynesian knickknacks, and riding round the exquisite hothouse garden avenues, they rather surprisingly picked up cheer.

Transferring our baggage from the *Tahiti* to the *Fisherman* was a job I would not care to undertake again, in this latitude. It took about all day, a Papeete day at that, if you know what I mean.

That night I was too tired to do anything but sit in a deck chair, and rest, and watch the twinkling lights of Papeete, and feel the cool breeze. Next morning we rose early to bid R. C. good-by. The early morning was glorious, bright, golden green, and cool. The S. S. *Tahiti* sailed at seven, with R. C. waving good-by from the bridge, and the Australian girls leaning over the deck rail with sad eyes on the boys. R. C. waved and called down to me: "Say, I've left you in many hard places, but this is the limit. Good night! Good luck and good-by!"

He may have had a lot of fun out of this, but it was not funny to me. We all felt stranded, and stood there until R. C. was a mere speck upon the bridge of the steamship. Then I went back to the *Fisherman* and watched the *Tahiti* until she disappeared round the green palm-fringed cape of the island.

There were a hundred things to do, and it was hot. I did not forget that in New Zealand I longed for the sun and vowed I would not care how long or how hot it shone. So now I did not complain. I welcomed it. All the same I nearly melted and worked until I grew dizzy. The harbor crew moved us from dock to bay, and from bay to the oil-ship *Beulah*, which last was not so bad, even if it was a blast furnace for heat. For we took fuel off the tanker, and it was the first good fuel the engineers had seen since leaving San Pedro. The tanker was a Panama ship that had happened in there.

Later in the afternoon we cleared, and ran up several miles inside the reef, and anchored in a tranquil bay, with the rollers just outside, and the dark shiny sandy beach behind. It was bordered with cocoanut palms, and in the openings where lawns of beautiful residences ran down to the sea there were magnolias and bougainvillæa in bloom, and other flowering foliage I could not name. I missed the flaming flamboyant trees in that scene of tropic color. We had seen them in January, in full bloom, most exquisite and lovely. I shall never forget the fire-shadowed aisles through the jungle.

This was my fourth time in Tahiti and I realized I was going to endure the sordid and hot Papeete with its sloe-eyed Chinese and the hordes of sad-eyed, smiling natives, from the sense of a growing enchantment in the amethyst sea and the emerald isle that towered up and up into the azure blue.

On the voyage from New Zealand we had met an old trader who had spent fifty years in the South Seas. He was intelligent and communicative. Captain Mitchell cultivated his acquaintance and later introduced him to me. Mr. Y —— had a vast store of South Sea experience, legend, romance, and history. I wondered why some of the South Sea writers had not exploited him. He talked to us hours on end. But his knowledge of fish was limited. He had seen sailfish among the islands, swordfish from Raratonga to Samoa, and from the Marquesas to the Paumotus. However, he did not know one kind of swordfish from another. He had heard, though, of swordfish ramming ships and schooners, and that, of course, meant old *Xiphias gladius* was in evidence. According to Mr. Y —— the Paumotus were most noted for fish—something which bore out the impression I had gathered from various sources.

Many significant things we learned from this trader, and some of them cleared up mystifying rumor that had drifted up across the Pacific to the States. I learned a great deal of interest about adventuring schooners that had at various times fared forth from California, with tremendous publicity at departure, and less than nothing or worse than nothing upon an unheralded return. I found out all about the fortune-making motion pictures, where and how they had been taken—for instance, certain cannibal pictures lately so startling to American audiences were taken within sight of a mission-house!

Mr. Y —— said that no white man had even understood the Polynesian, and never would. His fifty years of study had left him more in the dark than ever about these strange people. He talked fluently about Stevenson, Melville—all the South Sea writers. I was more than surprised to hear his opinion that the novel, *Numerous Treasure*, by Keable, came closer than anything to a true conception of the native mind. On the other hand, Mr. Y —— named recent books on the South Seas that I had carefully studied, as not safe to stand by. My own motive in coming was primarily to fish unknown waters, and in the main I meant to stick to that.

The most astounding thing Mr. Y —— told me was that the native Polynesian either cannot or will not tell the whole truth about himself, and will invariably tell you what will please you, without regard for veracity. These two things might have saved many a writer future embarrassment, had he but known them. I certainly made up my mind to profit by such revelation. What pitfalls for the narrative author! How hopeless for the novelist to get at the verisimilitude of life in the South Seas! For that reason alone I would deliberate long before daring to undertake fiction with this setting.

Nevertheless, I was very keen to see for myself if the fabulous color and beauty and romance of the South Seas really existed; and if so what they really were. Every one in the world, almost, has formed a conception of the romance, the enchantment, the idyllic life of these lonely isles separated by so many leagues of sea from the world of civilization. Tennyson wrote of them without ever having seen the Pacific. When a mere boy I dreamed of the South Seas. I longed to sail down the endless lanes of this vast ocean and visit some of the islands. But I never had any hope of doing so. And I have read many books about them. And when I found myself there I realized it would take a great deal more than a few cheap pearls, and half-naked, half-savage native women and fine French wines to be had for nothing, to constitute the glory and the dream that have emanated from the South Sea islands.

We interviewed ship captains, traders, and natives, to learn what we could about the fishing round Tahiti and the islands. It was all very interesting, but discouraging. We could get so little upon which we could rely. Then many opinions conflicted with others. Not until I met Mr. Charles Nordhoff, a Californian writer, who has lived on Tahiti for seven years, did I begin to get accurate and authentic information. Mr. Nordhoff was not a salt-water angler, but he was greatly interested in Polynesian fishing and had been studying it for years. He knew very little about our methods, but he was a keen observer, and he spent part of almost every day on the ocean, and was able to answer the questions with which I plied him.

Only a yachtsman here and there had ever fished around Tahiti, and these trolled leisurely to and fro with ordinary spoons and lures. Their luck had been as indifferent as their zeal and method. A few small tuna, bonito, and an occasional barracuda were all they caught. The possibilities of the waters around Tahiti and the Paumotus were unknown. Nordhoff welcomed the advent of anglers experienced in pioneering new waters, and showed tremendous interest in our tackle, especially the teasers we trolled behind the launches to bring fish up to the surface.

Broadbill swordfish, marlin, and sailfish were numerous in these waters, and also big tuna. The natives fished outside of the reef on still days, and had come to know each species of these fish. Large tuna had been hooked in what they called the tuna holes, and sev-

The "Fisherman" at Tahiti

ZANE GREY WITH FIRST SWORD FISH CAUGHT IN TAHITIAN WATERS

eral over one hundred pounds in weight had been brought in. The heavier ones, of course, broke away. The natives were afraid of the swordfish. One native had been killed by a broadbill. This was near Raratonga. He washed ashore with a hole in his head. Next his canoe was found. It had a piece of the sword of a broadbill impaled in it. No one could figure out what had happened. My theory is that this native happened upon two pugnacious swordfish, and hooked one of them. They capsized him, and while one speared him the other attacked the canoe. Of course one swordfish might have done both, though that is not very likely. Or he might have hooked a swordfish which came up to attack him. The natives were equally afraid of the round-billed swordfish, or marlin, better called spearfish, which is the correct name. The one objection to this name is that it does not include the sailfish, which has a bill almost identical with the marlin. Very large sailfish were sometimes seen; also big tuna, which I believed must have been yellow-fins.

The bait proposition did not worry Captain Mitchell and me until we tried to catch some. It was impossible. Small fish appeared mightily scarce. On our first day out we ran across several schools of bonito. We located them by the wheeling gulls and boobies. They were feeding on small fish like sardines. They surfaced for a moment, threshing the water white, then they were gone. We could not keep track of them, and when next the birds located them they were far off. These bonito would not look at any kind of spoon or artificial lure we tried. Late that same day we struck a school of tuna feeding. If anything, they were warier and faster than the bonito. I saw several tuna leap. They were almost silver in color, and entirely different from any tuna I had seen. One that leaped would have weighed sixty pounds, and some that ploughed up the water might have weighed more. Nor would these tuna strike at a lure.

We turned shipward, late in the day, worn out with the heat, the lumpy trade-wind sea, and the discouraging prospect. The sun had seemed to burn a hole in the top of my head. It had been a hard, uncomfortable day. The sea was as blue as indigo, and the mountains, crowned by white clouds, grand to gaze upon. I made the most of them.

That night we interested the natives in our bait problem. We learned they fished mostly at night, and the best time was in the dark of the moon. I saw lights out on the reef, torches made of palm leaves, probably. Next morning I was up at dawn, and the dawn surely was wonderful. Soft, cool, fresh, so still that the boom of the surf on the reef came loud, like thunder, and with all the colors of pearl, changing to opal, and then the golds and pinks and reds of sunrise, bursting over the great green slope of mountain upon blue sea and sky. There was a rich and rare fascination in the moment.

I saw natives fishing out on the reef, standing in the water up to their knees, wielding long bamboo poles, and casting into the white surf. It looked entrancing to me.

After breakfast a native came in his canoe—a queer little narrow bark with its outrigger—and fetched us a string of small fish, green and shiny, with big dark eyes and soft protruding mouths. They were too small as well as not the proper shape for trolling. Nevertheless, we took them and started out again.

The glory of the early morning had given place to high light, glaring sea, obscured peaks, and down-dropping veils of rain on the horizon. When about two miles out we saw signaling from Captain's boat, and got to him in time to observe the last leaps of a long slim bronze sailfish. We heralded the catch of the first sailfish at Tahiti with shouts and yells to the lucky Captain. "Same old story!" I added. "Lucky Mitchell! . . . But it's great. Go on!"

I had a blank day. Again the sun bored into the top of my skull, like a fiery worm, and I was glad to run in early. My New Zealand boatmen, Francis and Peter, were likewise affected by the heat.

Captain Mitchell soon returned, and we eagerly listened to his report.

"I didn't see the first sailfish come up," he said. "There were two. I got a smashing strike. Thought it was a marlin. Let him run. When he jumped we saw it was a sailfish twice the size of the one I caught afterward. He threw the hook. Then when I was reeling in my bait a second fish took it, and I hooked him. By Jove! he was fast. He made five high leaps. We got him in, and went on. Late this afternoon I raised a big striped marlin. He was wonderful to look at in that water. Black or dark blue on the back, silver-sided with purple stripes, and a bright blue tail. Never saw such a fish! But he was leery of the little bait. Wouldn't take it. We had trouble keeping the teasers away from him."

"Well, that's all good news," I replied. "It's getting results. . . . It looks like new and difficult conditions to master. No surfacing fish. No birds. No bait. And that crystal-clear water. We've sure got a job on our hands."

Next day we had mullet for bait. The day began hot and sultry. Squalls came up. We welcomed rain, and soon were soaked through. I liked that at first. But after several hours I got tired of being wet. We ran across another school of elusive tuna. Romer got a hard strike, which took his leader. He was trolling a white feather gig. The tuna went down, and we saw them no more. It rained all kinds of ways, and on the run in, during a lull in the wet downfall, I espied a wavering gold shape far back in the wake of the launch. It was a fish. I yelled, and then all of my companions saw. The shape came on swift as a shadow. I never saw anything like its color or speed. Then it dropped back fifty feet behind the teasers. Finally I decided the wavering motion was due to the sail of a large sailfish. Suddenly it shot forward and crossed our wake. It was a sailfish, very long and slim, with huge sail and a blue tail. I called for the others to haul in the teasers, but the sailfish, charging like a flash, hit the teaser on the starboard side. Then he dropped back, wavered in the blue billows, and vanished. I believe if we had kept the teaser away from him that I would have gotten a strike. We ran in to find Captain Mitchell already there, and his report was a blank, tiresome, wet day.

You tire easily in the tropics. The energy of the northerner keeps him on the go when the languorous native or the experienced visitor does nothing. I have no idea how long that energy would keep up, but I imagine not long. I found what I liked best was to sit under the awning on deck in an easy-chair or under the rustling cocoanut palms and feel the cool sweet breeze and watch the crawling white-and-blue sea. To sleep was as easy as closing your eyes. Tennyson's "Lotus Eaters" seemed to haunt my mind. I found reading impossible, writing difficult, and creative writing harder than anything I had ever attempted.

The pearl-and-opal morning before sunrise, the golden flushing of the mountains, and the drenching of the sea in magical light were the glorious moments of the day. Sunset was warm, rich, sultry, smoky, a great blaze of red fire through massed clouds. Sunset over the island Moorea is famous. All visitors to Tahiti speak of it, and many writers have attempted to describe it. I shall not be so vain. And at that there are really few scenes I shall not try to paint in words.

Trolling out of the pass next morning, I raised and hooked a large white sharp-nosed fish that broke water and escaped. Captain Mitchell did the same thing, which I learned upon my return. This day he had Mr. Nordhoff in his boat, and he headed for Moorea. When we got in the lee of the point of Tahiti that jutted out to the westward we found smooth water. The sun was hot and the sea glassy. "Broadbill swordfish weather!" I exclaimed, and could hardly make myself believe I could not see one of the king of fishes.

We ran across boobies and terns wheeling and sailing over schools of bait that were driven to surface by bonito. The boobies were mostly light brown; some were white and black, like the great boobies of the Galapagos and the gannets of New Zealand. The terns were white, which species I well knew, but the black ones, with white heads, were new to me. These sea-fowl traveled fast, and we could not keep up with them or catch them until they circled.

Mr. Nordhoff showed us the Polynesian method of fishing with a pearl gig. He used a long bamboo pole and skittered the gig over the surface of the water. I saw him get one smashing strike, but he did not hook the bonito. It illustrated the method of the native, however, and appeared a skillful and artistic manner of fishing. The gig was a work of art. Nordhoff said he had made hundreds of these, only a few of which would raise tuna and bonito. The shade of pearl appeared to be the most particular point. The gig was a curved piece of pearl shell, with barbless hook tied on the concave side, and with short whiskers of cocoanut fiber at one end. This

Polynesian lure is a very old one, and was made, I am sure, to imitate a shrimp. The amazing thing about it is how very effective one out of a hundred can be. Nordhoff assured me that one with a slight yellow shade would raise fish when no other would; and at times a pink one would do likewise.

We caught no fish of any kind that day, and ran back to the ship about three o'clock. To don bathing-suit then and row to the beach and cool off was something too good to describe adequately. The natives appeared to have no concern about sharks inside the reef. I never saw a fin while we were anchored there. Nevertheless, I did not feel at ease for myself or anybody, and kept a sharp lookout. I had heard some terrible stories about sharks of the South Seas.

There were a number of picturesque native houses up on the palm-shaded bank, and nearer town many beautiful residences belonging to Papeetians. We walked inland some distance, and up and down the shady lanes. Flowers, foliage, color, perfume, languorous warmth everywhere, and always in the background, golden-skinned dark-haired Tahitian maidens. The magnolia blossoms fallen from trees covered the grass—large white and yellow flowers, with most exquisite fragrance; bougainvillæa flamed its wonderful cerise from the shady green background; great trees, magnificent clumps of bamboo, always the whispering, rustling, moving, graceful, drooping palms. I looked across fields of cane to forests of palms and on up the gold-green slopes of Tahiti to the sharp cone-shaped peaks. An empire of the sun! The hot breeze fanned my face, the odors were almost sickeningly sweet. We sat down every place where there was anything to sit upon. In the shade it was always cool, always pleasant, always still, dreamy, peaceful, strange. I began to absorb Tahiti.

Near where the *Fisherman* lay at anchor lives an English artist —Macdonald—who had come to Tahiti to paint. He showed us his fine water-colors, rich in the gold shades and white shadows that make Tahiti so exotic. He had made a very beautiful painting of my ship. Mr. Macdonald was something of a fisherman himself, with trout tackle, and he interested us much by telling about the *nato*, a beautiful little fish inhabiting the Tahitian streams. He caught them on the lightest of fly tackle and claimed they were very gamey. Captain Mitchell and I were both of one mind—how could we ever find time for all!

We had a clear hot day, and then a wet hot day. If it had not rained so hard and so long I should have preferred the wet. But we could not keep dry, or keep anything on board dry, and it grew disagreeable. Captain Mitchell raised two sailfish and one marlin, and I raised one sailfish. To my amaze, I learned from the Captain that the second sailfish, a huge fellow twelve feet long, had been too quick for the Captain and his men, and it had charged the teaser, caught it, and jerked so hard that it broke off the yard from the launch and took the whole business. Of course they recovered the teaser. This appeared to me a very remarkable incident, and I cannot equal it with any of the same kind. I have seen tuna break off teasers and pitch them high into the air, but tearing off the whole rig was a new one on me.

The bait question was the puzzling and serious one. We fished with all kinds of artificial lures that had been successful in other waters, and had no success whatever. Then we tried hiring the native fishermen. This worked for a day or two. We had mullet, and a small, wide large-eyed blue-backed little fish that trolled fairly well. Bait would not keep long in this latitude. Mullet caught one night and put on the ice, fresh and frozen stiff when we started out fishing, would be spoiled in a few hours. We finally had recourse to the market at Papeete. This necessitated sending some one by launch before daylight, in order to get the pick of the rather scant variety of fish brought in. One morning I was amazed to find two small bonefish, and half a dozen small tarpon, in the bag from the market. I positively identified the bonefish, but was not so sure about the others. They came from the Paumotus, and were exactly like the small tarpon I had caught in the Florida Everglades. Mr. Nordhoff said there were the same fish in a little lagoon on Tahiti, and if they were not tarpon he certainly could not classify them. Imagine me using bonefish and tarpon for bait! Both of these great game fish I had glorified to the best of my ability. It reminded me of years ago on the Delaware River when I encountered bass fishermen using trout for bait.

All the same I trolled both bonefish and tarpon to and fro over the ocean for miles on end without a strike.

There came a cool morning with rippling sea and appreciably less humidity. I started out somewhat behind Captain Mitchell and when we reached blue water Francis yelled, "Looks like the Captain is hooked on."

I stood up the better to see. A white splash caught my eye. The *Sky Blue* veered round sharply. "Sure is, Frank. Let's see what the *Loren G.* can do."

Suddenly we jerked as if from a stationary position, and flew over the water ahead of great white furrows. The bow of the *Loren G.* stood up high; her engines roared and set to a purring drone. I had to get down from the deck to keep from being blown overboard.

"What's she doing?" I shouted in Francis' ear.

"A good few miles, I'll say. Sixteen or seventeen," he replied.

That was plenty swift for me. I do not care for speed boats as fishing-boats. Too many more desirable features have to be sacrificed for speed. At Catalina my brother and I found more swordfish and caught more than all the swift launches put together. You can travel too fast!

Soon we were up on the Captain, and when Francis slowed down I got up to look, camera in hand. He was hauling away on a fish that had out a lot of line. I saw heavy splashes and black fins.

"Looks like a marlin," yelled Francis.

"Reckon he's got a black marlin fin," said Peter.

I waited for a good sight of the fish before I made any conclusions. Then he leaped.

"He's got a black marlin fin," repeated Peter.

"But he's got a striped marlin bill," replied Francis.

Not only did the leaping fish puzzle me with his variations from the familiar shape and colors we knew, but he performed in a new manner. He was pretty big, around four hundred, long and round but not thick, dark green on the back, very silvery on the sides with purple stripes. He had a long slim spear. His dorsal strikingly resembled that of the black marlin. He leaped with a churning motion, like a projectile on end, but he did not come clear out. He would stay up a good while, covering rods, without showing clearly. In fact, he stayed on the surface longer than any marlin I recalled. Then he sounded.

Captain Mitchell warned us to keep a goodly distance away, from which I grasped that the fish was very fast and uncertain. He stayed down long, during which time Captain labored on him with powerful sweep. I waited, camera in hand, watching keenly, and very much elated over the prospect of seeing, and perhaps classifying, the first marlin ever caught on rod and reel off Tahiti. After a while—so long that I relaxed in vigilance—the fish came out pretty close to me, in a fine leap that I missed, much to my chagrin. The next one, however, I snapped, and Middleton on the other boat did likewise with the motion-picture camera. I had a good look at the marlin this time. Those two leaps were the only ones he made clear, but he careened like a crazy ballet dancer, and again reminded me of the wheeling surf-boards behind the speed launches at Avalon. He got several hundred yards of line, and I began to think Captain Mitchell was slow in following the fish. But Mitchell and R. C. are alike in that respect—they will not give in to a fish as quickly as I will. They risk more, they hold harder, on a stronger drag. And they lose more fish than I. In that case the marlin was so big and strong and fast that it was a wonder he did not break off. As it happened, he tore out the hook. My disappointment was intense. Specimens of new fish that have never before been caught by rod and reel are most desirable to obtain, first for scientific interest, and secondly for the pride of achievement and record. Naturalists, of course, are insulted at being classed with sportsmen. But all the same I aspire to a little of both.

It turned out that, so far as disappointment at losing a rare fish was concerned, I had nothing on Captain Mitchell. When we met on the deck of the *Fisherman* he looked the picture of woe.

"By gad, that was hard luck," he said, feelingly. "I never saw a marlin act like this one—so swift and savage. We all saw him flash at the same moment. I yelled. Edward dove for the port teaser, a green one. But the swordfish was quicker. He got it. Naturally I expected him to spit it out. Not so! He hung on.

" 'Careful,' I shouted to Edward. 'Pull easy. You'll break off the line.'

" 'He won't let go,' replied Edward.

HOTEL METROPOLE

Only in the mysteriousness of ♡ is "the mystery of logic" revealed.

Dreams need to be repeated to come to be

P.O. Box 1900, Avalon, Catalina Island, CA 90704
Telephone (310) 510-1884 or (800) 300-8528 Fax (310) 510-2534
www.hotel-metropole.com

CHAPTER TWO

TEN days of faithful scouting for big game fish up and down the west coast of Tahiti resulted in raising eight sailfish and three marlin swordfish. One sailfish was caught and one marlin fought for an hour. This may not appear to be good fishing at all, but in so far as finding these fish is concerned it was a distinct achievement.

From different sources we had heard and kept hearing about the wonderful variety and number of fish around the Paumotu Islands. So we decided to run over there and take a "look see," as the Indian guides say at home.

It was fairly early in the morning when we first sighted Rangiroa. A few low blurs on the horizon, dots thickening to a long green line, next a white flashing surf here and there, a wandering stretch of sand, and then the beautiful wild fringe of cocoanut palms,—what a thrill each and every one of these gave me!

For many years I had fished along coral reefs and waving palms —the Florida Keys in particular. I imagined I was back in the blue Gulf Stream, watching the islets form in a long green line of land. It seemed impossible that I was in the South Seas gazing at the largest atoll in the world. In fact an atoll did not mean anything. I had my conception, of course, which at first sight of Rangiroa, vanished as a dream of a place.

In an hour or so we ran close up to the reef, to find it extending in both directions as far as eye could see. Over the flat bronze and gray reef was visible the blaze of blue lagoon. Long strips of white coral were topped by graceful green and gold palms, waving gently in the wind, speaking a language only those who know these trees can read. We were on the leeward side and there was calm water, with scarcely any surf breaking on the blunt square reef. Flying-fish darted like swarms of bees; big fish splashed close to the coral; myriads of birds, gray and white, with black heads, followed the ship, uttering strange cries.

There was a sameness in the leagues of reef. Strips of bleached coral, dead black levels reaching a half-mile across to the lagoon, then a lovely golden palm grove on a higher ridge; here and there pools of aquamarine between sea and lagoon; great blocks of reef, large as houses, thrown up by hurricane, and little islands on the inside of the reef, lovely and isolated.

For hours Rangiroa was like this. Something grew on me, but I could not say exactly what. But part of it was surprise. I could not realize that this wandering reef extended in a circle on and on, endlessly on to surround a lagoon that was an inland sea.

Late in the afternoon we rounded a cape more to windward. The sea was blue and white, the surf breaking in a long heaving tumbled crest; and the cocoanut groves merged into one unbroken mass of green.

We came quite unexpectedly upon the pass. It was not visible a mile away. From the angle by which we approached, however, any break in the shore line could not be seen until we were right upon it. I had expected a narrow, calm passageway into the lagoon. What I saw was a seething tumultuous river rushing in like a millrace. Well inside, a little picturesque island, fringed with palms, lay to the right, with broad channel to the left. I saw some palm-thatched huts, a gleam of white through the trees, and then a church spire. That surely was a surprise, though I might have expected it.

The channel was a curve, and what with the current and the power of our engines we went in swiftly. Once well into the channel I could see the bottom through the clearest and strangest water I had ever beheld. It was a light green. I could not judge the depth. The width of the channel might have been a quarter of a mile. On each side the reef broke off abruptly and squarely, as if it had been chopped.

We sailed on into the lagoon. I knew it was a lagoon, though it looked a sea as vast as the ocean we had left. But I could see the lines of cocoanut palms curving for leagues, reaching out to surround the lagoon, and to disappear.

Natives ran along the beach in an excitement I supposed natural enough. Ships rarely visited that isolated little part. Then the church bell rang. It startled me. What a place to hear a church bell! To me it had a warning note.

Captain Kleibengat was forward, high on the port halyard. From my stand aft on the deck I could see how the water shoaled. Away to starboard showed swift rips and rifts, a sure sign of shallows. I wanted the skipper to sheer to port, nearer the village, and so I called to him. But he yelled back something about going behind the island for shelter.

Suddenly I felt a slight jar. I had felt such a thing before. We had hit bottom. In an instant I was paralyzed. We struck again, careened a little, went on, to the hoarse yells of sailors and others, and then stopped dead. The *Fisherman* keeled over and the bow began to swing to starboard. The millrace current caught her full and moved her fast. She pivoted back toward the outlet to the sea, and there she stuck.

It was a bad enough situation, without a horror of peril so common to shipwreck. After the first few moments I was calm enough myself, and resigned. I had prepared myself for almost anything. The *Fisherman* was my property and if there were to be loss it would be mine alone. For the rest I would hardly dare to describe the excitement on board.

Native boats put out, and then we learned that the natives had seen we were going aground and tried to warn us. The tide was running out—a most fortunate circumstance, because if it had been high we would have stuck there for good—a monument to the folly of a fisherman. The hours that followed were crowded with noise, action, and fraught with anxiety. My chief engineer feared to start the engines—which he had shut off the instant we struck—because if we were on hard coral there would be permanent injury. The sounding-lead showed ten feet aft, where we were aground. The *Fisherman* drew twelve feet. There was plenty of water under the bow, and to starboard, which was toward shore.

The skipper put out kedge anchors and with them and the engine endeavored to work her off. The natives came out to help in any way they could. Flood tide came after midnight, and sometime in the early morning I heard the ship groan and felt her budge. Little by little, in fact inch by inch, they worked her off the reef. By three A.M. she was afloat, and soon we anchored in deep water, nearer the shore. Everybody except the watch went to bed, worn out with worry and fatigue. I did not sleep much and was up before sunrise.

In the fresh dawn how different the lagoon and the wandering line of coral! I had an hour alone on deck and the serenity and sweetness and beauty of the scene were worth almost what it had cost to find them. It occurred to me, however, that this was the atoll at its very safest and best. There was treachery of sea, current, and wind here, and the eternal menace of the iron reefs.

Our interpreter, John Blakelock, went ashore to the village, Avatoru, and brought back some native fishermen. We interrogated them in the same manner as we had the Tahitians. They identified all the fish of which we showed photographs, except the broadbill swordfish, and they positively claimed him for Polynesian waters, averring, however, that his sword, instead of being an extension of the upper maxillary, was an extension of the lower.

This was a statement that seemed impossible to take seriously. But I was compelled to take it seriously. One of our visitors was the native governor of Rangiroa. He was intelligent and spoke English fairly well. He stuck to his statement about the swordfish with the sword underneath, and could not be shaken. The other natives were equally as positive.

This swordfish grows very large and the natives fear it. When they fish for bonito from the sail-boats—trolling the same pearl-shell gigs used by Tahitians—very often the school of bonito will mass under the boat and almost cling to it. This is a sure sign one of the great swordfish is about, and when the fishermen look down they are sure to see one, and often more.

Sailfish, spearfish or marlin, tuna, wahoo, and other large fish, were often seen outside the reef. Sharks were plentiful and ran very large. The governor said some sharks were eight fathoms in length. This statement was another hard one to swallow. But we were in unknown waters, unfished by anyone except natives with the crudest of tackle and method. *Quien sabe?* You can never tell. I, for one, believe absolutely in the fabled sea-serpent.

We put out to sea in three boats, with orders from me to hang pretty well together. Middleton, the camera-man, was in the *Red*, and he was to follow us closely. We trailed two teasers behind each boat. I forgot to say that the natives caught us a few mullet for bait before we left. We trolled both bait and feather gigs; and ran around outside of the entrance to the lagoon. The sea was just a little rough for comfortable fishing, but not bad. Birds were in evidence, though not in any large numbers. We sighted no schooling fish and did not see any fins.

Peter caught a small yellow-fin tuna, the same species we found off Mexico and South America, a wonderfully brilliantly colored fish, blue and silver, with yellow fins. Soon after that Peter hooked another on the feather gig.

He was hauling this up and had brought it somewhere near the boat when he let out a yell. I jumped up and instantly sighted a huge green shape looming up astern.

"Whale!" shouted Peter. As he was a whaler, I at once took his word for it.

But as the fish came closer, I saw it was not a whale, but a shark. Only in size did it resemble *Rhinodon typus*, from which fact I took it to be one of those most colossal of sharks. I was intensely thrilled and excited, but not frightened.

Francis yelled something, and Peter answered. I waved for Middleton to hurry close in the *Red* and frantically motioned that there was something to photograph.

The great fish passed astern of me, not far from the surface. He was yellow and green in color, had a square head, immense pectoral fins, and a few white spots. He was eight feet across the back, and considerably longer than my boat—conservatively between thirty-five and forty feet. The after third of his body and his tail were lean compared with the bulk of his head and shoulders. He went under us, out on the other side. Just then Peter's tuna, which he had kept winding up, came into view. It passed close to the head of the shark. He did not appear to see it. Then he turned, flashed a bright blaze, and went down shining until he faded and disappeared.

He had been with us only a few seconds. When he was gone we recovered wits enough to calculate upon what we had witnessed. The eye sometimes deceives one and excitement is no help to accurate observation. But there could be no doubt that we had seen an astounding and almost incredibly huge shark.

"He was forty feet long and had more beam than our launch," declared Peter. "When I first saw him I thought he was a fin-back whale."

"Some joker, that fish!" exclaimed Francis. "No one could have made me believe it. But I saw him."

These New Zealand fishermen were used to big fish, and not given to exaggeration. So I relied much upon their judgment. And presently I figured out that the fish had not been a *Rhinodon*. He was not a harmless whale-shark, but one of the man-eating monsters of the South Pacific. Then I was more frightened than I remember for a long time.

We returned to the ship. During our absence the sailors, the engineers, Reuben and Harry, the cabin boys, and Romer and John, the "go-getters," had been busy. Our aquarium was full of the most amazingly colored and beautiful fishes I had ever seen. These had been caught by hook and line from the ship. Schools of fish surrounded us, and would bite upon anything. I spent some enjoyable moments watching the fish in the aquarium. Three species of angel-fish, and a trigger-fish, were all I could identify. The angel-fish were gold in color with a black spot on the tail, and a black bar across the nose, and long streamers. They were exquisitely lovely. Another angel-fish was deep dark blue, with tiny bright glints of yellow, and he had two long blue streamers on his tail. A third was black as ebony. The trigger-fish was a mass of bronze streaks and stripes, not so beautiful as astounding.

After supper we compared notes. It was hard to get the others to credit our shark story, but at last they did. Captain Mitchell had caught a small tuna.

Early next morning, before anyone was up, I caught a big fish from the ship. It was one of the blue-green bass-like fish I had seen swimming around. Catching it was no great matter, but landing it on deck was. I required assistance and had to yell for it.

Once upon deck, the fish turned out to be remarkable in all details. The weight was around a hundred pounds. It had a bass shape, with a hump back, long snout, and big lips, with wide fins and tail almost meeting above and below. The color was aquamarine blue from head to gills, and the rest appeared to be a green blue, and was wonderfully marked in a maze of circular lines on a brown background. It had large white teeth. There were black dots and wide wavering lines, like etchings, on the head. The dorsal, pectoral, and anal fins were lined cross-wise with the irregular markings. The even pattern did not begin until behind the pectorals. This fish had green eyes. We skinned it to find the green color permeating all the flesh and bones, even the blood was green. It had immense scales, like those of a tarpon in shape, half of which were green with longitudinal black bars. The native name was *mara tear*. This huge fish grew to weigh several hundred pounds, and was rank poison.

Another strange fish I caught that morning was an *avai*, an oval fish, without scales, shiny, silvery, with six small yellow spots on each side. Its dorsal and anal fins were fringed to its wide sharp tail, and the pectoral fins resembled long silver feathers. It had two small white butterfly fins under the pectoral. This fish undoubtedly belonged to the crevalle group.

Romer, of course, had to partake of my sport, and manifested a very sudden scientific interest. He caught an *onai*, a large fish almost round, with spots on its nose, a wonderful deep purple on the body, yellow fins, and very long dorsal and anal fins. It had sharp spurs at the juncture of the tail, no inconsiderable weapon. The tiny mouth was a striking abnormality. No wonder Romer had snagged this fish! It could not have gotten even a small hook into its mouth. The eyes were small, black, with gold rings round them. Each lobe of the tail was ornamented with a long narrow streamer, like a ribbon. Altogether this was an extraordinary fish, and like the others, one we could not classify.

Romer's next addition to our aquarium was a mottled gray-greenish fish, with very long head like a pig—an ugly, hungry, vicious-looking customer. It had a red mouth, very low dorsal fin red at the back where it widened. It was called *utura*.

But though we caught various multi-colored fish, we could not get any that suited for bait. The mullet would not troll well, and besides grew soft in a very few hours. Needlefish would have been good, but we could not catch them. We tried all sorts of lures, and finally had to go without bait. What a beautiful, fascinating, and dangerous place that channel was! Once outside, Peter, using a feather gig, promptly caught a small tuna. It was not a yellow-fin. It had long fins, yet was not an albacore. I just as promptly put it on for bait and let it go. There was a feeling of anticipation and apprehension accompanying this venture. Sure enough, my hunch was right—I had a tremendous strike. How good to feel and see and hear the line whiz off the reel! When I could stand it no longer I put on the drag and struck, and I came up on a very animated coral reef or whale or something. I never saw the thing and it soon broke my line, to my relief. I had visions of one of those enormous sharks.

Then we went on trolling. This was fine sport. The azure sea, the white surf, the green coral isle, all so exotic and strange, were more than enough to keep me distracted from the worry and zest of fishing. It was my luck, presently, to catch a small tuna. He looked the same as any other tuna, until we had him on board. Then I saw that I had landed a new species, and undoubtedly one of the kind Nordhoff had mentioned. It resembled a blue-fin, only the fins were pale. It had no discernible yellow. The head was not so trim and gamy as that of a blue-fin, and its eyes were larger. Most markedly it had teeth like a dog. "Well, here's a dog-tooth tuna," I remarked. He was not a pretty fish, but, considering his weight—about thirty pounds—he had put up a strong fight. The importance of catching him, however, consisted in the fact that he was new. This tuna, Nordhoff claimed, was frequently caught by natives, and sometimes extraordinarily large ones were hooked and broke away. Upwards of four and five hundred pounds! These large ones appeared to travel alone. At least no more than one had ever been seen at one time.

After that Peter caught three small yellow-fins, and then a large bonito. This fish had stripes like a skipjack, common at Catalina in August. The largest on the California coast weighed fourteen pounds. This one approached thirty. Not to be daunted by lack of bait, I put the huge bonito on my hook and let it down. Indeed, it shot down, fully three hundred feet before slowing up. And I said to the boys:

"If something takes him—good night!"

But a drift of an hour or more did not gain a strike. So I resumed trolling. We tried to keep up with the wheeling, shrieking sea-birds, but could not do so for long. At sunset we turned toward the reef and met the Captain on the way in. He cupped his hands and yelled to me: "Hooked a big marlin! On a feather gig! . . . Enough said!"

Events appeared to be multiplying. I had not needed any more evidence, however, to assure me that fishing among these South Sea islands was to prove a very difficult, exasperating, and almost fruitless task. The water was too clear and the great game fish too scarce. Still, the fishing had singular attractions, perhaps owing to the many obstacles, and the conviction that but few anglers would have the will and endurance to stick at it.

We reached the entrance to the lagoon at sunset, and if it was not purely a place of enchantment I did not know what to call it. Words are inadequate to express some things. They must be seen. The sky was a mass of broken white and purple clouds, the west a blaze of gold, the atoll a shining blend of sea and reef. The sun sank, and all changed as if by magic. Indeed, magical lights, dark, luminous, exquisite, lit the channel and the wild wind-spread palms, and the vast lagoon.

The following morning I called a council of war against the bait difficulty, with the result that we got out the flying-fish net, and hiring half a dozen natives to take us where there were some small fish.

We ran several miles up the lagoon, along the inside. The scene was like a painting to me. I could not realize the actualities. The color of the water and the long line of coral and cocoanut palms, wandering leagues away across the lagoon, were so extraordinary that I could not accept them.

The launch drew too much water to be taken near shore, so we anchored it and took to the skiff. The natives took to the water like ducks.

They had brought us to a break in the reef where at high tide

Zane Grey and Son Romer at Rangiroa, in the Paumotus

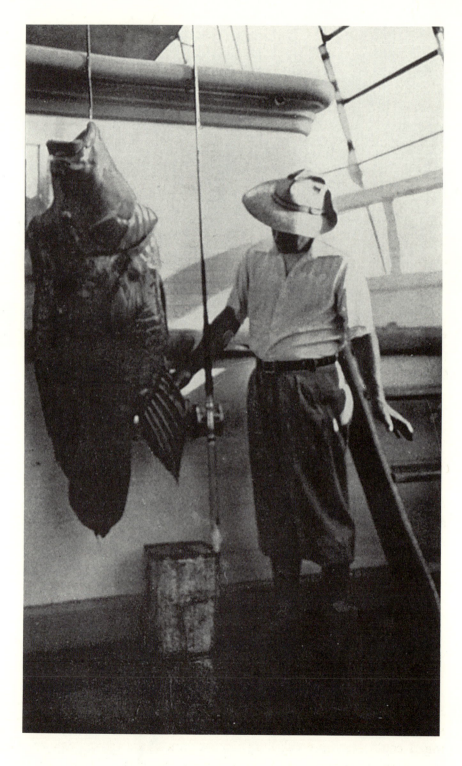

Strange Green Fish, Unclassified, About 100 Pounds in Weight, Caught by Zane Grey. It Had Green Scales, Flesh, Blood, and Eyes; Very Poisonous

the water overflowed and ran in. It was then low tide, and a long channel of smooth water lay in the rent. No palms or clumps of brush grew on or near this break. Far across the reef, half a mile at least, I could hear the surf pounding and see the tossing of white crests above the blue. The natives stretched the net across the narrow inlet into the lagoon, and while several of them held it the others splashed and threshed in the water to scare the fish. They scared them all right. And what mullet did not escape under the net leaped over it. I saw at once that no bait could be caught in this manner. The coral bottom was as ragged and rough as lava.

The natives next tried another place, inside the channel, and corralling a few fish in a corner they lifted slabs of coral and caught some little fish with their hands. These were not large enough or suitable in any way for bait. I gave up then and left the gang puddling around in the pool, having a fine time even if they could not catch any fish.

I started to walk across the reef, conscious of thrilling and profound sensations. It was as bare as the rock floor of flood-swept desert, the color of gray stone. In places it was smooth, and in others rough. Dead coral as hard as iron! Once far out on the reef, I could see miles of it stretching on toward the horizon, bounded on the sea side by the white wall of waters and on the lagoon side by the green line of graceful palms. The circle of the atoll was scarcely perceptible. Here again the enormity of the atoll struck me. How vast and mysterious the sea that could develop this atoll as a mere atom!

At last I got to the edge of the water. It came lapping and shallow to my feet, running in over red and yellow coral, smooth as marble, except for knots and ruts in places. I was still two hundred yards from the edge where the surf broke. This was the lee side of the atoll. I wondered what the windward side would be like. There was an incessant pounding and splashing as the green waves dashed to destruction and came tumbling over in sheets of seething froth. I waded to the highest point of the roof, just to the limit of safety, and there I stood for a long time, watching, listening, feeling. I could see three miles up the reef and more down; and the line of white showed breaking, changing, heaving, like an army advancing with banners. After I had indulged in an orgy of sensorial perception, I fell into the most delightful mood. This reef was a stupendous thing. The whole atoll incomprehensible!

To me the most acceptable theory of an atoll is that of Darwin. Coral-building animals, or polyp, can live only in water from thirty to forty fathoms deep. The incredible fact of their constructing reefs 7,200 fathoms deep, as Darwin found at Bora-Bora, can only be explained by the sinking of land through the ages. Barrier-reefs, such as surround Tahiti, show a gradual submersion of the land. The live corals work and build at the depth of around a hundred feet, and build as the land sinks. These amazing animals die and their structure becomes as a wall of iron. Some day the grand mountains of Tahiti will sink under the surface of the sea, and the barrier-reef of today will become an atoll.

But that did not satisfy me. The scientists, after they have explained a phenomenon of nature to the best of their ability, stop with the physical or material. You must take their cold expositions or leave them. Mostly I have to take them, for I recognize their truth. Still, are they not only half-truths?

The atoll was there assuredly. The reef had been millions of years rising sheer from the depths, or sinking, whatever the case may be. To think of these infinitesimal coral creatures, in countless trillions, building up that colossal band of iron rock, half a mile wide, and perhaps far more in depth, was to my consciousness simply staggering. It is one thing to read about an atoll; it is quite another to stand on one and see it, feel it. For me the beauty, the grace and dream and romance, were here secondary. I was tremendously concerned with its being. Most of it was dead, but part of it was alive. That was the most incredible aspect of the atoll. I stood on a wide band of coral that extended over a hundred miles in a circle. Outside, the sea had vast depths; inside the lagoon, it was shallow.

All nature is wonderful. It is the new and striking features that seem incredible. We take mountains, deserts, as a matter of fact. Perhaps this atoll staggered me mostly because it was so different from anything I had ever seen. Still the manifestation of death and life was here unusually prominent. I held in my hands bits of coral, pink, lavender, white, very beautiful to see. I had broken these pieces from the reef, where they had stood out like blossoming flowers. What I wanted to know was where the life came from? Who are what breathed life into those crystalline cells? The scientists did not tell me that. They cannot. And they never can. This is where science fails and where the Infinite steps in. Whoever can solve that will make clear the riddle of the universe. The origin of life has been the mystery of the ages. The nebular hypothesis and the subsequent heat, moisture, chemical combinations, electricity, etc., as developers of life on a planet, are plausible enough and fascinating to study. But who made the nebular hypothesis? Who created the endless space of universe that existed before? Here we are baffled. And it seems easier to me to lean more toward a spiritual faith in omniscience than reel blindly in materialism.

CHAPTER THREE

OUR anchorage at Rangiroa was not only unsatisfactory, but on a certain tide, when the trade wind grew strong, it was dangerous. The current ran like a millrace. All that enormous body of water appeared to be pouring down to get out of the channel. The launches bobbed around as if in a rough sea, and it was unsafe to try to get on them. Moreover, they tugged and chafed at the ropes, bumped into one another and the schooner.

When I looked at the angry waves of this lagoon I had to laugh. The word lagoon had no more significance for me. Its power was gone. It had meant blue water as still and tranquil as the sky. Many other of my South Sea perceptions were becoming disillusions.

We employed the native pilots and ran the *Fisherman* eight miles up the lagoon to another deep-water channel. Here we anchored in the lee of the reef and enjoyed smooth water. It was too deep, however, to see the bottom and the fish—which was a circumstance to be regretted. Our position lay opposite the native village, which extended for half a mile on the inside of the end of the reef.

This village, Tiputa, was larger than the one at the other passageway. We went ashore to be met by the whole population of several hundred natives, who welcomed us most kindly. The *Fisherman* was the largest ship that had ever touched there. A shady, white, coral-walled street divided the picturesque village. The gold and green palms dominated the place, standing loftily above the broad-leaved breadfruit and other trees. These breadfruit trees were planted in pits dug in the coral, for which soil from Tahiti had been brought. Only the marvelous cocoanut palms could find root and sustenance in the living coral.

Tiputa was more civilized than I had expected to find an atoll. There were stores kept by Chinamen, a tiny white church, and many bungalows, the materials for which had been brought from afar. The native governor spoke some English and he showed us around with great ceremony. While we were ashore a trading-schooner arrived. We were informed presently that an itinerant motion-picture exhibitor was to show a picture that evening. This appeared an opportunity not to be missed. We went. After dark the native village was a place of dark shadows, rustling palms, sweet odors, velvety sky full of white stars, moving figures, like spectres, and always the booming sea on the outer reef. We were conducted to the governor's office—a large room, whitewashed, and decorated in French design and Polynesian words. Here a miscellaneous crowd gathered—a very interesting crowd. Little tots and boys and girls sat on the floor before the screen.

The picture operator worked for two hours getting his projector so it would project. The motion-picture technical departments ought to have seen that job. It was marvelous. He built a fire outside of cocoanut hulls, and heated a brass receptable, which I was given to understand generated the motive power. A long hose ran inside to the contraption of pipes, boxes, cylinders, etc., on the table. This appeared to be the projector. Finally the lights were turned out and the picture shown. It was Texas Guinan in a Western of a very early period. I shall never forget that picture and the screaming, wildly-applauding natives.

Next day we started out to fish from one channel to the other—eight miles—outside the reef, of course. The day was perfect. We ran into flocks of wheeling boobies and terns and schools of bonito. I tried one small bait after another. No good! Then I used a strip of a bonito that Peter caught. Every once in a while Peter would sing out—and we had to stop the launch for him to land a yellow-fin or bonito. But at last he hooked something different. It meant business. I knew it was not a tuna. Soon it broke water and turned out to be a long, slim, racy marlin, almost black and white in the blazing sun. We were all elated. A marlin hooked on a feather gig! He got going hard and leaped all over the ocean, and presently left us for good.

"Gosh! Bad luck dogs us!" I exclaimed, blankly. Peter expressed himself in a blankety-blank manner. And Francis, who seldom used bad language, burst out with, "Damn!"

We trolled all the way down to the other channel, and found the water there nice and smooth. Meanwhile the sun had been westering, and soon it began to set. Beautiful clouds changed from white to purple and from purple to gold. I never saw any color approaching pink or rose. Flocks of gulls and boobies screamed and circled above the leaping bonito. The place surely looked fishy. But I hardly expected a strike on that piece of bonito hide—that had been trolled to a frazzle.

Nevertheless, I did get a strike—a violent one that jerked me round in time to see the unmistakable swirl of a marlin. I let him run off line, fully two hundred feet, then struck him. He felt solid, and I thought the hook had gone in. But as I was hauling hard to get in line the hook came out. Pretty tough!

Sunset made up for disappointment. I watched the sun lift the sea, then sink swiftly out of sight. The darkness came on apace—a wonderful thing to see on the water. Captain Mitchell appeared in no hurry to run in. He was half a mile outside, and I got the impression that he was busy. But I knew he would come presently, so I ran in. Once in the channel we found it swift and heavy, with great seas running in the middle. They heaved up, black and white, and seemed to roar. We kept close to the inside. But when we entered the lagoon we found the current could not be avoided, and almost before we knew it we were in the heavy sea chopped up by tide and current conflicting. It took us half an hour to beat our way out into the lagoon. Night had now fallen. We could see the fringe of palms and had that to guide us. And no sooner did I have no more cause to worry about our boat when I remembered Captain Mitchell. We waited an anxious hour, going slowly, until to our relief the *Sky Blue* sped down upon us. Then we raced toward the beacon light on the *Fisherman*. Like a star out of the darkness it guided us.

Upon arriving I was to learn what had kept the Captain so long in catching up with me. I had waited fully an hour before entering the Avatoru passage. Nothing much! Only twelve tuna! He told a tale of remarkable interest. And Harry, our cabin boy, who had accompanied him burst out, "Some fishing!"

They had about decided to join me before sunset when a flock of boobies circling near attracted them. They ran over to get among tuna, both hooking on at once. Then began a merry time. The fish were thick, and at length appeared to mass under the boat for protection from large fish that could be dimly seen flashing to and fro. Some were sharks, for Captain Mitchell caught two, and hooked another which broke away. All the tuna caught were yellowfins, around thirty pounds. There were plenty of bigger ones, but the small ones snapped the bait before the others deeper down could get into action. Captain said it was a wonderful sight to look under the boat.

"Those tuna were scared so they came right under the boat. Big fish after them. I am sure I saw one of the long-billed swordfish we've heard about. He had a long sharp snout, but I couldn't see whether or not it was an extension of the lower jaw. Longest fish altogether I ever saw. Fully sixteen feet! And he sort of wavered and blurred in the water. Changed shape, as it seemed."

"Cap, that sounds like sailfish to me," I replied, thoughtfully. "The big sail moves, floats, and gives the fish a changing wavering shape."

"Well, by Jove! he was some fish!" went on Mitchell. "The whole experience was thrilling. You know we doubted what the natives said about bonito and tuna seeking protection under a boat. Well, it's a fact. And these tuna did not appear to fear the sharks, either. I saw that plainly. There was a devil of a fish around and I'll bet it was one of those new swordfish."

We fished several days out of Tiputa, taking natives with us each time. We raised two of the striped spearfish to the teasers. They refused the baits offered. In fact, we could not get good bait, and with big savage strange fish out there to catch, the lack of proper bait to offer them was most exasperating. Captain Mitchell hooked a marlin on a feather gig—light tackle—and on the first run it broke the line. So our angling misfortunes multiplied.

There was an Armenian living at Tiputa. He had been there thirty years—had seen prosperous days once in copra and pearl trading, but was now reduced by changed conditions to a bare living. He was an educated, intelligent man, and spoke English and French fluently. What was of more interest to us, he had been a fisherman for years. And he had a visitor at this time, a German—who also spoke English well and had fished a good deal. The method of these fishermen was, of course, to use hand lines and troll from canoes and launches, and even schooners.

Both men absolutely had seen the under-billed swordfish, not once but many times, and the Armenian had hooked one on his hand line. He had stopped among feeding bonito, and was hauling one in when the school ran under his boat. He said they could be scooped up by hand—that they actually quivered with fright. Then he saw four enormous fish with long bills. They had no fear of the boat. They flashed to and fro under it—great purple fish fifteen feet long and thick-bodied in proportion. The fisherman threw the hooked bonito overboard, and as it sank a few feet one of the strange swordfish rose to it. When it opened its mouth he saw that the upper jaw was the short one. The under jaw was yellow bone, not smooth, but covered with small knots or protuberances. This weapon was formidable, but did not run to a sharp point. He hooked the fish, which broke the hand line. And he did not have any desire to hook another.

This man appeared to me to be sincere and truthful. He was convincing, and I believed him. I had myself seen one of the forty-foot sharks of Paumotus waters—sharks that have never even been mentioned in scientific fishing-books; and neither Captain Mitchell nor I saw any further reason to doubt the existence of a swordfish with sword a development of the lower maxillary. What would I not have given to catch one!

Then we had for three days what the skipper called heavy trade winds. I called it gale out of a clear sky. Anyway, we could not run outside to fish. We fished from the ship, and spent a good deal of time on shore, mingling with the natives. I had some lonely walks along the beaches.

But it was not easy walking. In most places it was rough broken coral, cast up by the sea, that afforded loose footing, and soon became wearisome. The outer reef was hard, but sharp and ragged, most hazardous in places. My dream of golden beaches of the South Seas, long winding slopes of lucent sand, shaded by palms, was soon dispelled. There were none. The white beaches that looked so beautiful and enticing from ship deck turned out to be beds of broken coral. Shells were few and far between. The only thing about these beaches that was attractive was the tinkling metallic music of the sliding broken bits of coral. The cocoanut palms, however, made up for a lot. I knew cocoanut palm trees, from so many sojourns on the Florida Keys, and in the Caribbean Sea. But I had a great deal to learn about cocoanut palms. I was learning it.

Apataki lies seventy-five miles southeast of Rangiroa. We left one morning early and sailed for hours along the lee shore of Rangiroa—a most enjoyable and memorable sail, filled with glimpses of tropic beauty—and then, when we got round the corner of the atoll to windward we had to buck a heaving white-billowed sea for some hours further, until we got in the lee of Apataki. Far to the north lay another atoll, an endless green-fringed belt along the horizon. Slowly it sank into the blue. Then, gradually, as we drew near Apataki, I had more added to my impressions of the vastness of these Paumotuan atolls. We sailed along the reef of this one for twenty miles, and at last, toward sunset of a day that had been wonderful, we reached the narrow entrance.

No ship with the length and tonnage of the Fisherman had ever gone inside this channel. The reef appeared cut into islands, gold and white, with lofty palms leaning away from the wind. The channel, dark blue and deep, was placid at this hour, and narrow compared with the others. Our native pilot assured us we could go in safety. How I ever consented to the idea I never knew —but we went, and dropping anchor in mid-channel we fastened hawsers to the palms on the village side and soon had the yacht moored securely along the rude dock of blocks of coral. A few lone natives, and Monsieur Herve, administrator of some fifty atolls of the Paumotus, welcomed us on shore. The Frenchman was certainly a very cordial and courteous gentleman.

"I look out my door," he said, with expressive gestures. "I see zat ship. I never see her before. I know not what to think. But I was ver' glad. We air much alone."

If Apataki was not a lonely Pacific atoll I could not imagine what one would be like. Moreover, it was beautiful in a way hard to name. But there it was, with channels on all sides of the village —a few palm-thatched huts and some pretty white bungalows— reaches of white and golden coral, with the outer reef so far away that the surf could not be heard.

The inhabitants, some two hundred in number, were away on different sections of the atoll, gathering copra. Monsieur Herve, with his wife and eighteen-year-old daughter, and the several natives we saw, had been alone for weeks. This village was the best protected of any I had seen. The islands on the windward side, with the reef outside them, and on the lagoon side, with shoals of coral reaching far out, appeared to me to make this place safe from the devastating sea, if not from the wind of the hurricane. A shady pleasant lane divided the island upon which the village stood. I walked clear to the water edge at the end, and in the moist hot shade expected to find mosquitoes. But there were none. Fresh water was very scarce—a matter of concern to Monsieur Herve. He said, however, that it did not worry the natives. Nothing ever worried them.

Soon the *Fisherman* was surrounded by many-hued little fish, and some large ones deep down. And the "Go-getters" got busy! There were flocks of angel-fish; and each flock were of different hues. Such an aquarium I had never dreamed of. I saw little fish the color of magenta cactus blossoms; others that resembled sunflowers; and innumerable others that were just brilliant sparks of light. There were queer fish, too; one of which was a long, slim, gray creature with head and snout just like a pipe. I imagined this fish used his pipe-like snout to stick into holes in the coral, in order to suck out those forms of life upon which it subsisted. The reward of watching was really beyond estimation. No end of fish! They passed by under the ship, an endless, varying stream of movement and color. Many lingered, but the majority went on.

We fished three days off Apataki, with the same kind of luck we had encountered in the other places. Some large bonito, small tuna of different kinds, a grouper or two, several marlin flashing at the teasers and refusing our poor baits, a huge *ono* as large around as a telegraph pole that took a vicious lunge at Captain's teaser, two white sharks, the first about twenty feet long, that hove up from the blue depths to look us over, and a few strikes from fish which never showed—these made the sum of our experience at Apataki.

Next morning early we set off for the nearest atoll, Arutua, twelve miles across the blue arm of sea. We took Monsieur Herve with us, in Captain Mitchell's launch. I trolled about the whole distance.

Green clumps of palms rose up from the horizon, then streaks of white surf, and then coral beaches. The channel into Arutua permitted only small boats to enter. It was a maelstrom of a place, and scared me so I did not get to appreciate the marvelous beauty of this entrance into one of the loveliest and most beautiful of all South Sea atolls. But when we were once inside, with clear green water underneath us, like a transparency over the pearl-hued coral, and the tiny green aisles ran out from the shore toward the intense blue lagoon, then I had at last the realization of my dream. Arutua seemed as rare as a pearl. I saw one tiny isle with a single cocoanut palm rising slender and graceful to unfold its fern-like branches to the wind. There were other isles and points of reef that called with strange and insistant lure. Come—rest here—gaze over the lagoon—let time and the world go by! It was there—this mysterious South Sea enchantment.

We ran in and out of green channels, around to the back of the large grove of palms, and approached shore to find a picturesque group of natives assembled, awaiting us. Here was a white beach, and pretty thatched huts in the shade of palms, with crowds of naked and half-naked children, stalwart native men in *pareus*, and golden-skinned white-clad girls and women, not forgetting the large population of pigs, chickens, and dogs.

We were welcomed ashore with great dignity by the chief, which fact, no doubt, was owing to the large French flag that Monsieur Herve had put up in the *Sky Blue*. Johnny, our interpreter, was acquainted here. And it was very easy to see how seldom visitors came and how welcome they were. The whole population escorted us under the palms, down the shady lanes, so colorful in green and gold, and bright red with hibiscus, into the capacious and airy meeting-house, where we sat on benches with our feet in cool sand, and listened to the natives sing. How weird, monotonous, low and strange they chanted! The dominant note was melancholy.

Arutua was exquisite. Civilization had not yet marred its beauty or corrupted its natives. Here, though, as well as everywhere, I saw a little eleven-year-old girl, quite beautiful, carrying an infant in her arms. I asked Johnny about it, and he said nobody but the kids' mothers ever carried them around. This baby was white.

In one palm-thatched hut we came upon death. A baby had just died at birth. It lay shrouded in white on the floor. The mother was up and around. She had large liquid eyes, somber, resigned. The natives accept death with tranquillity, as they do all the slings and arrows of outrageous fortune. We passed on to other scenes of the village, but I did not soon forget that mother and child. The little cemetery was a strange place. One grave was decorated with bottles buried in the sand, and strings of beads around the coral stone.

Through the beautiful grove on all sides shone the blue of sea, on the lagoon side an endless deep smooth blue; on the outside, contending tides and pounding surf. You could never forget the ocean here. It was supreme, yet the sun appeared to be a rival. Green lights, white flashes, blue spaces! Out from the sweet shade the heat was intense. The sand burned through my shoes. The least exertion brought the perspiration freely. We watched the natives sail their outrigger canoes. Romer and John took a ride and raved about the speed and ease of the crafts. They were going to have one at Avalon, etc, etc.!

Monsieur Herve arranged to have a diver go down for pearl shell. We went out into the lagoon and watched the proceedings. It was what I had seen in the movies and not particularly more thrilling, despite the natural background of Arutua. I was amazed and quite concerned about the diver staying under so long. I thought he was surely drowned. But the fact is, when you are watching and waiting for a diver to reappear, a minute is a long time, and two minutes an eternity. Some divers, however, can stay under much longer than that. One thing struck me that I had not gotten in the movies, and it was the loud moaning sound the diver made inhaling air before he submerged. The shells that came up from the depths of Arutua lagoon were large, and beautiful on the inside, but did not contain any pearls.

Across the lagoon, or on one end of it, was a nesting-place for sea birds. We visited it. What a wonderful ride across the blue lagoon! Before we drew near the land I made out a dark cloud moving above the green. We soon discerned that it was composed of birds, black and white terns. There appeared to be endless numbers of them, wheeling, darting, circling low, soaring high. Thousands flew out to meet the boats, these noisy invaders of their peace, and they uttered plaintive notes of protest.

When we went ashore a cloud of birds arose that darkened the sky, and an almost deafening roar made it necessary to shout to be heard. The strip of coral was half a mile wide, overgrown with green brush not unlike desert greasewood, and here and there cocoanut palms. You could scarcely find place to step for fear of crushing eggs. Eggs were as thick almost as bits of coral. They resembled the coral, too. Gray and pale white with faint specks of brown. Johnny told us that a week before three schooners had visited this nesting-place, and had packed away one hundred cases of eggs to sell. The natives eat these eggs, and like them a little ripe, so to say. They claim the birds lay again as soon as they are robbed.

I went off alone up the beach and found places inside the brush, wide patches of coral, literally black with birds. The heat was intense and the odor very unpleasant. Some of these birds would not leave their eggs. There were no nests. The eggs were deposited upon the bare coral. I imagined they would have hatched without the aid of the mother, so hot was the coral. What a marvelous sight it must be when the eggs are all hatched out and the ground covered with little birds!

It seemed useless to try to estimate numbers, but there was a mile of reef, a half-mile wide, absolutely covered with birds, and as many in the air. Millions, no doubt. It struck me forcibly that as they lived by the sea there must be endless schools of little bait fish there.

This visit to the nesting-place of the sea birds was a very great privilege and a remarkable experience that I shall never forget. It must rank with my trips to the Isla de la Muerte of the Caribbean

Sea, and to the White Friars off the Mexican coast, and the Perlos Islands off Panama, where millions of sea birds live lonely, peaceful lives. As the years go by—the commercial years of this age—more and more does wild life, both feathered and furred, become scarcer. Only far from the beaten tracks can it be found in any numbers.

On our return toward Apataki we ran into a heavy sea, rolling blue, with white tips, and for some miles were uncomfortable. Then as we neared the lee of the atoll the sea smoothed out to good fishing water. I trolled all the way, unfortunately with bait not tempting even to a hungry fish.

When about in mid-channel Francis let out a wild yell just as I caught a flash of gold behind the left teaser. It came from a sailfish, and he was so fast that before we could move he had seized it. He held on, too, and we dragged him. Francis had to jerk several times to get the teaser out of his mouth. My, but that was a mad sailfish! While I reeled my bait in closer the sailfish kept darting at the teaser. He would hit it with his bill, then rush on, evidently to seize it in his jaws. But the boatmen fooled him until he grew desperate and charged so swiftly that he got it again. Whereupon Francis pulled it loose shouting, "Let go, you hungry joker!" Personally I did not think the sailfish was joking. He made a magnificent sight in that clear water, and in his eagerness came clear up to the boat. He got hold of the teaser again, at a moment when I dragged my bait right over him. But for this I believed he would have taken it. Anyway, Francis pulled so hard to get free of the fish that I was sure he would break something. The teaser came loose, however, and as Francis drew it in the sailfish came alongside, his slender golden shape very distinct, his wonderful purple sail cutting the water. Even in the thrilling excitement of the moment I thought to take a close look at him. In shape he resembled other sailfish, though decidedly longer, slimmer, more delicately, racily built. And he was about twelve feet long. He had no fear of the boat. We could easily have gaffed him, or almost lassoed him; and considering our ambition to collect specimens of new species it assuredly was a temptation. As long as Francis dangled the teaser over the water—of course the launch was running fast all this while—he struck and lunged at it, sometimes touching the boat.

He paid no attention to my bait. Then as Francis lifted the teaser out of the water the great golden sailfish flashed away and vanished. Perhaps this incident was really more remarkable than the actual catching of him might have been. Certainly we had close and amazing touch with him without doing him any harm. I had a longing to hook and catch him quite incompatible with any idealistic appreciation of his gorgeous color, his falcon-like symmetry, his wild spirit of the sea.

We fished several more days out of Apataki; the only striking out-of-the-ordinary incident was the raising of a giant barracuda. This happened to Captain Mitchell, so I did not see the fish and can judge only from the Captain's very vivid impressions. The fish leaped at the left teaser, coming half out of the water and startling Captain M. He missed the teaser, turned in a roaring surge, with alligator-like jaws open, and came again in a rush. He got the teaser and spat it out. I saw the great teeth-marks in that teaser, and most devoutly thanked goodness he did not get them in me. This fish was gray and silver in color. I identified it as a barracuda from the long sharp head and huge teeth. He was a big fish, over ten feet in length.

One day betweentimes I took a stroll and a wade, across the islands, the channels, and out on the reef. It was not very long until I was Robinson Crusoe on his lonely isle. What attracted me most was the green surf breaking on the outer reef. It was not so very high or rough, but singularly beautiful in its rise and curve and color. So I waded across the wide red and orange coral, through the shallow rushing water, out as far as I dared. Then to my amazement and delight I saw schools of small fish rising in the green curling breakers. This made me venture still farther out, where the white froth seethed round my knees. And then I watched the green billows heave and mount, and curl high to let the sunlight through.

As the waves rose fish appeared in the crystal water, shining, floating, rising, even swimming; and of all aquarian spectacles of beauty and life that I had seen this was supreme. To the left of me, and perhaps several hundred feet distant, there was a point where a school of black angel-fish rose within the wave. Next and closer were numbers of tiny fish like opal sparks from a camp fire. Directly in front of me and closest was a school of dark-blue oval fish with vivid spots and bars. I could see each school only for the instant when the curling breaker rose. The fish went down with it in the white crash and could not be seen again until the next rise. Not all waves were large enough to lift them up. Sometimes I had to wait. But in the main I saw them every few moments. To the right of my position the waves appeared highest, and here dark-green fish, quite large, floated to the very curling crest. How incredible to see dark-green fish in bright-green water, each the clearer for the contrast.

All along this reef schools of fish were rising in the waves, and each species kept to its own kind. They were playing. I could detect no other reason for this beautiful activity. Enemies did not appear to be near. I must have stood there fully an hour, so absorbed that I did not realize it until from the strain of standing against the surge I tired. Then I waded out and sat in the shade of rustling cocoanuts, and my thoughts fitted the scene. I could not conceive of anyone wanting to leave this wonderful world. There are compensations for all save the appalling tragedies and griefs. A love of nature must be some kind of religion. For happiness it is incomparable. The sea and the desert and mountain are there, waiting to reward anyone who will watch with wide slow eyes.

The morning we moved to leave Apataki was an anxious one. No ship the size of the *Fisherman* had ever before moored at that quaint dock. We had hawsers out fore and aft, beside the anchor in the middle of the channel, with a hundred fathoms of chain.

No doubt we waited too long before starting. Anyway, a breeze started up which augured ill for our enterprise. But Captain Kleibengat said he could make it. All lines but that on the stern were cast off. We steamed slowly out and up channel, hauling in the anchor. The *Fisherman* slowly swung till her bow pointed at the reef opposite. The breeze freshened. The foresails were run up, and this egregious blunder, with the letting go of the stern rope, caused us to drift with the wind and current towards the reef opposite.

I was up on the forecastle with Peter, who shook his head dubiously. The bow swung clear round and pointed out to sea. But

TROLLING OFF VAIRAO

The Cocoanut Climber

owing to the short turn we had no headway, and all the time wind and current bore us broadside toward the reef. The foresails were let down with a run. But that was too late.

Peter studied the slow movement of the big hull. "She'll just make it," he said once. Then a little later he added, "No, she won't!"

I could see no peril as yet, and thought we would clear the reef. We were still over a hundred feet, but we were drifting inevitably closer while at the same time making headway down channel. Closer and closer we neared the coral. How yellow and treacherous! My fear was simply that we would drift on and stick!

"Too bad!" muttered Peter, sorrowfully.

That caused me to believe we would be wrecked surely. I had a vision of the white *Fisherman* stranded forever on the coral. Closer! When we drifted to within fifteen feet of the reef I was gripped by a sudden nausea. What a slow, torturing process! Why could we not crash on and be done with it?

Presently the dark gap of water between the hull and the reef narrowed and closed. We struck gently, gratingly against the reef. And in a moment it dawned on me that we had not hit bottom. The water was deep, the coral straight down. Wind and tide held us there, but there was absolutely no danger. I could not realize it, believe it, until Peter assured me we were very lucky indeed.

Two small schooners that were moored below the dock put out to our assistance. The long hawsers were thrown off. We tied up to cocoanut trees again, this time to get leverage to pull off. What with all this aid and our own engines it appeared we might get away from the reef. But what looked so easy to me turned out a task for a mariner. We would get the *Fisherman* away from the coral and she would drift and blow back. The native crews of those schooners worked like beavers and, like beavers, were in and out of the water. At one time we had five cables out. My anxiety prohibited any thrill in the proceedings, but I certainly had them etched indelibly on my memory.

We were four hours getting away from that coral reef. I had some conception of how tenacious coral is. It jealously held on to the hull. But at last we worked free and in the channel. The two schooners escorted us outside and took Monsieur Herve off, and also all the native population of Apataki, who had gotten on board the *Fisherman* during the excitement. They had lent themselves whole-heartedly to our rescue.

We steamed away to the southward, over a blue rippling sea. I watched until white reef and green, drooping palms of Apataki sank below the verge.

CHAPTER FOUR

OUR sojourn of several weeks in the Paumotus was certainly not long enough to be satisfactory so far as capturing big fish was concerned, yet as a pioneering venture it was a success. We raised and hooked several species of game fish, besides the many small ones we caught. And we left there convinced of wonderful possibilities in those blue waters. The swordfish with the long lower jaw really existed, I was convinced, and I wanted earnestly and seriously to have another go after him. That, however, had to be left to the future. The *Fisherman* was too big a vessel to be risked any longer among the treacherous reefs of the Dangerous Archipelago.

We ran back to Tahiti and dropped anchor at Taaone. This was around the first of July, and the S. S. *Makura* was soon due at Papeete, northward bound. Romer and John, after six months away from home, and very much restricted as to their liberties, began to manifest unmistakable symptoms. So I suggested that they take the *Makura* for California. At once they were torn by conflicting desires—the longing for home and friends, and the thirst for more adventure in the South Seas. Naturally the former won out, and the last I saw of them was on the bridge of the *Makura*, from which John waved good-by to a dusky Tahitian maiden, and Romer divided his time between farewells to me and his interest in the manœuvres of the ship as she worked out into the channel. A month before the *Makura* had struck the reef going out. This time, I dare say, Romer saw that they navigated the ship right.

Captain Mitchell and I went fishing as usual. We could not be stopped. We kept trying the market for bait, trying to hire the natives to catch it, trying to catch it ourselves. But half the time we did not have any at all, and seldom did we have fresh bait. That was a drawback which had to be overcome.

We learned from natives that there were more bonito and fish round on the other side of the island. We had also been strongly urged by Nordhoff, McDonald, and other of our acquaintances to make a visit to the eastern half of Tahiti, beyond the isthmus. We were assured that here was the most beautiful scenery in all the South Seas. So we decided to go.

But before we left Taaone I had two heartbreaking experiences with swordfish, one each on the two days we remained there. This first morning we had fresh bait for a change—barracuda just the right size, which we had procured at the market. And we took as guests on the fishing-launches two officers from H. M. S. *Diomede*, which was anchored in the harbor.

By way of a change that morning, Francis, running my launch with both engines full speed, struck the inside edge of the coral reef and leaped high up on it. I was thrown flat, but though unhurt, I had scare enough for one trip. I expected the bottom to fall out of the *Loren G*. But evidently we had not smashed her. Francis and Peter piled overboard, and the other launches came to our assistance. We got off, marvelously, with only a bent propeller and a roughened keel. Then we ran on out, and across toward Moorea. I gave Lieutenant-Commander Farquhar a rod, and a feather gig to troll—we had been having most of our luck on the gigs—while I put on one of the barracuda. I put the bait out, and set the rod in the chair socket, with drag lightly on, for only a moment, while I fixed up the other heavy tackle. The barracuda weaved and flashed just back of the left teaser, a very attractive bait. Suddenly there was a smashing splash, and I wheeled in time to see a big blue marlin take the bait and surge away. I nearly killed myself getting around Farquhar's chair to that rod. But too late! The swordfish ran a few yards, and feeling the strain of the drag, he let go the bait. It was sickening, yet served me just right. The idea of a fisherman of my experience pulling a stunt like that! But when fish are scarce and strikes come seldom, vigilance relaxes. It cannot be helped. The unexpected always happens. We had a fine day on the sea, but we did not catch any fish. That unlucky incident, happening right at the onset, colored the whole day with regrets. Lieutenant Farquhar could not get over the fact that he might have released the drag on my reel the instant I yelled. But he never thought of it, and that caused his poignant regret.

That was nothing, however, to the awful incident of the following day. I was off in mid-channel, with Captain Mitchell somewhere on the horizon. Peter caught a fresh bait, a bonito, and we greeted the rare occasion with lusty whoops. I put the fine shiny, kicking bait on my hook and dropped it overboard. It shot down. Francis ran the boat slowly, over closer to the school of bonito. The birds were circling, screaming. Little white bait fish were leaping frantically. I saw a huge dark curved fin cut the water. It gave me such a thrilling, surprised start that I never told the boatmen I thought I had seen a broadbill swordfish.

Very soon after this something hit my bait a violent whack and ran off a little line. I tingled to my very toes. The boys had seen the strike, so I didn't need to tell them. The fish stopped. I waited with palpitating heart. Suddenly off he shot and all was well. It was a real old broadbill strike. My mind was full of visions of battle, success—and a wonderful South Sea swordfish—a new kind —to hang up and photograph and write about.

Then I hooked him. I jerked with all my might half a dozen times, and each time when I came up on his enormous weight the rod bent almost double. He took a short run, then sounded a hundred feet or so. All seemed okay. I knew he was big. I had him well hooked. And when he batted the leader a few times, I knew, from the familiar old feel, that he could be nothing but a broadbill swordfish.

Suddenly he gave a quick jerk, so swift and powerful that but for the rod-socket and harness he would have snatched the tackle out of my hands. I never before felt such a tremendous jerk. The strain slackened. And so did my heart! I reeled in a limp line. He had broken off, and again I was plunged into the despair that I knew so well. My old giant, Bad Luck, had haunted my trail again. But it was not bad luck, only bad fishing. The drag on that big Coxe reel was very sensitive and it took only one turn to set it tight. It was too tight for such a sudden and powerful jerk. It would have broken anything. I had forgotten, after hooking the fish, to ease up on the drag. Vain, vain regret and bitter, bitter disappointment! The rest of that day was one endless fight with myself. Toward sunset, as we were about to turn islandward, I saw a big white splash in mid-channel. I leaped to my feet, shouting and pointing. Then a huge fish showed. Francis yelled, "Black marlin!" He came out again, higher. The third time he stood on his tail, a broad-shouldered shiny swordfish of some kind, and a thousand pounder if there ever was one. When he disappeared, leaving us transfixed and thrilling, I realized that there were other great fish in the sea besides the one I had lost. So I pulled in my line, and gave the word to go back to the ship. I watched the sun set in gold and purple over Moorea, and found my tranquil self again.

Under the guidance of Captain Lucca, the genial pilot, we steamed down between Tahiti and Moorea, and round to the leeward side of the island. We ran forty miles before we came into the bay that cut into the isthmus. The south side of Tahiti was so magnificently beautiful, so infinitely more wonderful than the Papeete side, that I thought it would be long before I attempted description.

We ran through a wide passage in the reef, up under the lee of Vairao, and anchored just off the coral, in deep water, almost under the shade of lofty cocoanut palms. The shore line was colorful with thatched huts, and outrigger canoes and groups of curious natives. When the engines stopped I became aware of the most solemn and tremendous volume of sound I ever heard from the sea. It was the great swell of the Pacific breaking upon the reef a mile out. The beauty of Vairao and the marvelous melody of the deep kept me on deck a long hour when there was much work to do with tackle. If only off this bay of Vairao there were a few fish, how perfect it would be!

I instructed our interpreter, Johnny Blakelock, to round up several of the best native fishermen in Vairao. There was only one course left, and that was to take natives with us and give them such a good time that they would catch the bait we needed. Bonito were what we had to have. No use trying to hire the natives! They did not love hard work and showed no greed for money. So we tried kindness and friendliness. The natives round Papeete were sullen and somber, ruined by whites. But around on this south side of Tahiti, far removed from the evil and contaminating influences, they were still unspoiled in some degree.

Next morning I was up before sunrise. It was a pearl-and-gold dawn, exquisitely cool and fragrant, and the light on the mountains, the reflection in the water, and the deep, mournful music of the reef made it a place of enchantment. Three native fishermen arrived with their long bamboo poles and pearl-shell gigs. So we started out in three launches, as keen and hopeful again as if failure and disappointment had not dogged us, renewed by that everlasting spirit which is the splendid thing in all true fishermen.

As we neared the corner of the passageway through the reef I felt a shivering atom of humanity appalled by the mighty forces of nature. I could see three green rollers at once—the first crashing thundering to white chaos on the coral barrier, the second lofty, awesome, beautiful, curling its silver crest so that I could see down a long green tunnel—and the third coming grandly, rising, swelling, dark green and ponderous, close on the heels of the wave just breaking. The sound was voluminous, ear-filling—a deep-toned rolling roar.

I wondered how we would ever pass that corner. The middle of the channel, however, was safe, smooth, though it lifted us on mountainous swells. A few hundred yards outside the reef we turned to the left, and running parallel with the reef we began to troll for whatever fish might strike. Outside there it appeared calm. A white line, like a wall, defined the position of the reef. The sea heaved gently. Yet mysteriously out of it, in those few hundred yards, rose the great billows. Seen from behind, they were not frightful, though they made me gasp when they broke. A ship drifting on them to the coral would be kindling-wood in a few moments.

Presently my rod was almost jerked out of my hands. Strike! With a game fish tearing off line I was reminded that the work at hand was fishing. I soon pulled in a small yellow-fin tuna—most brilliantly colored. We ran on. Soon needlefish, large and small, like silver shooting arrows, began to leap across the water. It was most beautiful, even extraordinary, to see. Some were four feet long. They would show at times fully a hundred yards from the boat. Of course they had sighted the feather gigs. These gigs, by the way, had silver heads, and shone far through that transparent water. Then their leaps were prodigious. Some of them thirty feet! Half a dozen needlefish would charge my bait at once. But not even one hit it! When they reached it they discovered the deception. Needlefish make good bait, and their perspicuity was most irritating, especially when the question of bait was so serious.

Soon, however, I had a bite from some kind of hungry and fast fish. He was small and I landed him quickly—a tuna of some species, surely, and absolutely new to me. He was tuna-shaped, though a little thinner and longer at the tail, silvery-white all over except the back, which was blue, and he had very large black eyes. The native with me had a name for him which I did not understand. What was more important to me was the fact that this little fish would make a fine bait for a swordfish.

So we ran out to sea, with me trolling this bait between the two teasers. Captain Mitchell was already far out. I could just see his flag. The swells were large, but not breaking, and they were nice to ride. We had started out to scout for flocks of birds and schools of bonito. The native and Peter were forward on the lookout. But it did not surprise me to be the first to sight dim sea fowl on the horizon, wheeling, circling. We ran out to discover boobies feeding over bait driven to the surface by bonito. Our native got out his long bamboo pole and his shell gig, and began to dance it over the water. He did not raise any bonito, and soon birds and bonito vanished.

Four miles out and somewhat to the eastward of our anchorage I had my first view of the most beautiful part of beautiful Tahiti. Nordhoff and McDonald had not exaggerated the magnificence of the scenery. The eastern end of Tahiti was cut into sharp peaks and deep gorges, all mantled in exquisite soft green. There was not one bare spot of rock. Some of the high peaks held the oncoming tradewind clouds, that resembled grand wreaths of white. For the most part, however, the peaks were bare, clean-cut against the sky. It was a big country, and I knew I could not grasp its true range. But some of the mountains were high, fully five thousand feet, and all spear-pointed. Green shafts towered into the sky; cone-shaped peaks pierced the clouds; knife-edged foothills raised sharp ragged edges to the dominating heights. Some of the clouds were letting down misty veils of gray rain; some of the canyons were full of golden light, others dark in purple shadow. I gazed until my eyes ached, and forgot I was fishing.

Here indeed was the strangest, weirdest, most beautiful, the wildest and grandest background to any sea I had ever fished. I admitted it with reluctance. I hated to uncrown the Galapagos, and rare exotic Cocos, the tropic peaks of Ecuador, and the yellow stepping ranges of Mexico. Not to mention the cold, gray, broken skyline of New Zealand! But I had to do it. This eastern end of Tahiti stunned me.

The hours fly on the ocean, when one is fishing or watching. I did not raise a fish. We did not sight another flock of birds or any more bonito. My eyes were strong, but they were tired from looking. Sunset overtook us on the way in, and it appeared one gorgeous blaze of gold with flecks of silver. I looked right into the sun, until it seemed a molten lake of silver.

Captain Mitchell was in, and full of enthusiasm. "By gad!" he said. "I raised a wolloper of a marlin. But he wouldn't take."

"Did you have any bait?" I asked.

"We caught some bonito. Had to try several schools before we found fish that would strike. These natives can catch them. I think taking them was a grand idea."

"Well, Cappy, old top, if in the end we don't raise and catch fish we'll have the satisfaction that no one can. I think it's some place!"

We got out my books on fish, and my photographs of tuna, three kinds of swordfish, sailfish, wahoo, and others. And we went over them very carefully with the native fishermen, using Johnny Blakelock to interpret for us. I never before had such a bewildering experience. These natives calmly identified every one of the species we presented and did it with no show of excitement or exaggeration or mistake. When they identified the broadbill I threw up my hands, and when they voluntarily informed us that there was a swordfish off Vairao with bill forming the lower jaw—then I simply threw a fit.

The native I had taken with me—a smiling, keen fellow—could speak a little English.

"All same feesh here," he vowed, indicating my photographs. "Not many now. October—November—December—plenty big feesh!"

I could not stand much more, so sent them forward to get supper.

"Johnny," I said, to our Tahitian interpreter, "I'm afraid these men are telling us these fish stories—just to please us."

"Natives like to please, I know," admitted Johnny. "But I advised these men to tell the truth—that they would profit by it. I'm sure they didn't lie. I believe them."

"Why then have the traders—and white men—no knowledge of these great fish?"

"They never saw them. They don't know anything about them," said Johnny. "But the natives have seen them while out in their canoes. They tell me once in a while they spear a big fish and hook one on their hand lines. These fish always break away."

"Well, by gosh!" I exclaimed, baffled. "It's too good to be true. . . . I wish R. C. had not gone back to Avalon."

Next day, July 4th, we left the schooner flying streamers of flags, and these, with the white hull against the background of golden green, made a brave and bright picture.

This time I took Harry, the cabin boy, with me and let him hold a light rod. He was not only wild to catch a fish, but also quite wild in his handling of a rod. The swell on the reef was low this day, allowing us to run closer. Right off Harry began to have strikes. Then he hooked a fish that got away. Presently he was into another, something which flashed like a bright silver shield when it hit the gig. It leaped, disclosing the long, slim, silver shape of a wahoo. Our native fisherman called it *ono*. It was a big one, eight feet long, and I was about to take the rod from Harry when it tore loose. We went on, and I began to have that comfortable pleasant thrill occasioned by the discovery of fish. A few hundred yards farther on Harry had another fine strike. The fish hooked himself and ran off line. By dint of much patience and force I kept Harry connected with this fish, which turned out to be another wahoo. He landed it—a fine wahoo of thirty-two pounds. Harry was white and shaking, and wet with sweat, and his eyes stuck out so you could have hung your hat on them. His language was incoherent.

This wahoo was almost identical with the wahoo of the Gulf Stream, called *peto* in the Bahamas. In 1912 I caught the first one ever landed at Long Key. It caused a sensation. Several years later another was caught. In 1917 I got two more. Of late years these are not so rare and a few are caught every year. The wahoo is a member of the mackerel family, and he is built for speed. He is the swiftest fish in the ocean for short distances, even beating the *coryphene* (dolphin), which is certainly going some, as Romer would be wont to say.

Harry hooked another, and when it ran close to us and poked its head out of the water he pulled so strenuously that he tore loose the heavy silver-headed gig. This came toward us like a bullet, and struck me hard in the chest. Funny and singular things happen while fishing.

"Harry," I said, "if you are going to shoot at me with fishing-tackle and endanger my life, I shall find it advisable to leave you on the ship."

"Oh, Mr. Grey!" he exclaimed, tragically, "I—I didn't do that on purpose!"

Shortly afterward I hooked a fine wahoo on my bait tackle, which was light for such a fish, but it gave him freedom enough to run and jump, which he did most spectacularly.

Next Peter got tangled up with something big and had to work hard to land it. Before we saw it I was sure it was a tuna. It turned out to be one of the species I had named dog-tooth tuna, a splendid specimen of sixty pounds, the largest we had taken. The natives told me this fish, as also the *ono*, grew very large. It was a fascinating thing to have these natives corroborate what we had learned in the Paumotus.

We worked out to sea, keeping a lookout for birds and bait. I trolled a rotten mullet that any fish would have scorned. In the afternoon Captain Mitchell ran up on us, and his men threw me two fine fresh bonito.

"Caught nine," he called. "Lots of fun. I got one myself. . . . Raised a marlin, too."

The late afternoon was not only the most beautiful time of the day for fishing, but it seemed the best. There was the pageant of peaks and clouds to entrance me, and flocks of birds and schools of bonito showed up at intervals.

It seemed to me that I was looking right at my bait as it slid over the water, when it disappeared in a sharp splash. Then as I dropped my rod the line whizzed off my reel. *Strike!* Francis threw out the clutches, we glided to a stop, and my line paid out. The bait was large and I wanted the fish to have time enough to get it in his mouth. But suddenly he shot up some hundred feet astern, a good husky marlin, white and black in color, and most marvelously swift and savage. Frantically I pumped and wound to get in the slack line and come up on his weight. But he was sliding toward us, two-thirds out, and coming like an express train. He gave his head violent jerks. I knew he would throw the hook before I could get it fast in him. And he did.

"*Mucho malo!*" I said to the native. He understood my tone, if not my words. The remarkable thing about this incident was that the marlin, after coming up, never went down until he had rid himself of the hook.

It was late that evening when Captain Mitchell and I compared notes. He had had a strike and had missed it clean.

"We may just be having unprecedented bad luck," I said. "But I've begun to think otherwise. The conditions are different here. The fish are not the same we have had experience with. I suspect we are up against a harder game."

"By gad! we'll get them, anyhow!" he exclaimed. "We're raising them."

"It's a case of running the wheels off the boats, and sticking at it. That's all."

Next day of nine hours was a blank one for Captain Mitchell, and he looked fagged. I had to report that late in the afternoon I had raised a marlin to the teasers, got him to take a bait, and was just about to hook him when he came out, swinging the bait round his head. He had spat it out, but the leader was still between his jaws. Coming toward me, he plunged down, then lunged up, swinging the bonito higher and farther. He was over two hundred pounds, silver underneath and black or blue on the back. I observed a straight, clearly defined line down his broad side where blue and silver met.

"Run the other way, you joker!" yelled Francis at the marlin as he threw the launch into full speed ahead.

I simply could not wind the line tight. If I could have done so I would have pulled the leader through his jaws and hooked him on the outside, as we very often hook marlin. But it was not to be. That agile and cunning swordfish in a final splashing flurry threw the bait and hook a mile. I wound in ruefully.

"Well, as long as they show us up this way we can't kick," I said, forced to admiration.

On July 7th, I took Harry with me again. He was a most terrible fisherman, but he coaxed to go and averred he would bring me good luck.

On the way out by the reef we trolled our feather gigs. I was watching the needlefish leaping like slim greyhounds when I heard a peculiar sliddery sound and then a whiz. Harry screamed. I looked up to the left, and I saw my green teaser tumbling in the air, higher than my head, and above it a magnificent wahoo, level, with curled tail, wolf-like nose and gleaming black eye. Fifteen feet above the water! He was not a fish, but a bird. Down he dove slick as a knife blade. He had bit the teaser hard, with such force that it and himself had gone high into the air.

"By gum! When am I gonna quit being surprised round here," I said, facetiously.

We caught a bait early and I dragged it all over the sea, fully seventy miles. After early morning we never sighted the *Sky Blue* once. Late afternoon we ran shoreward. The sun sank behind Tahiti, wondrous to behold. The swift cold shadows enveloped the mountains.

I was not looking at my bait when something hit it viciously with a great splash. But Harry saw. "Big black fin!" he yelled.

Grimly I bent over my reel and watched the line as it slid swiftly off into the water. It was hard to choose the right instant to strike. These Tahitian swordfish had us guessing. I did not let this fellow go so far. And when I struck him the solid weight lifted me from my seat. I did not look up until I knew I had this one hooked for keeps. And when he began his aquaplane stunts I was not worried, though I kept the line tight. Harry yelled all through these pyrotechnics. He was quite demented. They did not last long. Then this marlin sounded deep—several hundred feet—and he stayed down, which was certainly a new way for a marlin to comport himself.

While I was fighting him Captain Mitchell came up and yelled: "Hand it to him, old man. He'll be the first one for these waters."

"Put a bait over," I yelled back. "There might be another one."

Cappy did so and let his line out, while his boatman ran the launch slowly, evidently meaning to make a wide circle round me. But he scarcely got started. Something happened and I guessed it.

"Hey, Doc! I got a bite!" yelled Captain.

"Fine! Fine!" I yelled back.

It was now nearly dark and I had my own troubles. So I could not watch Captain Mitchell. Francis told me presently that Cappy had hooked and lost the fish. I had all I wanted pumping my swordfish up. He was stubborn and strong and fought in a circle, which was another new one on me. But soon I pulled him up and held fast, and while he was plunging and ploughing the water into caldron Peter gaffed him, and that was the end of that. We hauled him on board and ran shipward over a darkening sea, with a lovely afterglow softening the west.

"What do you think?" queried Cappy, seriously, when we reached the *Fisherman*. "I sure had one on. By gad! I'm glad you landed that plugger. Shake, old man, on the first marlin caught in these waters. It means a lot to Tahiti."

"What happened to you?" I asked.

"Well, when you told me to drop my bait over I did so, just for fun. Didn't expect anything. But I had a dandy strike. A slow, heavy, easy take. You know the kind! He loafed around. When I hooked him it felt as if I had the bottom. Slowly he came to the surface, stuck up a short, heavy, club-like bill, gave his enormous head a wag—and sent the hook flying back to me. He was like a black marlin and at the very least five hundred pounds."

"Good Heavens! Cappy, what *are* we up against?" I ejaculated, elated and aghast.

"By gad! I don't know, but it's a lot."

"Well. . . . Let's look at my fish," I said.

The marlin weighed 170 pounds. We laid him on deck in the bright lights and studied him closely. He was short and compact, very shapely and round. His bill was short and slim; his fins delicate and small; his flukes wide and powerful. His back looked jet black and the line where it met the silver was straight down the center of his broad side—the median line, in fact—surely another species of the class *Tetrapturus*.

CHAPTER FIVE

THE morning was delightfully cool, fresh, sweet with odors of fruit and flowers. Native canoes flocked around the ship, and numerous natives came aboard to give us presents of ferns and cocoanuts and bouquets, and to sell *hula* costumes made of colored fiber from trees, and pearl shells, native trinkets.

When the sun peeped over the high green hill that hid the mountains from my view the day changed. It grew hot and bright. Already I was tanned to the hue of a native, and liked the feel of sun and rain on my bare arms and shoulders.

We went out at the usual hour and began our scout for birds and bait. They were scarce. We had to waste all morning up until one o'clock before I had anything to troll. Still the time passed swiftly. By afternoon the veils of clouds had reached from the peaks out over the sea, and we had rain and sun alternately, and wind and calm. There was always a glorious procession of clouds and shadows over mountain and canyon, and everywhere I chose to look rainbows—rainbows—rainbows. There was one grand rainbow that sheered down from the purple clouds right into the midst of the depths of the mountain canyons. On the horizon rainbows short and long, shone dimly. The mountain kingdom held me for hours. I was fishing, but every moment I gazed up at this spectacle, always different, always tropic, always a marvelous varying combination of tropic hues—green and gold, purple and pearl, white and gray, of the most perfect softness and richess. Sometimes I could see three waterfalls sliding like downward lace from dark green notches. The deep canyons lured with their verdant mystery.

I got back to the *Fisherman* after dark. So far as fish went it had been a blank day for me. Captain Mitchell had hit it lucky. He had raised three marlin, the first of which, a large one, had savagely charged his bait, utterly fearless of the boat, and had smashed it off in one bite. When he put over a second bait almost immediately he had another strike. Captain hooked this fish, but it made such an amazing and powerful run that it tore free. Then he put on his third and last bait, and dropped it over. The leader was still in his hands when he saw a third marlin loom out of the blue depths. The fish took the bait and made off with it. Captain Mitchell hooked this one so that it could not get away. It made a tremendous display on the surface, and then sounded deep and stayed down. He had an extremely hard fight with it, upward of two hours. "By gad! I wouldn't like to tackle more than two of these birds in one day."

The swordfish weighed 206 pounds, and appeared to be perfectly built for speed and endurance. We had not marked a single blemish or parasite on either of the two swordfish we had caught.

This day ran our score of raised or sighted large game fish to twenty-nine.

Next morning was cloudy and wet. We stayed aboard, working over tackle, hoping it would clear toward afternoon. After lunch the showers ceased and we went out, the three boats manned as usual with anglers, boatmen, natives, and camera men.

The wind came from the southwest, something new for us there. But the sea was fairly smooth and birds were working. The prospects looked good. While my boat worked round a school of bonito, Captain Mitchell drew away some little distance. Soon then my sharp eye caught the waving of a flag on his boat.

"Boys, something doing on Cap's boat. Hook up!" I called.

If there was anything the boatmen, especially Francis, liked to do well, it was to hook up those two engines and go like the wind. But it always scared me, we went so fast. In less than five minutes we sped down upon the Captain. I found him fighting a fish. As it was straight down and deep, we ran up close.

"Hey, old top, why all this excitement?" I called.

"I've been into three swordfish here," he replied. "This is the third. The first was an enormous fish. He didn't run. He just crushed my bait off. I hooked a second, which threw the hook.

Then I got fast to this one. Looks like I'll hold him. Troll around. There are fish here."

"You lucky son-of-a-gun!" I shouted. "Three fish again! I've begun to be crazy about this place."

"If you see a swordfish like that first one you'll jump overboard," he replied.

"Well, Cap, a fish on your line is worth a lot of loose ones. Hang on to him."

Whereupon I went to trolling. My bait had been on ice all night and was fairly good, but not fresh enough to satisfy me. Presently I raised a medium-sized swordfish that took a sniff at my bait and refused it. We circled, trying to raise him again, and hung in that vicinity until Captain landed his fish—a fine marlin larger than his first.

We then made the discovery that a storm was sweeping down upon us. The mountains were hid in a black pall and a wall of gray rain came roaring at us. We headed for the ship, and in a few moments were overtaken by such a torrent of rain as I had never seen before anywhere. We could not see fifty feet ahead, and completely lost sight of Captain Mitchell for some time. The sea was beaten down flat, for which I was grateful. We went so fast that the spray flew aft and wet my face. It was warm and salty. But the rain, in great contrast, was cold and stinging, like sleet. Soon we were drenched to the skin. Rubber coats were no protection against that downpour. It took an hour to run to the ship, and when we arrived we were a pretty miserable bunch. The storm, of course, let up as soon as we got back.

After changing into warm dry clothes I went out to see Captain's fish. It was a beauty—238 pounds—with all the features noted in the others. Captain Mitchell waved an emphatic hand at the fish.

"That marlin isn't one-third the size of the first one," he vouchsafed.

"Cappy, please be serious," I expostulated. "This thing is getting on my nerves. I'm afraid this Tahitian climate is affecting you."

"Nonsense!" fumed Captain Mitchell, who always took me literally. "I'm as clear-headed as a bell."

"How do you know that swordfish was three times as big as this one?" I asked.

"By gad! I *saw* him, that's how. He sailed up behind the teasers slow and easy, like a big barge. He had his pectorals spread. Oh, he was a sight. He mashed my bonito off and came on for more. When I got another ready I lost sight of the big fellow. Pretty soon I had a strike—we never moved the boat—and I hooked the fish. He leaped and got away. But he wasn't the first one by a long shot!"

"Was your bait fresh?" I asked.

"No. It was pretty soft. But these fish were hungry. And they wanted it."

"I'm half convinced that we've discovered another great fishing-ground."

"By gad! I'm wholly convinced. I *know* it. Why, these natives on my boat were not even excited when I raised those fish. They are used to seeing them. And they kept saying: 'Plenty big feesh. October—November—December!' We've struck the off season. What do you suppose the right season would be like?"

"I'm afraid to think," I replied, thoughtfully.

The next day was beautiful. The sea was one huge dark-blue ripple. I trolled a fine fresh bait—small tuna—for three hours. Then I laid my rod down to take a photograph of the mountains. Splash! Strike! I dove for the rod. I had removed my gloves, and when I hook a fish I always need gloves on. It takes violent action. In this case the fish came up before I tried to hook him. Nevertheless, I pulled tight on him and he started off with a rush, to shoot up on the surface, turn toward the boat, and slide on his side, wagging his head until he had freed himself from the obnoxious hook. Lost! I had to admit to the boys that owing to the desire to take a picture I had balled-up this fine strike.

Every day at Vairao seemed different. The sea changed like the sky. Never, however, was there a moment without the moan and boom of the surf on the reef. This morning such a storm of sound rolled in from the coral as I never heard equaled in my life.

Outside there was a heavy sea running. The great swells resembled hills of a rolling prairie or ridges of the desert. Several miles out they spread and lengthened so that we found it possible to fish. Yet it seemed perfectly absurd. The oncoming upward slant of a league-long swell looked like a mountain bearing down upon us. Yet slowly we rose with the invisible force of the wave, up and up, high and higher, until we rode the very top.

Clouds drifted out over us and let down a little mist of rain. We trolled out and in, everywhere, and about noon the boys yelled in unison, "Swordfish!"

I saw it pass us some fifty feet away, clear in a wave. He turned and followed the boat, evidently attracted by our teasers, but he did not come close, and wavering in the blue he faded out of sight. This was a bigger swordfish than any our boat had sighted. We kept on trolling.

About mid-afternoon Peter yelled out, "Flag waving in Captain's boat!" Indeed there was—a frantic flag. We flew over those tremendous swells as if our boat had wings, and soon bore down upon Captain, who was laboring on his rod.

George, his boatman, who had waved the flag for us, stood up and called:

"Thunderin' big fish of some kind. Think it's a shark. It was yellow. Followed us way back an' wouldn't come close. We stopped an' let the bait back. It sank an' the fish took it. We've not seen him since."

This statement from George had to be taken for what it was worth. But it was not convincing to me. I had to see for myself. The Captain's incredible luck was a factor always to be considered. I saw that he had hooked something heavy, and I was very sorry to see that it was on the English Hardy steel-center 39-test rod, which had been designed by Alma Baker. Now Baker is a theorist, not a practical angler. He had never fought any giant fish. I did not trust any of these Hardy salt-water rods. The light ones were too thin, the heavy ones too stiff. It took only a glance for me to see that Captain could not bend this steel-center rod to any advantage. What little it did bend was near the tip—bad for a heavy fish.

"Boys, if that fish is really big—good night!" I said to my boatmen. And to the Captain I shouted: "Play safe. Wait till we see what it is. And don't trust that rod."

"It's an old shark," called back Mitchell, hauling away.

"But, Cappy, if you didn't see it you can't be sure," I protested.

Here Francis chipped in, "Bet it's an old reremai."

Captain heard this and perhaps it offset my caution. The reremai is a nasty shark that occasionally we hook in New Zealand waters.

"Peter, what do you think?" I appealed to my elder boatman, who as a whaler had been years on the sea.

"Reckon they're right. Fish stays down deep and he's slow," replied Peter.

I was chagrined. For a few moments I stood up and watched Captain Mitchell's rod. Then I bent keen eyes on the line. After a little it swept out and up toward the surface, and slowly sank again. Presently the fish repeated this movement, and for a moment I believed he might come up to the surface. But he sank again. All the time Mitchell was hauling strenuously.

"How long has that fish been on?" I shouted to George.

"Half an hour or more. I waved the flag several times before you saw it."

"Has the fish been acting that way all the time?"

"Yes, except for a big run at first."

That decided me, and I had Francis run closer to the *Sky Blue*. I cupped my hands to make my voice carry.

"Cappy, you're on a thundering big swordfish. For Heaven's sake play safe! Let up. Ease the drag. That damned rod is no good. It won't bend."

My earnest, almost authoritative words did not convince Captain Mitchell. He was red in the face, and angry at this stubborn fish, and bent on pulling his head off. Nevertheless, he ceased to work so violently, and for a little while I was hopeful. After a while I repeated my advice. There was need of it. Captain Mitchell was a powerful man, and in pumping up a fish he would raise the tip of the rod too high, and he never looked to see what his rod was doing. It was this fault that had broken dozens of rods for him.

"Nipper," said Peter to Francis, who was his nephew, "Mr. Grey is right. That's no shark."

Francis laughed. "Wait and you'll see."

So we were a divided lot of anglers and boatmen. I deplored this and intuitively sensed calamity. And I fought against it.

"Cap, please listen," I called. "That iron rod is N. G. You'll break him off. Maybe this is the very fish we want so badly."

Captain kept on hauling, nay, pumping hard, with a solid drag and a crowbar for a rod. I could hear the line screech and rasp on the reel. The sea was heavy and the fish difficult to hold. No need for us to be told that Mitchell was in trouble.

I watched the line. Again it swept out away from the boat and, lengthening in our sight, began to rise to the surface.

"By gorry! the joker's coming up!" shouted Francis, suddenly awakening.

Then came a bulge on the surface, a sort of swirl, and then a large round spout of water, out of which heaved a bill and a head that might have belonged to a rhinoceros. In fact, the long spear, curved upward, was decidedly like that of the African beast.

"Oh—he's a monster marlin!" screamed Francis, wildly.

The swordfish heaved out slowly, two-thirds of his length. He was a gleaming blue on his broad back, as wide and round as that of a large horse. His dorsal was short and long. His sides were green and white with wide bars of purple. I was speechless, paralyzed. Such a swordfish I had never even dreamed of. It took only a glance to see he was far larger than Captain Mitchell's 976-pound marlin, captured in New Zealand. With tremendous sullen surge the swordfish sank and sounded. I found my voice.

"What did I tell you?" I roared at Mitchell. "*Now* will you be careful?"

By this time Captain looked scared. His eyes stuck out. "Hey!" he panted. "Did you see—what I saw?"

"See? I nearly fell overboard!" I shouted. "Cap, it's the chance of our lives. That's a new kind of swordfish."

For a while we were an excited group. Middleton had run up close in the *Red* and his face was shining as always when he had turned his camera on something good.

"Nailed him on the film," he yelled.

"Careful now. Watch. Don't get close. You might run over the line," I replied. "And listen. I'll yell when the fish is coming up."

Picking a favorable opportunity when the swordfish was down deep, we ran close to the *Sky Blue* and put Peter aboard with his big gaff. For a moment this procedure inspired me with hope, because there never was a cooler and stronger man with a gaff than this whaler Peter. We hung off a hundred yards or so and I got out my camera. But even with the prospect of an extraordinary picture in sight I could not keep from worrying. In half an hour Mitchell was working as wildly as ever. I had to run close to warn him for a last time. I cussed the rod fervidly, and when I saw that the reel was also the Hardy Alma type holding only 450 yards of thirty-nine line, I cussed that, too. I bit my tongue to keep from including Mitchell. He had a Coxe reel holding 600 yards of thirty-nine, and one of the great Murphy hickory rods, which I had given him; and here he was tied up to the grandest of swordfish on tackle hopelessly inadequate. It was sickening. I sensed disaster more and more. I knew he could never land that fish, and I never wanted anything so badly. Perhaps if I had not been so poignantly affected I could have used my fishing wits to better advantage and have prepared for any contingency. But I lost my coolness. Everything tended to make me do so. Francis almost wept as he said, "Oh, if you only had that fish on your big tackle!"

"Look, Frank! He's coming up," I cried, bending to my camera.

When the swordfish broke water I was bending over the finder and did not see what made my companions yell madly. I snapped the camera. Then the swordfish swished again on the surface, this time with head and tail out. The distance between that head and tail was incredible. The upper lobe of the tail was all that showed. It was scimiter shaped, dark blue, and four feet high. When I saw that powerful sweeping half of tail I swallowed hard and found my mouth too dry for speech. The next break of the swordfish I did not see. The bow of my boat obstructed my view. But Francis saw, and he actually let go the wheel and waved his hands in gesture more eloquent than any words. Then he pointed: "Look at the blood! He's hooked deep. It must be pouring out of him."

As he moved the launch around I saw a dark cloud in the water. It spread to an enormous size, discoloring the surface for many yards. I tried to encourage Captain Mitchell by calling attention to this. No swordfish could bleed like that and stand it for long. Presently he would sound and then ——!

The swordfish, like the others we had fought, milled round in a circle. He did not appear to have an objective, unless it was the bottom of the ocean. He would go down several hundred feet and then change his mind—no doubt owing to the terrific strain—and slowly come up. It was a slow, terrific battle, yet the time flew. We kept dancing about to stay and still avoid any risk of hampering the other boatman.

For a new hand, George, who was the chief engineer, certainly did well. But he might have made it easier for the Captain if he had had more experience. This aspect of the situation bothered Francis, and he kept calling my attention to George's failure to ease the position for Captain Mitchell. But Cappy was ignorant of this. All he knew was that he had on a terrible fish. I tried not to watch that rod. I shrank every time the tip bent. There was no spring whatever. I had no idea what Alma Baker meant by thirty-nine-test curve, but it was plain that the middle of the rod was stiff and the tip gave a little. Every time it bent I groaned. The grand swordfish came up again. He was too ponderously heavy to leap. He could not get out. We never saw the depth of his gleaming sides. We could see the wide round shoulders; we could guess at his length. But no doubt the magnificence of this fish made us inaccurate. We were far more likely to underestimate his size than to overestimate. I saw a flood of dark red blood pouring from his gills. When he sank he left the water red.

Then he began to sound. I saw it and had Francis run the boat close. Captain could not stem that steady descent. Down and down the swordfish went, until I feared to ask how much line he had off. Peter waved a hopeless hand at me. But the swordfish stopped. Again the doughty angler labored to raise him, and in due time he did so. I began to be hopeful in spite of all the array of facts against success here. It is impossible to be a true fisherman and not be hopeful.

Cappy performed so valiantly and the swordfish helped so materially that the leader was hauled up until the swivel touched the tip. Mitchell could not wind the line farther. I saw Peter stretch out his hand to grasp the leader. He drew it back. Then he stretched it again, as if impelled. But he did not take hold of it. He looked down into the water, and his posture was so intense and stiff that I realized he was gazing at a marvelous fish. I was dumb myself. The thing to have done was for Captain Mitchell to tell Peter to haul on the leader, bring the fish up within reach of the gaff. It could have been done. Swordfish, once they are coming up, will come, or can be drawn to the surface for an instant before they dive. I understood Peter. He dared not take the responsibility, and either the Captain failed to recognize the opportunity or feared to take it. The moment was heart-rendering for everybody, me most of all. This time when I longed to command Peter to take a chance —of course there was risk of breaking the hook loose—I could not get the words out. I too was inhibited by the fear of losing the fish. Nevertheless, even at that precise and poignant moment I knew it was the game to take the chance.

Perhaps for ten seconds the swordfish was still. Then he got his head again and dove. He sounded by slow stages—that was to say, he would take a few yards every move, and as these grew slower and shorter the loss of line was less. At last he must have had out half the line when Captain tried to hold him. This would not have been my procedure. I would have let him go. No doubt, Cappy, owing to his short line of only 450 yards, was afraid of this.

Anyway, suddenly the rod broke off squarely. I saw the six inches of tip slide down the line into the water. I threw up my hands in despair. Captain was now hopelessly up against it. He labored as before, only he seemed a pretty tired man. The rod was now a stiff straight poker. He could not recover any line with it, and every instant, as the fish kept sounding, there was more danger of breaking it.

I awoke to the crisis. Something had to be done quickly. Many great fish I had saved in extremities, and though this case seemed utterly hopeless, there was still a chance.

"Peter," I yelled through my hands. "Get hold of the line. Hold hard, but let it slip through."

Peter was quick to do as bidden. Captain lowered the broken rod on the gunwale. I began to tear line off my reel, calling at the same time to ask how far down the swordfish was.

"Three hundred yards," shouted Cappy.

I spun my reel to get the line off. It back lashed. How slow I seemed getting line off! I wanted to run off four hundred yards, then hand the rod to Mitchell, and tell Peter to cut the Captain's line and tie it on to mine. This would work, if I could be quick enough. I worked frantically.

"Hang on Peter," I called. "We've got a chance yet. Hold just hard enough not to break him off. I'll have another rod for Cap in a jiffy. . . . How much line has he off?"

"Three hundred and fifty," came the answer.

"Francis, this will never do. Hook up and run off fast, then come back," I said, desperately.

In an instant we were shooting full speed away from Captain's boat. I had thrown the coils of line I had reeled off into the water. And as we raced away the line on my reel appeared to melt.

"Fine, Nipper. Now run back!" He made the water fly on our return, and when we slowed down to go alongside Captain's boat I cut my line, and handed the rod over to Peter, who reached it to Captain.

"Now, Peter, cut Captain's line above where you're holding it and tie it on to mine."

"Aye sir. Reckon we'll have time," replied the whaler, coolly. "No better man for that hazardous task could have been found!"

"Cap, how far is he down?" I queried.

"Four hundred thirty yards."

"Over twelve hundred feet! It'll kill him! If only ———"

Then I grew mute. Peter held that fish momentarily with one hand, and cut Cappy's line and tied it to mine with the other. Deftly, swiftly it was done. I would have whooped if I could have found utterance. Peter let go of the line. I saw the dry white line where it was tied on to the wet slip down into the water. But scarcely had I drawn a breath in recovering from that breathless moment when the white line broke.

If there ever was a supreme tragic fishing moment that was it. Captain stood up like a soldier to take his sentence.

"Too late, old man. He's beaten us. . . . My God! what a fish!"

"Oh, Cappy—how awful!" I returned, hoarsely, and fell back into my chair.

Upon my arrival at the ship I found Captain had gotten there ahead of me. He looked composed, but I could tell what a blow this defeat had been. I had not yet recovered, and doubted that I ever would.

"Mitchell, how big was that swordfish?" I asked, bluntly.

"Fifteen hundred pounds. He was very much larger than my black marlin."

"I hope this will be a lesson to you."

Captain was silent. Evidently he had fortified himself. I hated to lecture him, but felt forced to do it.

"Naturally, as an Englishman, you prefer English things, fishing-tackle especially. But that Hardy Alma Baker outfit was far from being up to this fight. With the Coxe reel and Murphy hickory, you *might* have got this swordfish."

"I know it, old man. And it hurts like hell," he said, feelingly.

That softened me. "Well, even as it was I could have saved your fish. In the excitement and hurry I gave you the wrong rod. I had not used the line on that rod for days. It had not been wet for days. It was weak. I should have remembered this. I think I did remember. But it ran through my mind that the guides on the big rod might not have let a hurriedly tied knot pass through. That was my mistake. And it hurts *me* like hell."

"Mr. Grey, we all made mistakes," spoke up Peter, in his calm way. "Reckon that was natural. We never had any fish like this one. Even that twelve-hundred-pound mako Captain Mitchell hooked in New Zealand was a baby compared with this fish. I never dreamed of a swordfish so big. Mind you I had a good long look at him, in clear still water, not very far down. He was eighteen or twenty feet in length, not counting his bill, and thick as a barrel all the way down to his tail. With that length and width he must have been comparatively deep. He made Captain's nine-hundred-pound black marlin look small."

"Is—it—possible, Peter," I gasped, faintly. I had great confidence in this whaler's coolness and judgment.

"It's a fact, Mr. Grey. I've had time to think it all out. I wouldn't make a guess as to his weight. But he was a new species of swordfish, far larger than we had any idea swordfish grew."

"Peter, you said we all made mistakes?"

"Yes. I made one. When the leader came up I should have asked Captain to let me take it and have a go at the swordfish. I think I could have pulled him up within reach of the gaff. But I was afraid to suggest it, because if I had lost him ——"

"We understand, Peter," returned Captain Mitchell, putting a kind hand on Peter's broad shoulder. "The fault was not yours, but mine. I should have ordered you to have a go at him."

"Peter, he's right," I added. "I saw the chance just as you saw it. But I was dumb. It was Captain Mitchell's place to tell you to take the risk."

"Too bad! He was some fish," sighed the whaler.

We talked long after dark. The loss had affected everyone on the ship except our native boatmen. These were not in the least upset.

"Come back, October, November, December. Plenty big feesh!" they repeated until that became at once a joke, an inspiration, a solace to us. To me it was almost a fetish.

As I walked away to be alone I overheard one of the bright wits on board deliver this remark: "Well, it must have been tough on the Captain to lose such a fish. But it will cost the boss one hundred thousand dollars. He'll come back here and catch one or die. Pretty expensive fish, I'll say."

As I leaned over the rail aft in the darkness I had to laugh. I was sorely afraid the speaker had the situation sized up correctly. Yet what a magnificent thrill the idea stirred!

A heavy sea and a full tide thundered out on the reef. The grandest of grand music! I listened for long with nothing except the delight of sensorial perception. Then the sound provoked thought. This night there came a far louder and deeper detonation, owing to the full-moon tide and the swell from windward. I could not realize it. The reef was a straight wall of coral, just awash at high tide. From the bottom of the wall the sea floor sloped quickly into very deep water. When the wonderful swells rose, backed by the vast Pacific, and rolled with stupendous volume and motion in upon miles of reef, they gave rise to a breaking, cutting, cracking, booming, hollow thunder. It ran along the reef here and there. But somewhere it was always terrific, shaking the coral shore. It was an appalling sound, most mighty and infinite and awe-inspiring of anything I had heard in nature.

A full moon soared over the dark hills. It rose into a green sky and spread a lightness as of weird day. On shore the red fires of the natives, burning cocoanut shells and leaves, shone out of the black shadows. The palms clustered along the shore, silent, drooping, graceful, beautiful.

If there was singing on shore, as usual, I could not hear it for the strife of sea and reef. Likewise the ship seemed silent as a tomb. The line of surf shone like a rising, falling wall of pearl. And steadily from it rolled the mighty rhythmic music, with its note of eternal melancholy.

CHAPTER SIX

IT WOULD be impossible to describe the feelings of an angler for big game of the sea who had hooked or seen a swordfish such as this. I called it a long-speared marlin—giant Tahitian striped marlin. Where there was one of these fish there would be more, and always a bigger one. How tremendous the impetus and stimulus to go on fishing!

July 12 was a hot, glaring, clear day. The swell had moderated. I did not put up the beach umbrella we had in the *Loren G*. In fact, I had not used it lately. I burned up. My naked arms, shoulders, neck grew blacker. Yet that sun felt good.

After nine hours of trolling I saw a bit of blue flash behind my bait. The light was bad. I had caught just a glimpse, as of the tip of a swordfish tail. I leaped up. Nothing in sight. But I stopped the launch and let my bait drift back and sink down deep. Something took it and shot off like a bullet. He came up with a bounce —a fine swordfish—and flung my hook back at me.

The following was a perfect day, like the weather at Zihautenejo, on the Mexican coast. We had no bait. After hours of fishing, Peter caught a tuna. I put it on alive and let it down. Soon I had a moving, tugging fish as heavy as a submarine. Presently it bit through the leader. Shark! I would like to have seen him.

Captain M. ran off shore miles. Raised four marlin, one of them over 500 pounds, all of which refused rotten bait. On the way in the natives caught a bonito. Cappy trolled that in, to raise a marlin, and catch him—204 pounds.

We had now increased the number of seen or raised large game fish to forty. This was the off season. In view of that it seemed a remarkable showing. Better than New Zealand!

July 14.—We went out before sunrise this morning. No bait.

The seas were heavy again. We ran around until two o'clock before we caught a fresh bait. At five o'clock I raised a swordfish. He was small, very swift, yellowish in color, leary of the boat. And he quit us. But I let my bait out, and manipulated it so he struck. When I hooked this one he catapulted himself into the air, and in as wonderful a run as I ever saw on the surface he took 400 yards of line, went down, and gave me the very devil of a time fighting him up. My fish weighed 130 pounds. It was difficult to look at his small size and believe he made the fight he did.

July 15.—This was the same kind of a day, only somewhat rougher. No bait. I wondered how many fishermen would have gone out day after day, into all kinds of weather, without bait.

About 1.30 we ran upon a school of bonito, and the two natives in the *Red* caught fifteen bonito. They sure were good to look at. As we went on trolling the sea roughened until it was pretty bad. All the time the spray came over. It was warm, and there was nothing in being wet. I stuck it out. As far as the Captain was concerned, his middle name was stick. I often told him he did not know when to quit. But there are virtues or gifts or hallucinations imperatively necessary to the angler who has ambitions to catch great game fish.

At 4.30 I had a fine strike. None of us saw the fish break as he took the bait, but he surely made a fuss about it. I let him run. Then jerked too soon. It was a case of being afraid he would shoot up quickly and fling my hook. However, he got my bait. As I was putting on another bonito a large swordfish flashed by under the boat. He did not come back for the bait. I was inclined to believe this fish was a second one.

The boatmen were weary of the long drill, and I decided to call it a day and go in. The sunset turned out to be the most gorgeous I had watched. Great masses of gold clouds overhung the peaks. A rainbow shone resplendent through the mists of golden rain. Around the horizon a vast fleet of trade-wind clouds, like ships, seemed to be passing in review. Soon the sea was one golden glory of marvelous light.

Captain Mitchell reached the ship after dark. He had raised four marlin, remarkable to state, just outside the reef, and just after sunset. He had only two baits, and he had four strikes on these. Both baits were torn in half by the voracious swordfish. He hooked only one, and this one did not stay with him long.

July 16.—It was a cloudy day, with the mountains draped in veils of gray rain. What was left of the rough yesterday was a sea of high heaving swells—the kind that make fighting a heavy fish something torturing.

Early we raised two swordfish. I was looking right at my bait sliding over the water. I saw the splash when the first fish struck, but I did not see him. It was a mystery to me how that big marlin could be so swift and slick as to evade a sharp eye.

This swordfish took my bait and ran off slowly, came back, ran under the boat so that Francis saw my line, circled us, came on, and showed his purple fin.

The second fish took the other bait, but the native who held the rod could not release the drag in time, or else he inadvertently put it on. Anyway, the swordfish did not have a free line and he let go.

I hooked my fish until I knew he never could shake the hook. Then I waited for developments, expecting the usual rush to the surface. He swam around slowly, and once we saw him. I took him to be pretty large. He sounded to a depth of seven or eight hundred feet, and there he hung for two hours and forty-five minutes of toil for me.

At last I brought him up, and both Francis and Peter, at sight of him, let out yells of wonder and pleasure. It was a bronze-colored, dark-striped New Zealand swordfish—very long and big-framed, but thin. I thought he would go 400 pounds and so did Peter.

We went on fishing and soon raised two more, one large and one small. The smaller stayed up and rode the swells, while the larger vanished. We stopped and let my bait back. No good. The swordfish would not take it. Then we ran on. He charged my bait again, ran all around it, darted, sailed at it, and suddenly actually snagged himself under the bill. When I felt the tug I snapped on the drag. Up he wagged in a bloody spray. Then he was off like an express train, and we had to chase him all over the ocean. This was the first fish I ever had on that jumped at a distance of 400 yards from the boat. With that much line to drag, he displayed

NATIVES DRAWING NET

In the Tahitian Jungle

exceeding power. Indeed, he ran so fiercely that he exhausted himself and I was not so long in landing him. This was another of the silver-and-blue swordfish.

Soon after that I raised still another marlin. As he sheered away with my bait we saw a companion swordfish, or took something for one. It disappeared. Then my fish let go the bait. But soon he took it again—or I thought so, for I had a good hard strike. Soon I was fast to him. A heavy sea was running, and this fish, staying down deep, punished me for over two hours without my making any apparent progress with him. He stayed down deep and plugged. The rising of the launch on the swells kept me from gaining line. The last hour, which was my sixth hour of toil that day, all but finished me. It is torture to fight a strong, heavy fish deep down in a sea that helps him with every wave. The fight ended with the expenditure of my last bit of strength.

And I dragged up a 500-pound shark! Francis and Peter, in their wrath, literally cut that brute all to pieces. I should have saved him for study and photographing, because I had never seen his like. But I was so sore that I did not think of this.

The thing which had happened was easy enough to figure out. We had seen a swordfish take my bait. We had also seen a second fish, which we took for another swordfish. But this was the shark. He had rushed the fish with my bait, and made him drop it. That was when I felt the slacking of the line. When the second strike came it was, of course, the shark that took my bait.

The New Zealand swordfish weighed 311 pounds—light for his large frame—and the second marlin weighed 152.

Captain Mitchell raised and hooked one, a long, wonderfully built fish that leaped until it gave out. This one weighed 194 pounds.

July 17.—The day was fine, partly cloudy. Again I trolled nine hours. No birds—no bait—no fish! It had to go as a blank day. I was so tired that I staggered up the gangway of the ship.

Mitchell raised one large swordfish that made three lunges at his bait, then quit it.

July 18.—Storm. Wind and rain. We started out, but were frightened back by the monster seas. It rained all day and all night.

July 19.—This day was clearing and cool. The seas were abating, yet still the highest I had ever dared to troll in. I hoped I would not raise a fish in that rough water. There would have been little hope to land him. But of course I did raise one—the largest I had seen so far. He refused the three-day-old bait and I was glad.

Captain did not come in until some time after I got back to the schooner. It was still early, before sunset. The instant I saw him I knew something terrible had happened. He had a long face and harrowing eyes. He carried the big tackle, with the Coxe reel. I observed then that half of the line was gone.

"Cap, please have a heart. Don't tell me!" I implored, weakly.

"You see this tackle you gave me?" he demanded.

"Yes, I see it," I replied.

"Well, it wasn't equal to the demands made on it."

"O Lord! Don't say you got fast to another of those long-speared birds!"

"By gad! he got fast to me," returned the Captain, with feeling, as he laid the rod on the deck. "I raised a fish that looked huge. But he was deep and far back. He disappeared. I stood up to let my bait back. But before I could do so I saw a swordfish right down in front of me. George had thrown out the clutch; we were gliding to a stop. The water was still. I saw this swordfish much closer than the other big one. I was scared so I shook like a leaf. Big! He was every bit as big as the other—the most remarkable sight my eyes ever beheld. When George got the teasers in, this swordfish saw my bait back there. He shot at it. He looked like a blue flash. By gad! . . . Well, my bait went out of sight in his huge mouth. He ran straight off, faster and faster. I put the drag on. It made no difference. He got going like lightning. My reel smoked. When he got off between four and five hundred yards there was a jerk. The line stopped. I reeled in fully two hundred yards. It had broken clean. Too much speed and strain. . . . But what could I do?"

"Nothing. Absolutely nothing," I returned, dejectedly. "We may as well face the truth. We have the finest, biggest reels ever built. We have the longest, strongest lines. But this tackle will not stop and hold these monsters. . . . Say, old man, you ought to have had your drag off!"

"That swordfish simply showed me up," replied the Captain,

miserably. "On that other big fish I certainly gave a rotten exhibition. But this one—why, he made a child of me."

"I wonder what the twenty-four-thread-line anglers would say to such swordfish," I mused. "Or the nine-thread champions!"

"Great Heavens! They'd never believe. Even if you showed them one they'd say 'there ain't no such animal!'"

"Somehow I always had faith that there were greater fish in the sea than had ever been seen, let alone caught. You remember how the New Zealanders ridiculed me for claiming there were thousand-pound swordfish. Then you caught your nine-hundred-seventy-six-pound black marlin. These long-speared marlin here are much larger than that. We *know*. And we have the gigantic task of catching one or two, and proving it to the world."

On July 20, after spending half the day catching bait, I raised two swordfish, one of them about 400 pounds. They took the baits, swerved a little, and threw them out. Then a third marlin, in size about halfway between the other two, and he did precisely the same thing as the others. We trolled over this water, to and fro, without raising one of them again. But when we ran out a mile or so I had a smashing strike, hooked a marlin that appeared undecided whether or not to turn into a bird. Anyway, he spent his strength in surface work. After which I held him from sounding and soon brought him in.

Captain Mitchell had an empty day. My swordfish weighed 140 pounds.

This day, unfortunately, was to be our last fishing, and we hated to quit. I had not even raised one of the huge fellows. We were to run in to Papeete on the morrow.

The night was so clear and calm and beautiful that I began to think we might risk fishing all the way back to Papeete—forty miles—half of which was out in the open unprotected water. The barometer was steady. The skipper assured us there was no weather reason why we need not try it. I yielded to temptation and decided to fish around outside the reef, while the *Fisherman* ran east and north, round the other side of the island, giving Middleton opportunity to photograph her from shore, when she was close in under full sail.

The Southern Cross was particularly brilliant this evening. I always looked for it, and watched it when possible. Here at Tahiti it was not high in the heavens over my head, as in New Zealand, but about midway between zenith and horizon.

Northward I saw the three stars forming the handle of the Dipper. That was the constellation of my own hemisphere, and while down in the antipodes I had not seen it once. How it thrilled me! It seemed somehow to put me nearer home. But California was still 3,600 miles away.

Next morning the weather was fine, and we were off early, in the *Sky Blue* and *Loren G*.

As we ran down to the westward outside the reef we saw the *Fisherman* working in the opposite direction, soon to disappear off the east end. For two miles we had a nice sea, and I trolled a bait expectantly. Then, as we reached a point opposite the isthmus, a breeze sprang up from the north and soon chopped up a nasty sea. We could not go back, so we took our medicine.

Clouds rolled up and hid the peaks. The wind strengthened, and the sea assumed a threatening aspect. It was a following sea, and often angry waves rolled over to half fill the cockpit which held my fishing-chair. The swells grew higher and longer, and they raced us forward at tremendous speed. When we glided down a wave the water sheered from the bow in two beautiful curved sheets. But for the risk involved I would have enjoyed that ride. Now and then I had a scare, and always it dismayed me too look across the white water to the *Sky Blue*. She was a shorter boat, and in more danger. We ran fifteen miles in something over an hour, and rounding a long point of the island, found smooth water again.

Once more we began to fish. Captain Mitchell soon raised a swordfish. There were flocks of boobies and schools of bonito. It looked fishy round there. The sun did not shine, but enough light filtered through the clouds to make watching for fish fairly good.

Suddenly I saw a shadow far back. It was wide and yellow. It moved forward. I stood up. Shark, I thought, and a whooping big one. Next I made out the stately side sweep of a blue tail, proving the fish to be a swordfish. He came on like a barge. Vehemently I shouted to the boatmen. They just got a glimpse of him behind the slow swell. I had let my bait back and he had probably come to it while the swell hid it and him from my sight. When the water leveled again he was gone. We slowed down and I let my bait back, and waited in most tense longing. But no strike! The bait was too old. I trolled around there for an hour, loath to leave. That was the biggest swordfish I ever saw, not excepting the monster Captain had fought on July 11. But I would not dare estimate his size.

Our attention was soon called to a threatening storm. The sky over Moorea and to the north was black as ink. Captain Mitchell came up and informed me he had raised another marlin. That made three for us this day. We all agreed that the imperative need of the day now was to get inside the reef. I was glad I had fetched the three natives. We headed north and ran fast until rough sea made us slow down. Soon the storm struck us, and of rain and wind I never had seen the like. But we had just enough protection from the reef to save the boats from being swamped.

Eight miles up we ran through a narrow break in the reef—and my hair stood right on end—and had only rain to contend with the rest of the way. We reached Papeete safely, and as wet as if we had swum the distance.

There we waited patiently for the *Fisherman*. She did not come. As it continued to rain, we remained wet. At eight o'clock we found rest, if not comfort, in a dingy Tahitian hotel. Next day it rained cats and dogs. The afternoon was a flood. There was a gale, too, and the sea was black. The *Fisherman* did not come. What a miserable day that was, sitting on a bench or walking in the rain! The second night was worse. We could not get anything that was fit to eat. After the first meal I did not try.

Next day at noon the storm lifted, and soon after the *Fisherman* came in to anchor. She looked a haven of refuge to shipwrecked mariners. I never had appreciated her enough. The skipper had run seaward to ride out the storm.

The sum of our efforts in these South Sea waters turned out to be nothing short of extraordinary, considering the conditions so vastly different from other waters we had fished.

We had discovered a wonderful new fishing-place. Without

actually capturing one of the incredibly large marlin we could not prove our claim to a doubtful angling world, but we had proved it to ourselves. We had caught nine marlin swordfish, of which there were at least two new species never caught or heard of before. We had raised or sighted sixty-seven great game fish.

At Papeete we became acquainted with a Dr. Wilder, botanist of Honolulu. He was interested in fishing, though only an angler for small fry. He had been around Hawaiian waters a good deal, and he assured us he had seen very large swordfish and sailfish and tuna brought into the market by Japanese fishermen. He hesitated about giving weights, but promised to send me the market fishers' reports from Honolulu. At Raratonga he had seen an *ono* (wahoo) weighing 110 pounds. Such data from him added to our interest.

Mr. Nordhoff was delighted with our success in establishing records of swordfish at Tahiti. He confessed then that the native bonito fishermen had convinced him twenty-foot swordfish, and larger ones than that, were not rare. These great fish were seen in the rainy season.

Different people, some of them American tourists, going out in glass-bottom boats to see the coral, had reported seeing small swordfish, about three feet long. The native boatman said these were common around Tahiti. But I do not put much credence in these claims. I have seen needlefish and garfish, also a pipe-nosed fish mentioned earlier in this chronicle, and any one of these could be mistaken for young swordfish.

Summing up, it seemed to me that there was nothing for Captain Mitchell and me to do but say very little about our discoveries and beliefs—to go home and plan bigger, stronger, finer reels, rods, lines, and come back to Tahiti and catch some of those marvelous new swordfish.

PART TWO

1929

CHAPTER ONE

AFTER a year of thrilling anticipating and careful and endless planning we sailed from San Francisco on the S. S. *Maunganui*, July 11, 1928, for the South Seas, with the avowed determination to land one of the monster fish we had been unable to handle in 1927, and to secure specimens and photographs of them.

The *Fisherman*, equipped and laden as never before, was dispatched, on May 14, from San Pedro for Papeete in charge of a new skipper, Captain Tobin. She carried a load of lumber, fuel, water, food supplies, eight portable bungalows, several launches, among them the *Skyblue*, and an assortment of fishing-tackle that beggared description. The *Loren G.*, remodeled and improved, two thirty-four-foot launches, especially designed and built each with two engines for South Sea fishing along the dangerous reefs, and a sea sled were put aboard a Union Line freighter bound for the same destination. Tom Middleton, motion-picture photographer, went on this freighter with his equipment. Captain Laurie Mitchell, with the New Zealand young man, Reuben Moran, who had spent a year in United States, sailed for Papeete on May 16, to take charge of the outfit and build a camp at Vairao.

My brother R. C., of course, accompanied me, and Romer's pal, Bob Carney, and the others of my party. My son Romer saw us off at San Francisco. He was a disconsolate lad. He had lately been commissioned by my publishers, Harper & Brothers, to write a book of his experiences on our trip to the Galapagos in 1926, and it was incumbent upon him to finish the story of that adventure before beginning another. In May, with the time of our departure far off, it did not seem momentous to him, but when he met us in 'Frisco and saw the *Maunganui* he simply "blew up," as his uncle

R. C. put it. We arranged for him to sail on September 5, and meet us at Tahiti, September 15, and take the rest of the trip with us.

Romer swallowed hard, but manfully, as he bade Bob, his uncle, and me good-by. "Pretty tough, Rome," said R. C., "but you've got to finish that book." All I exacted of Romer was that he would surely do it and meet us in Papeete on the date set. He was the last to leave the ship, and on the crowded dock, a gala sight with the streamers of bright colors stretched down from the passengers on board to friends and relatives below, he paced to and fro, his pale face and dark eyes uplifted. At last the fragile strings of colored paper broke and flapped in the wind. These had been the last connecting ties between ship and land. I waved until my arm ached, and the last thing my intent sight distinguished was Romer's figure, foremost on the point of the pier. It vanished, and I was reminded of Tennyson's poignant lines about the watcher and the ship passing out. Perhaps, surely it was so with Romer.

Outside the Golden Gate the sea was rough and gray, overhung by a heavy fog. Soon the land dimmed and disappeared. The *Maunganui* headed on her course southwest. I had two surprises, as I watched from the stern. I saw fair-sized tuna striking at bait and breaking water, and soon after that a small black albatross wheeling in our wake.

There was no sunset and thick fog soon brought the night. I awoke several times as the ship careened and rolled me against the wall. Next morning was cool, cloudy, misty. The albatross still stayed with us. I wondered why he did not tire. The sun shone very little, and that palely, during the day. The wind went down and the sea. Friday morning was clearer, but still the sky hid under clouds. I saw a flying-fish dart from under the bow.

Sometime Saturday night we ran into the trade-winds, and next morning there was a breeze and white-capped sea, with occasional moments when the sun turned the gray waves blue. Sunday marked an appreciable difference in temperature, with a return of the old familiar languor and reluctance to move. I noticed it first in the aching of my legs, a rather tired sensation that disappeared under exercise.

I met a Monsieur Rougier, nephew of Father Rougier, to whom

I expect to sell the *Fisherman*. He spends six months at home in Paris, and six months on Christmas Island, where they have developed a wonderful business in cocoanuts and pearls. When Father R. bought the atoll—which is the largest in the Pacific—it was generally believed that cocoanut trees would not thrive there. But he proved the fallacy of this and made himself a fortune. Monsieur R. told me that large game fish abounded in the waters about Christmas Island, which is a line island—under the equator. He told of the capture by some one of a three-foot broadbill swordfish. This was interesting news to me. This atoll lies halfway between Tahiti and Hawaii, and I shall visit it some day.

Last night a large flying-fish flew aboard. It was about the size of a Catalina flying-fish, but the wings were shorter and the scales smaller.

Sunday as we neared the line the weather grew warm and muggy, with threatening squalls. Monday morning I was up early and had the deck to myself. Silver-gray trade-wind clouds, dark and rainy in patches, circled the horizon. But I had a couple of good long stares into the sun, which violet-ray treatment I find wonderfully beneficial. I do not wear dark glasses any more to protect my eyes from the glare.

I went forward to the very apex of the bow and sat by the rail, enjoying a perfect exhilaration. The sea was rough and the great ship ploughed and roared through the billows. Blue swells, white-crested, raced from behind and destroyed themselves in hollow boom against the iron hull. We dipped deep and anon rose high and higher, until I felt lifted to the skies.

Tiny metallic-looking flying-fish darted across the waves, and a flock of dark-winged, white-breasted gulls flew about the bow. They impressed me with the remarkable velocity of their sailing, swooping flight, not unlike that of albatross, but much swifter. They must have been engaged in play, because I saw no evidence of their hunting for food. The flight of wild sea birds in midocean is a marvelous spectacle, and gives man a glimpse of restless spirits.

Far ahead a gray squall crept across from the southeast, in the track of the trades. Presently I made out a dim outline of a rainbow, and then another. I could distinguish only the faint pink, yellow, and purple. One of them slowly rewarded my watchfulness by growing vivid. Then it faded as slowly and was lost in the mist. The squall came on apace, driving me to shelter, and soon the ship was enveloped in a tropic downpour, which made a flood on the deck. Presently the squall passed, after the habit of rainstorms near the equator, and the sea and sky grew light again.

Next day we ran into a heavy southeast trade that rolled the sea into huge billows and spread white tufts all over the blue. That was not a very comfortable day, and at night, when the portholes had to be closed, it was sweltering. But I soon slept.

On the morning of July 18, about eight o'clock we crossed the equator and were in the Southern Hemisphere. The night before I had seen the Dipper turned upside down, with the pointers close to the water, and Polaris out of perspective, so that it looked closer to the Dipper. Soon it will be good-by to Polaris, at least, and the Southern Cross will shine again.

On the evening of July 19, which was clear and bright, I saw the North Star going down into the sea and the Southern Cross rising high and brilliant. This was somewhere in the neighborhood of the Paumotu Islands.

The sea this trip was more prolific of fish than heretofore. Besides flying-fish we saw a giant ray, a black orca, and a school of tuna. The last was a most welcome sight and delighted us. We made pretty sure that they were blue-fin tuna, as they were feeding, and some of them leaping high. I saw several over one hundred pounds, and no doubt the school contained larger ones. Like old times at Avalon it was, to see the big blue-and-silver fellows shoot out and dive so clear and sharp. They ploughed the water and sent up the familiar short spouting splashes.

Mr. Wilford, a Minister of the New Zealand government, told me a terrible shark tragedy which he saw years ago at Napier. He went in bathing at 6 A.M. with a friend named Wright Cooper. After a little, Cooper, who was an expert swimmer, went up the beach where some other men were bathing. Suddenly Mr. Wilford heard yelling. He looked to see a great commotion in the water. Men were shouting, "Shark!" He ran up the beach. All the men ran in to Cooper's assistance, scaring off the shark. But Cooper was dead by the time they got him ashore. His hip was half bitten off, and part of one leg and shoulder.

M. Rougier, the nephew of Father Rougier, who owns Christmas Island, told me that if I would come to Christmas Island I could photograph many natives who had been bitten by sharks, and could learn some facts about fatalities there. Sea fowl are there in great flocks—boobies, terns, frigate birds, boatswain birds, etc. There are sixteen old wrecks around the atoll, many graves and tombs. In one place there is a sealed tomb and beside it a hole in the ground with a skeleton in the bottom. Presumably two castaways lived there on the island. One died and his companion buried him. The other, when he found he was dying, probably from thirst and starvation, lay down in the hole. What tremendous mysteries connected with the sea!

We arrived at Papeete on July 21. The magnificent green, rugged peaks of Tahiti were shrouded in gray clouds, and rain roared on the ship. But over Moorea the sun sank in a golden and purple splendor. By the time we ran in to the dock it was clear again, and the *Fisherman* swung white and beflagged in the harbor. The sight gave me a thrill. In two hours we were on board, with all our one hundred pieces of baggage, a remarkable performance. Then I learned things.

Captain Mitchell had come down two months ahead to build a camp for us at Vairao, which he reported progressing wonderfully, with six cottages, dining-cabin, cook-house, electric-light plant all up. My launches and car had been sent on May 16, by a New Zealand freighter, and had arrived in good shape. It had been a hard day, standing, walking, waiting, and my feet were dead. The hot hours in the sun had been trying. How the sweet, strong odor of copra went to my head! But I slept like a log, and was up at dawn, out watching the clouds turn rose and gold, and then silver.

We were to tarry until the *Beulah* (a freighter from Los Angeles) arrived in Papeete, so that the *Fisherman* could take on fuel. We had five days' wait. And anyone who has been aboard a schooner in a port like Papeete will appreciate what I mean by five days of hell. Papeete has a demoralizing effect upon sailors and ship men generally. There were a few of my men who did not succumb to the banal lure of Papeete, and these I shall remember gratefully. So the less said the better. However, a fisherman who wants to explore virgin waters cannot do it without these trials and afflictions.

On July 27, towing the sea sled, *Flying Fish*, our fleet was off for Moorea. Captain M. in the *Loren G.*, R. C. in the *Moorea*, and myself in the *Tahiti*. The peaks hid in white clouds; the surf piled on the reef; the patches of green and gold shone on the slopes. Outside we ran into a flock of boobies and gulls feeding over bonito, and we were soon fishing.

Bob Carney, a chum of my boy Romer, was in my boat, and my New Zealand men, Peter and Francis. We let out gigs to catch bait, and soon Bob was fast to a small tuna. He caught two (while we laughed at his awkwardness), and finally a bonito, which I put on for bait. No sooner had I done so than something began to tug at it. Peter saw a big dolphin behind my bait. So we had Bob slack his gig back. The bonito struck, and showed once, a good husky fish around sixty pounds. He came head out, and broke the leader short.

We ran into a heavy swell from the northeast and found the new boats pretty good, though a little wet forward. We trolled all the way across to Moorea. The *Fisherman* ran up to megaphone to us that we would have to go round to the west side to find safe anchorage. We ran into another flock of birds, and turned to follow. Soon Francis yelled, and we saw a flash of gold behind my bait. "Sailfish!" But he would not strike. My bait was too large. We ran on.

An hour later, round the point of Moorea, I had a smashing strike, saw a long black fish that I took for a marlin. He shot off like a bullet, and when I shut down on the drag to hook him the leader broke. Pretty bad, but also good luck for the first day out, and only a couple of hours at that.

Captain M. saw nothing, and caught only one bonito. R. C. had precisely the same luck. We found the *Fisherman* anchored under the pointed peaks of beautiful Moorea, in a bay that seemed a blue-and-green entrance to paradise.

We stayed a day at Moorea, in the second western bay. The island is not nearly so large as Tahiti, nor so high, but it has some ragged peaks that stared up superbly. That night the wind blew hard, and next morning it bade fair to be rough. It *was* rough. We should have turned back. But I raised a marlin the very first thing, and that roused me to anticipations. We kept on, and round the north end of Moorea ran into the biggest sea I ever rode in a small boat. It was frightful. I had given Captain Tobin instructions, in case he found bad going for the *Fisherman*, to head for Papeete. He did so, and with relief we followed his example. But when we got across the channel the wind changed and Captain Tobin put the schooner about for Vairao. We turned and ran on. I raised another marlin—that refused the bait— and that added more zest. Then we got so far around that we kept on, and headed into a stiff wind and heavy seas, and finally storm. The *Fisherman* rolled on in our wake, gradually falling back, until she was a mere phantom of a ship. We reached Vairao about 4.30, in a gray storm. But we could still see the schooner eight miles down the reef. When it got dark we decided to run out to meet her and guide her in. This we acted upon, and I do not want another experience like it. Half moonlight and half storm gave us our trouble keeping track of the reef. The opening was wide enough for daylight, but extremely dangerous at night. Thundering surges piled on the end. We reached the schooner, hailed the Captain, and he said he would follow us in. How the ship loomed up stately and weird! She pitched deep and rolled from side to side, her lofty spars leaning far on each side. That was an anxious hour for me. I strained my eyes to keep that ghostly white reef line in sight, and I did it. Before we reached the entrance R. C.'s boat set off a flare, and that helped. When the *Fisherman* headed through that channel it was a great relief to me. She ran in close and dropped an anchor, and we were soon aboard, noisy and glad. The storm clouds broke above the mountains, letting the moon shine through. The scene was majestic and somber, and fitted the thunder of the reef.

Next morning was beautiful, calm and cool, until the sun rose. I went ashore to visit my camp on Flower Point. It certainly was a wonderful site. Captain Mitchell had cleared off a bluff, except for the large palms, breadfruit, and other trees, and had put up a number of bungalows, four on top of the bluff, and as many more below, including a bamboo-and-palm dining-house and kitchen. A little stream ran merrily down out of the jungle. When this camp is finished and the flowers blooming all around it will be an ideal spot. The view from my cabin porch was something I was in no hurry to describe, for fear of a confusion of wild and whirling words.

We moved the schooner to her anchorage, and all morning worked on tackle. After lunch we started out to break in on our long fishing sojourn at Vairao. R. C., in the Moorea, with his boatmen, Sid and Thad from Avalon; Captain Mitchell, with two native Tahitians, in the *Loren G.*; and I with my New Zealand boatmen, Peter and Francis, in the *Tahiti*. These launches had certainly given a good account of themselves on the forty-odd mile run from Moorea in a stormy sea.

We could not catch any bait along the reef, so at last we ran out to sea to catch bonito. This turned out to be the same hard job we found it last year, and we had to persevere. But at length we all had bait, and started to troll. It was not smooth, by any means, but good fishing-water, especially running with the sea. I did not raise a fish. I kept track of the other boats, and thought they seemed rather active once or twice, but not until we were back on the schooner did I learn that Captain M. had begun with his old trick of breaking off a big swordfish. This one he said looked like a black marlin, and would have weighed over 500. R. C. did not see anything.

On the way in, the sun began to sink, and soon the heavens were transcendently beautiful. Vairao Bay reached from the mountains in the east twenty miles across to a lovely point that ran out southwest, and all this vast expanse of water was a heaving amber and rose. Above the Vairao mountains the clouds were great white and pearl masses. The green slopes shone exceedingly rich and vivid. Across the bay the huge peaks of Tahiti were lost in cumulus cloud, and the canyons yawning between were choked with deep dark purple. High up the heavens were transcendently afire. To the east and south glorious trade-wind clouds reflected the color of the sea. It was not possible to put the spectacle in words. Too grand, too unreal, too stupendous to be credible! The impression made upon me was so great as to be stunning. I shall require time to appreciate the splendor of Vairao.

A Native Maiden

R. C. WITH HIS LARGEST TAHITIAN MARLIN, 357 POUNDS

Next day it rained. We ran out into gray misty squalls, passed them into rich sunlight and sparkling blue sea, with rainbows all around and the jagged peaks of Vairao shrouded in mist. There was no sunset that day. But after dark the moon broke through the clouds and cast a lunar rainbow across the bay. This was a perfect bow, like a ghost, yet the colors were perceptible. Very different from the other lunar rainbow I saw once in New Zealand.

This afternoon R. C. raised one of the huge swordfish. It followed slowly after the boat, a wavering shape, but refused to take a rotten bait. I had a long, hard, blank day. We must have run fifty miles, and saw only one flock of birds. Captain M., however, caught ten bonito.

August 1 dawned misty and cool, with low clouds over the calm sea. Fortified by our ten bonito for bait, we ran out, following Captain M. for eight miles and more offshore. The sea was rippled, blue, and ridged with great vast swells. Captain followed a flock of boobies and terns all the way out. They were on the track of bonito.

But we did not find any fish far out. We ran in, and the boats became separated, though not out of sight of one another. It was hard work to troll a heavy bonito, and after six hours of it I had my reward in Frank's yell, *"There he is!"*

Sure enough, a dark shape appeared back of my bait. It was a swordfish and a large one. He seemed wary. But at last he came in to my bait, took it, and just as I let my line run free he dropped it. From thrill to blank disappointment! He followed us, left us, came back again, so that we had plenty of time to estimate his weight at 600 or 700 pounds. Finally he vanished. I believed he did not want the old bait.

Soon after that we sighted frantic waving from R. C.'s boat, and we raced over, expecting to find him hooked on. But it turned out that there was a marlin right under their boat and following them, to their great excitement. R. C. pointed down and yelled: "Come over. Big marlin. We've no bait." And all the rest of his crew were yelling.

We ran close, and soon the marlin left their boat to flash over to ours. What speed! He was about 400 pounds. Pretty soon the native on our boat saw that this marlin was chasing bonito. They had taken refuge under our boat. So there was high old jinks for a while, but it did not develop to anything. We threw R. C. our last bait, and went on trolling.

Soon after that we saw they were milling around and acting queer again, but before we could get near they had started up again. And just about then we raised a twelve-foot sailfish. He came on like a dart. What a scramble to haul in the teasers! But he had hold of both. He came right to the boat, and could easily have been gaffed. He would drop back and strike at my bonito bait, which of course was too large. At length I drew it in, took it off, cut out a strip from its side, and putting that on my hook, let it back to him. Did he want it? Precisely and exactly he did. All on board yelled. But I did not expect to catch him on account of the large hook. And it turned out I could not hook him. That concluded a day of pleasure, a thrill, and excitement for my boat.

R. C.'s report was stronger than that. He had hooked a marlin on the last bait I gave him. Then to cap the climax the propeller on their boat killed a bonito, which floated back, bleeding profusely, and sank. Thad saw a monster swordfish, as wide as our skiff, take that bonito.

Captain M. raised one marlin, a fair-sized fish. We held an interesting conference, most of which related to the difficulty and necessity of getting fresh bait.

CHAPTER TWO

THE launches *Loren G.* and the *Sky Blue* I had on the *Fisherman* in 1927, and consequently had seen good use in these waters. For the longer, more complex fishing in the Society Islands and the Paumotus I had built two thirty-four foot boats, designed especially for dangerous currents around reefs. They were each equipped with two powerful Red Wing motors and two propellers. I also had a sea sled, the *Flying Fish*, shipped down with the large launches, which we named *Tahiti* and *Moorea*.

All the tackle used in former trips was replenished, and a considerable amount of entirely new rods, reels, lines, lures, and apparatus was planned and ordered. My personal array of tackle was too numerous and formidable to record. An enumeration of what I gave to R. C. and Captain M. will furnish some faint idea of our preparation for what I considered would be the hardest and most remarkable fishing experience so far undertaken.

Two new Z. G. Special Coxe 12° reels, holding 600 and 1,000 yards of 39-thread line.

Two Hardy-Alma reels 12°.

Two Hardy-Zane Grey reels, 500 and 1,000 yards 36 and 39 thread.

Two heavy Kavalesky reels of 1,200 yards capacity.

Two dozen Shafer Dualwood rods, equipped with special bronze reel-locks, and extra heavy guides and tops.

Three dozen assorted rods, hickory and split bamboo, of varying weights.

Lines of the finest Swastika brand, made by Crandall, Nos. 12, 15, 18, 21, 24, 27, and 36, to the number of a dozen spools of each. Twenty spools of 600 and ten of 1,000 yard 39. For the largest reels we had a few 750-yard No. 42 thread, which we wished to try upon these exceptionally heavy fish over 1,000 pounds.

Three dozen special bonito Z. G. teasers made by the South Bend Bait Co., besides various tarporenos and other styles of lures to use as teasers.

The Pfleuger Co. made me a still larger swordfish hook, on which we counted greatly. Conspicuous among a vast assortment of artificial baits were some large Turtle Devil Bugs.

Perhaps the most formidable and remarkable of all this assortment of tackle was the trunk of leaders. They were of all sizes, from six-foot piano-wire gig leaders to thirty-foot double airplane wire mako-shark leaders. These latter, by the way, had to be made within three feet of the hook, of case-hardened links of heavy Japanese wire, so that the mako could not cut through them. It remains to be seen whether he cannot still do it. Captain M. was a month in making these leaders, and they presented a wonderful array. Any angler for big game fish of the sea will appreciate the care with which we prepared wire leaders. A fisherman has to break a few leaders on big swordfish before he fully can understand.

Besides this collection we had a storeroom on the *Fisherman* full of all kinds of other tackle—nets, ropes, cords, leads, hooks, poles, gaffs, toggles, flares.

Last year here at Vairao we were at a loss in regard to bait. It was almost impossible to catch bonito, and when there were thousands leaping and darting around the launches the effect upon us was disheartening. Very few fishermen could stand this sort of pioneer angling. They would have to be men of long experience, who knew what rewards were possible and who had the stamina to stick.

We were all the morning of August 2 getting a bait apiece, and Captain M.'s expert native fishermen caught those.

R. C. raised and hooked a small marlin swordfish almost at once. Before I had my bait out he was fast, and we ran over to ply cameras. Toward the end of the fight, which was short, we had opportunity for a fine leaping picture.

I kept my lonesome bait on ice, and trolled only the teasers. Presently up sailed a sailfish, swooping in and out, but he would not look at my bait. He left us, and after an hour or so we raised a marlin. This fellow was shy and hung back. I let my bait back to him, and when both had disappeared I felt a tug—then a run. My thrill was all for nothing, for a short battle proved my quarry to be a shark. The way Peter and Francis cut this shark to ribbons was reminiscent of New Zealand, where the boatmen hate all sharks except the mako.

R. C. ran over to photograph my boat, but before he could reach us he raised a sailfish and got pretty busy. However, it was no go. These sailfish will not take swordfish bait.

Later in the day I raised another, a smaller one, all to no purpose. Upon running back to the ship I found that Cappy had had a blank day. R. C.'s fish weighed 180 pounds, a small size for this latitude.

I had sent for the best bonito fisherman in Tahiti, but my messenger was unable to locate him.

Next morning was dark, lowering, with a rippled sea. We had sent three Tahitians out in a canoe to catch bait for us, and when we finally located them, four miles out, we were highly entertained. We took the outrigger canoe in tow and soon located bonito. Then the natives cast loose and all paddled vigorously to keep up with the wheeling, darting terns and splashing bonito. It was some job. When they got among them the last man in the canoe laid aside his paddle, and taking up his long bamboo pole, he cast out with short line and skipped his pearl-shell lure, while he used his other hand to splash water ahead of him. Presently he changed the pole to that hand and splashed with the other. Suddenly the pole jerked down. He lifted mightily, swung out a kicking silver bonito and brought it to him, to catch it under his arm. A single action unhooked it and he cast out again. He missed one, then caught another. It was a fine performance. We yelled lustily. And when he caught a second it was jolly for us. "Atta boy!" "Yank, old Tahiti!" "Come to me, bonito!" and other like expressions. But out of seven bonito hooked and swung he saved only three. The canoe was very narrow and easy to miss with a struggling fish on a barbless hook.

With these bait, however, we set to trolling, and to make a long story short we ran all over the ocean, for seven hours, without raising a fish. First blank day for the three boats! Still the day seemed short. I got a glorious sunburn, though the sun appeared never to be out. And I saw rainbows to my heart's content. One was as wide as the slope of a mountain, a magnificent transparent veil of luminous colors, yet surely a rainbow. The sunset was silver and then pearl. There was no gold, and only later, in the far east, did I see a cloud touched with rose.

On the way in I sat up on top and faced the cool, moist breeze from off the Isthmus. Black terns by hundreds were wheeling above a school of bonito, and it was a pleasure to watch them. When a bonito splashed up a tern or two would dart down to pick at something, doubtless a tiny fish that the bonito were chasing to the surface. But though I looked sharply, I did not see a tern get his supper. They have to work endlessly. The scene was singularly beautiful—the broad, dark, ruffled bay, the horseshoe curve of white surf on the reef, and the looming grand mountain outline rising into the clouds. No boats had ever before cut up this bay with propellers. It was virgin water, free and broad and windswept.

Blank days at Vairao came with perplexing frequency and persistence. Two in succession upset our calculations. We had five blank days out of nine days' fishing. The natives had always said: "October—November—December—Plenty bonito—Plenty fish!" And it remained for us to find out. Big-game fishing is a game of stick. I had one strike in nine days. The long hours grew interminable.

One night under a cloudy sky I saw bright blue sparks flash in the water, die out, and flash again, in different places. Some kind of marine insect or fish was lighting his phosphorescent lamp for my edification. It was beautiful—the tiny brilliant blue gleams.

When, after two blank days, notable for the absence of birds, bonito, as well as swordfish, a heavy rainstorm set in and lasted all day and all night; we were relieved to attribute to the storm the desertion of our game from Vairao Bay. One of our natives said it might last three days, but if the wind veered as much as two points the weather would clear.

I had my work, and there is never anywhere enough time for me, but R. C. and Captain Mitchell and the others found the steady downpour monotonous and depressing. I walked in the rain along the beach for two miles, in which distance I passed by numerous thatched huts, and some frame houses with porches, where children appeared numerous and their elders lounged on the floor. These natives rested a good deal, it appeared to me.

Recently I read an article by a modern writer, now living in Papeete, on the joy of having little or no labor to perform, and the consequent peace and happiness of the idle Polynesian. The white man, the civilized, worked too much. Personally I think this theory is wrong. Any race, black or white, that ceases to work hard, ceases to progress. What happened to the marvelous Masai in Africa, after Livingstone stopped their wars? They degenerated and rapidly declined. I do not approve of war as a labor, but it proves the evolution of the physical man.

We did not see the sun on August 5, for a single minute, and rain—! Torrents! The ship reeked. And there was nothing dry outside. When I went to bed the stars were shining, yet upon awakening several times during the night I heard the rain teeming down. The morning promised fair, but outside we found a mountainous sea, and squalls looming gray from the east. Nevertheless, we chased birds and bonito all over the ocean. Not yet had I seen a school of fish travel so swiftly. We had to run ten miles an hour to catch them. Captain M.'s native boatman caught nine bonito and R. C.'s two—a most interesting performance. I caught one on a feather gig. We trolled awhile, but then the sea grew rougher and we were forced in.

I had a serious accident next morning, which might easily have been a fatal conclusion to the trip. Normally I am particularly careful how I step or jump round on the boats. Dew and rain and rubber soles are bad mixers. My launch lay about five feet from the *Fisherman*. I leaped from the rail. My foot slipped off the edge of the launch deck, and with all my weight I crashed on my face. If I had not broken that fall with my arms it would have been serious. The force threw me up and back hard against the side of the ship, and from there I was propelled down into the cockpit.

For a while I was stunned and did not know how badly I was hurt. I had a terrific pain in my head, my left arm hung limp, and I had numerous other hurts. I was afraid I had broken a rib or two.

Nevertheless, I went fishing, and for an hour or more held a rod. But the pain grew too acute and I had to desist. I began then to appreciate that I had suffered a severe sprain to my left wrist, and several contusions.

Meanwhile we raised a sailfish that would not bite. Next the violent waving of a flag on Captain Mitchell's boat sent us scurrying in his direction. He was indeed hooked on, and we remained near by until he captured a fine marlin swordfish. He yelled to me that he had raised two. Later he told me an unusual fishing experience. Two marlin rushed his bait, one twice as large as the other. The big one got the bait, bit it in two pieces, and dropped back in the wake. The smaller tried to get the head that was left on the hook. Captain drew it in, put on a fresh bait, threw the head to the smaller swordfish, and let his new bait back to the big fellow. No good! The smaller one was too quick. He nailed the bait, was hooked, leaped all over the ocean, then sounded. In due time Captain wore him out. At the ship this fish weighed 339 pounds. The larger one must have been superb.

Upon arriving I found that I could not lift my left arm and was otherwise in bad shape. It might easily have been worse. But the lesson could not fail to be valuable.

All the same, next morning, bandaged and lame, I laboriously got down into the *Tahiti* and went fishing. I hung on to one of the heavy tackles, too, until I could not do so any longer. We raised one of the large swordfish. He loomed back in the swells, a wavering shape, tawny, but with a little purple tinge, but he would not come on close to the teasers and baits. I slacked one of these last back to him, as he slowly faded; however, he would not take. We trolled till the trade-wind roughened up the sea, and then came in, not too soon for me.

The following day I felt better and could use my hand to some extent. Captain Mitchell went to Papeete by auto, and I put the three bait fishermen in the *Loren G.* and sent them out. We followed, my launch with two bonito fishermen, one the best in Tahiti, and one for R. C.'s boat. We ran up and down, for miles and miles. It was nearly noon before we espied any birds. When we got among them they scattered to the four winds. We went on and found more birds. They were working over bonito. Then began a chase. When the bonito were up the birds sailed screaming to them, and dove pellmell into the mess on the surface. By the time we reached them they were ready to move on. So it went for an hour before we caught one bonito. But we had bad luck in losing three. One hit the chair and bounced back, the next hit the boat, and the third pulled loose.

During this last hour we saw a large swordfish leap five times. Then we raised a sailfish. Finally I put a bonito on my hook and began to troll. We still followed the birds. At three in the afternoon we were still doing it. We lost the *Loren G.*, and R. C. was left far behind. Francis saw a dolphin behind the teasers. We put on a feather gig, and soon were fast to him, a fine leaper. We landed him. Then I had Peter cut a strip of bait from the dolphin, and I put that on my sailfish leader.

Bob was holding the other line, with the bonito bait on it. When a crash came back of the teasers I looked to see a black fin. Bob, in his excitement, held to the line instead of letting it run free, and of course the sailfish got the bait. Then I reeled in the sailfish bait and dropped my bonito bait astern. It had not slipped back forty feet until a purple blaze was at it. I let the fish take the bait and swim away. I saw the bonito between its jaws. Presently the fish started swiftly and I had to put on my drag. Then up he came, to my amaze, a most magnificent sailfish, fully fourteen feet long. He swung my bonito round his head. That caused my heart to sink. He crashed back, was out again, dancing toward us, to free himself.

Of all the luck! If I had left my sailfish bait back instead of dropping in the bonito, I would certainly have hooked that wonderful sailfish. But my course was correct, for the fish that took Bob's bait was a marlin. How could I guess there would be a sailfish with him? And why did not the sailfish show? This Tahitian fishing is something to conjure with.

On the way in we saw another swordfish chasing bonito. It was smooth in the bay, and dark, with a glancing light on the water.

Black terns were darting around, and bonito were everywhere. But we could not catch any.

We had seven blank days in a row at Vairao—southeast trade, white water, heavy swells, and a growing scarcity of birds and bonito. Nevertheless, we fished. Several afternoons we were driven in by such seas as only a crazy angler would try to fish in. Perhaps we could have landed a moderate-sized swordfish, if we had hooked one, but one of the big fellows would have swamped us. When a heavy fish goes down, which he invariably does, every swell that lifts the boat takes more line, until in the end it breaks. I knew this perfectly, yet such is the spirit of a fisherman.

We had several sunsets that were splendid, one especially in which the colors were mostly all gold, until the afterglow, which was a blend of rose and amber beyond description. The sun sets quickly in the tropics, but the afterglow lingers, sometimes for half an hour or more, and it is exquisite.

I received a wireless from my boy Romer, who was on the S.S. *Makura* and would join us at Papeete on August 18. This was wonderful news. Bob, who was on board, was simply stutteringly tickled. We decided, therefore, to send the schooner round to Papeete, and we would troll in the launches. The distance was forty-six miles. I have trolled farther than that at one spell, but never in such a sea.

We had a lot of fun watching the *Fisherman*, as we passed her. Roll! She stuck her booms under clear to the rail. And we surely saw some white faces on board. There was an Englishman and Princess Ina, a Polynesian of high degree as well as fame, and these two were going to be married by my skipper, Captain Tobin. They could not be married ashore, because there is a French law that prohibits marriage for foreigners within the three-mile limit. So I lent them my yacht. They were terribly seasick, but had the knot tied securely, which was the main thing for them.

When we got in the lee of the point we saw some birds working over bait, but we could not catch any. I trolled an old dead bonito until it fell apart. There were a number of canoes outside, with natives fishing at what they call a tuna hole. These tuna holes, by the way, are important parts of native real estate, as many pieces

TALES OF TAHITIAN WATERS

of property along the shore have tuna holes that go with them. I gathered that a tuna hole was merely a deeper place in the sea where tuna congregated at times.

We arrived at Papeete that night and were up before daylight next morning, and saw the bright lights of the steamer a few miles out. She was hove to, waiting for dawn.

When she came into the bay, a couple of hours later, we were out there in the launches. Bob was the first to espy Romer and he let out a great yell. Then the rest of us followed suit. We lay alongside and talked to Romer while the ship rested during official business. And when she docked we were there. I was the first on board. That was a fine moment for me. Romer seemed overjoyed to see us. He looked thin and had worked day and night upon his book. His arrival was a consummation for me.

While at Papeete Captain M. met an old native who spoke English well. He had lived long at Vairao, but was now located in the Paumotus. He was a fisherman. He told us that December was the best month at Vairao Bay, when bait and big fish came on thick.

He spoke of *espadon*, meaning swordfish, six, seven, eight meters long. And he laid stress on a great fish the natives knew little about. It had a very large, high fin and grew seven to eight meters. This surely was a sailfish. Twenty-one and twenty-four feet!

Captain M. drew a picture of a broadbill swordfish, emphasizing the bill. He drew it long, flat, broad at the base, narrowing to a sharp point. The native said this swordfish was found in the Paumotus all the year round, following the schools of tuna and bonito. He had a very large mouth, and a good-sized tuna would make the best bait. But—and here was the striking thing—Captain M. had drawn the swordfish upside down!

This absolutely corroborated the data given us last year at Rangiroa by an Armenian who had been there thirty years and who spoke English. He, too, was a fisherman. Natives also saw my pictures of a broadbill swordfish, and they identified it with one in Paumotuan waters, except that it had the sword underneath.

Captain M.'s informant claimed the sword of this fish was short and heavy, in contrast to that of *Xiphias gladius*.

We surely had enough remarkable information about large and new species of fish to drive us wild.

Father Rougier is giving me a translation of a letter written him by the governor of the Marquesas in reference to sharks in Marquesan waters.

A Frenchman, Levee, captain of a South Sea schooner, had more fascinating information for us. These Tahitians were slow to find out what we wanted. Levee assured us that he had seen many *espandon* swordfish, eight meters long—twenty-four feet! Incredible. He had often seen a number of them chasing bonito, lashing the sea white, leaping clear out. He had seen two after a school of bonito that sought refuge under the schooner. One of them rammed the hull, in his rush of fury. Very often a schooner will come in to Papeete with a swordfish bill imbedded in her. When a swordfish was able to back away without breaking off his sword, then the schooner would leak badly.

Levee also told about Paumotuan sharks, some of which were so large that they could take a couple of men in one bite. He mentioned a strange toothless shark, one that fastened to his prey by sucking, and he related how a native had a large piece of his anatomy literally sucked off by this queer marine monster.

CHAPTER THREE

WE LEFT Moorea at sunset for Raiatea, an island west of Tahiti. The two large launches had to follow under their own power, and this was an anxious consideration for me. Outside we soon ran into a light trade-wind and a heavy swell. Just a few white caps running. The moon, half full, stood overhead, and the sea was a silver heaving waste. We watched the launches rolling along astern, and the Southern Cross slowly sinking. Finally I went to bed. The ship rolled with a long lazy roll, from side to side, and as my bed was a wide one I did not get rolled out. During the night I awoke and heard the cries of sea fowl overhead. At 4.30 I got up, dressed, and went out on deck. There was a faint light in the east; all the other points were dark. The stars were unfamiliar. The Milky Way was absent, and so was the Southern Cross. But I saw Orion, the same old familiar constellation, as always sloping toward the west.

My launch, the *Tahiti*, was close to the ship, but R. C.'s, the *Moorea*, was just barely distinguishable astern. I surely breathed a breath of relief. The sea was rough, but not bad. Gradually daylight came, and then sunrise, a silver gold bursting from under the trade-wind clouds. Raiatea had been in sight for an hour, and also another of the Leeward group.

The wind came up with the sun, and soon a white sea boiled and heaved about the ship. The launches forged ahead and soon passed out of sight. We were two hours coming up to the reef, but every moment was worth while. Raiatea appeared to be two islands, sloping from coast to headlands and in some places high mountains—a vast green-yellow country wreathed by a wandering white line of surf. In places miles of pale-green lagoon spread smooth and tranquil from reef to shore. Outside the sea was a heaving dark blue, rolling in great crested billows. Small islands added further beauty to the scene. The entrance where the *Fisherman* went in was picturesque in the extreme, a blue channel, curving between yellow reefs and palm-bordered islets. Inside stretched leagues of calm water. We ran on down to Raiatea and anchored. Our advent created excitement in the little village. Captain M. and the boys went ashore, while I wrote. Later they returned, and Captain reported that the natives said bonito were plentiful on the lee side. They told about the *espadon*—a fish of which they were in dread—and they wanted to see the kind of rope with which we proposed to catch them. Captain M. could not convince these islanders that we proposed to do it with rod and reel.

After lunch we took a run out the winding channel, round to the leeward side. The shore line and the reefs were striking in the extreme. We found the outlet between two small islands, and here a school of dolphin were lashing the water in pursuit of flying-fish. They resembled the dolphin of the Perlas Islands, except they were brown instead of gray. They leaped like a whirling projectile, showing their long pointed noses. We saw schools of leaping shining bait inside the reef, and outside, birds working over bonito. Soon I espied some frigate birds, and thrilled at the first I ever saw in this latitude. They were up to the tricks of the species, robbing gulls of the fish they had caught.

We ran out and trolled. The sea was calm, a very welcome change from Vairao. Far across stood up the great sentinel peak of Bora-Bora, the most remarkable of the Leewards. We trolled along the reef for five miles. Captain M. caught a three-foot barracuda and R. C. a bonito. I did not connect with anything outside, though on the way out I had caught a fine bait. We met two sailboats outside, with natives fishing for bonito. They called to our natives that morning was the time for bonito. Wherefore we trolled back. It was a long, hard, wonderful day. When I was asked by Captain M. and R. C. about the fishing-water, I could only say it seemed bewildering to me. So endless! Yet I thought it looked fishy around Raiatea.

The second day, as blank as the first, and hot on the sea, in no wise changed my first impression. It was not pleasant, however, and that always made a difference in fishing.

On the third morning I decided we would try to find the place where Captain M.'s informant had claimed were endless fish. Personally I suspected these amiable gentlemen, who had admitted they were not fishermen, had seen this piscatorial spectacle in the bottom of inverted glasses. Anyway, we found the passage through the reef, between two coral islets, and there we trolled up and down for an hour. I had one strike, and the fish ran under the coral.

Inside the reef we sighted some natives along shore with a net. We ran over to find they had some mullet, and we procured a number of these. It was nearly noon and hot. But clouds in the north promised a squall. Presently we got back to the *Fisherman*. And soon we were running across the wide lagoon toward the other island. The schooner heaved anchor and followed us. As we neared this second half of Raiatea we discovered that it was beautiful, more verdant, and less rugged, with a cove-indented shore line. Meanwhile a squall overtook us. How pleasant to sit out in the rain! But it passed over all too soon.

Our next anchorage was opposite a wide passage in the reef, near shore at the southernmost point of this island. The reef sheered away magnificently to the west. It ran miles out into the ocean.

With our mullet, and a bonito each, we headed out of the channel, to find the sea most delightful and alluring to troll. There was a long easy swell, a ripple, and dark glancing water. Outside a few miles we saw the white sails of the native fisherman. Bora-Bora stood up grandly. What a superb single peak! It was like one of the monuments in Monument Valley, Utah, only vastly larger. The larger island of Raiatea held a gorgeous panorama of clouds along the summit. Rain was falling in dim veils and gray palls. The reef boomed and sent up league-long lines of spray. Rainbows appeared. At last one formed, that for size, purity, and beauty excelled any I ever saw before. It was almost incredibly glorious. The arch was perfect, and it rose out of the sea and spanned half of the lagoon. Broad as a street, and intensely vivid, it was something at which I gasped.

We trolled all over, I with a small bait and Peter with a bonito, I with a short line and he with a long. The light on the water made it almost impossible to see; nevertheless, I did see a pale amber shadow. Almost I decided I had been wrong. Then again it wavered there behind my right-hand teaser, and I yelled. Then it moved across the wake and toward us. We saw a thin fin. Francis yelled, "Shark!" And Peter seconded him. But I answered, "Well, I'll take a chance on this bird." Next we saw a fine long beak shoot out. I shouted, "Sailfish!"

He took my bait and sheered away. Peter had been pulling the bonito in. Suddenly a tremendously long sailfish nailed the bait and ran. My fish stole my mullet. Frantically I wound in to hook on another. And Peter shouted, "Mine let go!" I let my bait back. Jimmy, one of our natives, yelled something in Tahitian. Then I saw the amber color far back. I let my reel run loose. I saw a swirl, felt a tug—and my line paid out.

"O.K. here, boys," I said, gleefully, as I watched my line slip out.

"Look at my bait," ejaculated Peter as he held up the rejected bonito. Its head was smashed. "He was a monster."

My fish started to run, so I put on the drag. Before I could jerk he came up, a big gold and blue-spotted sailfish. Then I hooked him. While I yelled for Francis to man the camera the sailfish leaped four times, two of which leaps were prodigious. Meanwhile R. C., in answer to our flag-waving, ran up to point a battery of cameras at us. My fish jumped only once more, after which I soon brought him to gaff.

Through a megaphone I told R. C. the particulars. And we resumed trolling. Soon somebody saw Captain Mitchell on a fish that jumped once and escaped. Nothing more happened then for an hour, except that the gorgeous effects of color and light on sea and slope, and especially upon the magnificent cloud pageant, changed more beautifully as sunset approached.

My eye roved to R. C.'s boat, and then to Mitchell's, and presently I saw he was not running. I called to Francis to take a look with the glass, and just a second afterward I saw a fish leap. Then we hauled in baits and teasers and sped toward the *Loren G.* Long before we got there we saw a splendid sailfish in the air, and when we drew near enough to photograph he gave only one more leap, a weary plunge out. But that was long enough to see that he was a big sailfish. Presently we were to see that he was indeed big, and as wonderful. I saw my record go glimmering. But so long as some one in the outfit beat me I did not care.

We put up our flags and ran back toward the ship, sighting R. C. far in near the reef. The sun was about to set in a gold and purple sky; it shone with an exquisite luster of pale fire; the hills of fresh rain-drenched foliage rose to the clouds.

Excitement prevailed around and on the *Fisherman* as we ran up. Native canoes and sailboats were numerous. We hauled our prizes aboard and surely they were fish to dazzle anglers' eyes. The first ever caught in the Leewards! My record sailfish caught at Zihautenejo in 1925 was ten feet one inch in length and weighed 135 pounds. Larger sailfish had been caught since, but not what we call qualified fish—that is to say, fish landed by an angler alone, with correct tackle, and without breaking anything. I gave up my record right there, and congratulated Cappy. But to our surprise, though Captain M.'s fish was four and one half inches longer than my record, it balanced the scales at only 133½ pounds.

R. C. arrived to report a blank day and to stare with wide eyes at the two big sailfish. "Gee! Pretty poor, I don't think. All same Zihautenejo!"

"You bet, but this species is a little different from that on the Mexican coast," I replied. "These were spotted all over in blue—something new to me."

When fishermen have a good day they forget the past with its long uphill climbs and downhill defeats, and the future is bright. Perhaps that is one of the great lessons fishing teaches.

We went out next day full of hope and certainty. The day started fine. We got a few bonito. The sea was a dark-blue rippling plain. But that soon ended. The trade whipped through the pass between the islands and roughened the water. We trolled five miles toward Bora-Bora, then a like distance back, and finally east as far as the end of Raiatea, where at last we got in the lee. But we found no birds, no bait, and we raised no fish. I had a headache from the hot sun, and I ached with the rocking of the boat. I trolled a heavy bonito for seven hours, until it felt as heavy as a log.

Only one redeeming feature made the day escape being wasted. The cloud effects as the afternoon wore on became wonderful. All day the east and south had thickened until a dark storm bank spread along the horizon. But above Raiatea great white cumulus clouds towered like mushroom mountains. How exquisitely white and soft! Like the purest of snow or smoke. Suddenly high up in the largest of these I espied a sundog. A bit of marvelously blended pink and rose and blue and gold, in extraordinary contrast with the white background. It was so beautiful that it seemed unreal. That spectacle saved the day for me.

After dark on this day the wind blew hard and there appeared to be a storm brewing. But the glass was normal, not at all high, and a high glass in the South Seas means wind.

The storm I had predicted arrived, and that before day broke. A deluge of rain and gusty winds beat upon the ship. At daylight the clouds were dark and lowering. Frequent rain squalls, light and misty, came along one after another.

I sent the boys out to catch bait, while I worked. Before noon there were indications of clearing weather, and fortified by a fair assortment of bait we went out, and spread all over the ocean. A heavy rainstorm loomed over Raiatea, caught up with us, and drowned the launch. I trolled right through it. After it blew over, the sea was fine, dark blue, rippling, with a good light to watch the teasers. Then a gale swooped down. Soon the sea was white. I beat in toward the upper passage, while R. C. and Cappy headed for the lower, near which the ship was anchored.

When we got into the lee the sea was calm, the sun shining, and birds were circling over bait. It was a beautiful scene, rich and dark in coloring, with the east inky black. The big mountain was lost in a gray pall. To the north, the long slope could be seen through a rainbow that extended from sea to summit, so wide, so transparent, so exquisitely lovely that I paid it faithful rapt tribute until it faded. Of late I have seen several rainbows, each of which I never expect to see duplicated.

Jimmy, our native, caught a bonito, and I put it on my hook. Presently I had a strike that sent the thrills over me. I hooked a heavy fish, and for a few moments entertained a hope that it might be a swordfish. But it was a yellow shark, a mean customer about 400 pounds. We had become swift and efficient in the dispatching of sharks, which once occasioned us such irritation, not to say labor. Peter's big gaff went in as if the shark had hide of butter; Charley helped on the cable; then Peter leaned over with his knife. A few powerful slashes and that shark was ribbons.

We ran back to the schooner in another misty rain, cool and dewy to the face. What was my surprise and delight to find that Captain Mitchell had caught a sailfish 110 pounds, and R. C. had one of 104. They reported fine leaping fish. R. C. also caught a forty-pound dolphin and a fifty-pound yellow-fin tuna.

Thad, on R. C.'s boat, said they had raised two sailfish at once, both of which were ravenously hungry. R. C. pulled the bonito out of the mouth of one four times. Finally they got a bait over in time, before the fish left, and hooked one of them.

Captain's fish took a bonito and made eleven wonderful jumps, three of these right at the boat.

We sent the *Fisherman* on the way to Bora-Bora and we trolled over. It was about twenty-five miles. The weather was beautiful, cloud and sun and blue sea. Birds were plentiful, but we did not see any bait. All the way across the channel the great mountain that dominated the island loomed higher and clear. It was indeed a noble pile. When we drew near I made out the coral reef ringing the island, and then inside the lagoon many flat islets, fringed by cocoanut palms and lined by white beach. The water inside was a pale emerald green.

Bora-Bora consisted of green slopes rising from the sea, gradually growing ridged and sharp, until they merged in the grand bulk of the mountain, gray-cliffed and green-faced, rising to the clouds. The color was vivid and fresh, a wonderful verdant tropic mosaic of green and gold. Of all the islands I have fished around this was the most unique. Tahiti is too great to take it at a glance. But Bora-Bora, though spread out, was really not very large—perhaps twenty miles long, and narrow. It had the shape of a starfish, with the peak in the middle. A vast sheer of rock facing the south curved up from the shore, like the broken side of a crater.

I fished a whole afternoon along the lee shore of Bora-Bora, a privilege and a joy not soon to be forgotten, if ever. The waters had a fishy look, too. Birds and bait showed at intervals. Captain M. sighted two large flocks of boobies working. We saw a splash behind R. C.'s boat, and ran over to find that a sailfish had stolen the port teaser. Broken it off! R. C. said they had raised a marlin, too. I put on a mullet, and trolled that beside the bonito. Soon I saw a big white-and-black fish, that came like a rocket, smashed the water, and sounded with my bait. All aboard yelled lustily. Romer pronounced it a tuna, and a huge one. I rather inclined to the idea that it was a marlin. Anyway, the strike was tremendous. I should have known it was a tuna, but was some time realizing this. I fought the fish on a soft hickory rod and twenty-one strand line, and I had my troubles. Something short of an hour it took me to lift him far enough for us really to identify a tuna. He was weaving under the boat, and that is characteristic of tuna. I judged him to weigh between 200 and 300 pounds. At the very end the hook tore out. My old unfailing bad luck! Later R. C. said he could not understand it.

At five o'clock we ran in and called it a day. The bay was magnificent, almost landlocked. The schooner lay at anchor under the towering peak and made a brave sight.

Cappy came in reporting that he had raised a fine big marlin that refused the bait. He hooked a shark, saw some five-foot needlefish, and most remarkable to record he saw a boobie catch a flyingfish. This was something I always wondered about, but never had the luck to see it. No doubt they catch many. And I was sure the frigate birds did also.

At 8.30 that night I went out on deck. The moon was almost full and it soared white and grand over the colossal monument of Bora-Bora. The scene was almost too marvelous to be credible, until I remembered that I was some degrees south of the equator, among the South Sea islands. It is one thing to read about them, another to see them. I had read 'most all the well-known books about the South Pacific. Nordhoff and Hall were the best of the modern writers, as were Melville and Stevenson of the past. O'Brien's books are fascinating, until you visit the South Seas. I did like Stacpoole's romance *The Blue Lagoon*. When I gazed up at Bora-Bora I longed for the power and wisdom of Ruskin, the spirit of Hudson. I walked the deck, sat on the rail, stepped up the halyards, and looked until my eyes ached. That black dome overpowered the place. I thought that anyone who loved nature must be serious-minded in its shadow.

During the night I awoke. Roar of gale through the rigging! How it whistled and moaned! Then the rain pattered, as on a canvas tent, coming thicker and harder, until it outroared the wind. I felt cold rain blowing in my window. The time was midnight. Several times before dawn I was awakened by another deluge. Morning came, cool, wet, dark, with scudding gray clouds sailing low out of the east. No fishing this day! I did odd jobs with tackle and cameras, then sat down to my writing for several hours. When I came out of that oblivion the sun was shining, and upon going out was hailed by R. C. and Cappy: "So you came out, groundhog? Well, then we can fish this afternoon!"

And so we did. I was astonished at the fine sunny weather and the blue rippling sea. Clouds were not wanting, however; and as we got out beyond the reef, which was fully two miles beyond the ship, I could make out the edge of black clouds moving up behind the mountain. Then I saw them lift and spread and envelop Bora-Bora. The whole high part of the island vanished in a black streaming rain-cloud, while I was out in the sunshine. This squall swooped out to sea, and like everything in the South Seas it was on a grand scale. The water became flattened under the downpour, as sheets of rain swept on. I sat in my fishing-chair, with water pouring off my hat and rain coat. That squall roared away across the ocean; Bora-Bora stood up again clear of its gray curtain, and soon the sun was shining hot, and I had again stripped to my thin sleeveless shirt. I learned to revel in the rainstorms of this latitude.

Then a big dolphin charged the port teaser. It frightened him and he darted away as fast as he had come. We followed a flock of boobies for miles, and at last I espied a swift gleam of purple in the blue water. "Marlin!" I yelled, and all was excitement. He was a fair specimen, swift as a flash, curious about our teasers and baits, but, as Francis said, "too leary to bite"! We ran on out to sea, up and down, zigzag and crisscross. Leagues of trolling! Sometimes I wondered how many times round the world would my sum of trolling miles go.

I had out a feather gig for tuna; a sailfish bait on another tackle; and the big outfit trailing a bonito. Peter held that rod. Suddenly there came a smash. After long hours of trolling and watching, when attention flags, a charging fish surely puts us aquiver with action. I leaped across to take the rod. The line was paying out. The fish came to the surface—a monster dolphin fully six or seven feet long, his dorsal erect in anger, his gold and speckled body showing broad and deep. He was the largest I ever saw, and would have gone over a hundred pounds. The suspense of that strike was terrific. But he let go the bait, and I reeled it in, smashed to a pulp. I did not say anything, but the boys, especially Charley and Jimmy, our natives, made up for my silence. We trolled on, over the blue sea, until sunset. R. C. and Captain M. turned reefward with me, and we ran in. The *Fisherman* shone like a huge white gull against the gold of Bora-Bora. I stood and gazed, and could only breathe a deep breath of rapture.

We found bait almost impossible to catch at Bora-Bora, and the natives could not supply any. When we cannot get bait it is a sure thing that that necessary article is hard to get.

Our last day at Bora-Bora was one of beautiful sunny spells and ripply blue seas and swooping gray-white squalls. I enjoyed these immensely, sitting out through all four of the severe ones, with water pouring off my hat and coat. We sighted a very large flock of sea birds far out, and we ran for them. They made a dark splotch on the sky. We found a multitude of boobies and shearwaters wheeling and diving for bait. I concluded pretty soon that only the small minnow bait was present, as there were no signs of tuna or bonito.

I caught a fine sailfish in near the passage. I pulled the bait away from him several times before I finally hooked him. Then I had so much line out that when he leaped he was so far away we could not photograph him. But presently he sheered round close to us, and then we got some fine shots of him.

Some time later we raised a marlin which looked thick across the back; however, he would have none of my stale bait. And as we could not catch any more, though we ran ten miles trying, we returned to the *Fisherman*. My sailfish weighed 102 pounds. He had the dark spots, instead of bars, very pronounced, and I decided to call this species Spotted Sailfish.

R. C. reported raising a large sailfish that took the bait but ejected it. Captain M. had a heavy tuna on for half an hour. We all formed a most favorable impression of Bora-Bora as a fishing-ground, especially when the bonito came.

CHAPTER FOUR

ON AUGUST 31, while trolling from Bora-Bora to Raiatea, in mid-channel, I had an encounter with one of the great South Sea marlin.

The sea was choppy, but not uncomfortable, and as blue as indigo. For bait I was trolling a long slim silver fish that appeared to me wonderfully attractive. We had left Bora-Bora at eight o'clock. At 12.15 I thought I saw a golden shadow behind the right teaser. I stood up, and then I thought I had been mistaken. But then it flashed again—closer. I yelled.

A second later a gold-green monster rushed my bait, engulfed it, and with magnificent whirl turned back. The line whistled. A long thin splash shot up. I dropped in my chair. It never occurred to me to let the fish take line. He was going swift as lightning. I screwed on the drag.

Then he lifted me. Half standing, I jerked on the rod with all my might six or eight times. What tremendous weight! And I had hooked him. The run exceeded two hundred yards. Then he slowed to rise and leap half out. How wild a chorus of yells went up! It was one of the big marlin we had come to catch. Huge broad head, dark back, green-gold sides, deep, thick, and long—the same species as the monster Captain M. had lost last year.

We waved to R. C. to hurry back. The *Fisherman* was now bearing down on us. She sheered aside, but passed us with everybody at the rail, while my swordfish sounded. He appeared to loaf awhile. Then he took a run deep under the surface. But I soon got that line back. Next he shot out on a long hard run of several hundred yards, at the end of which he began to leap. We saw his full length and breadth—a wonderful fish of six hundred pounds or more. He had short black dorsal fin, a long bill, curved slightly upward, and he was silver underneath. On this dash he ran the leaps up to sixteen, by my count. Meanwhile R. C. came up, hailed us, and congratulated me. "What you on?" called R. C. through his megaphone.

Just then my marlin leaped again. Pandemonium broke loose on R. C.'s boat. I settled down to a fight. Bob and Romer, in wild excitement, were active with cameras, while Francis ran the boat and used the Imo moving-picture camera. Peter held the back of my chair.

The big marlin gave a fine exhibition of leaping, on and off, sometimes in series, until my count went to forty-one. Bob had forty-seven; Romer more. The last two were not so far from the boat, and were thrilling in the extreme.

All this took over two hours, and the fish was working us back into the channel, where the water was rough. The wind freshened and the swells grew larger. At two hours and a half the marlin started to sound, and he went down over four hundred yards. There he stopped. It took my utmost strength to hold the line then. But he had quit. No doubt the tremendous pressure of water soon killed him. There we were and the sea was rising. I was pretty tired. My hands grew weak, especially the left one that I had sprained in my fall two weeks before. And my feet were sore from trying to brace myself here, there, and everywhere on the floor and gunwales.

R. C. kept circling us. He called, "How deep down?" And when I replied he shook his head dubiously. I could gain only a few inches at a time. The swells lifted the boat, and of course that pulled line off my reel, favoring the fish. I lost more than I could get back.

After three hours and seven minutes I saw the futility of further proceeding on that tack. I had Francis run the boat ahead, until my line slanted a little, instead of straight down. Then after a few minutes of this I had him throw out the clutch and I began to heave and wind with all my might. But this soon got too desperately wearing on me. The heavy swell made fighting him impossible.

Nevertheless we went on, running the boat ahead, then stopping while I endeavored to recover line. Perhaps altogether I might have reeled in fifty yards. This with four hundred still out, a fish that felt like the bottom of the ocean, was simply heartrending. If the sea had been calm I might have lifted him, although Francis thought he had become entangled in the leader and had to be pulled up broadside. Peter agreed with him; however, I did not accept this theory. Finally I instructed Peter to take hold of the line with one hand and try to start the fish. I really had no hope of drawing him to the surface. But Peter worked patiently and slowly. He did not pull. He held the line, and when a swell lifted us he gained a few feet, then held on. How slow this was! Not for an hour did I have any hope. Then the reel appeared to be filling. The time came when Francis said we would get him. Peter, too, was sanguine. He came easier and easier, according to them. At last, with about a hundred feet to the double line, I could no longer resist hoping and believing we could get him. Then the line broke!

R. C. who saw, made a gesture. Romer yelled his dismay. But poor Bob, who had never seen one of our losing battles, could not be reconciled. Peter said I should have gone back to the rod pulling just before that accident, and I agreed with him. I had thought of it, and meant to, but I did not decide soon enough. Four hours and seven minutes! I had had many harder battles and more bitter. Still, this was a disappointment.

We were three hours running to the ship at Raiatea, where R. C. averred we had under-rated the size of the marlin. "Between six and seven hundred. And sure a game bird!" Francis said it might well be true.

Thad saw a swordfish breach on the run in and he declared it was all of twenty feet long. "I'm sold on these marlin now," he said, and claimed he had not at first believed they ran so large as we claimed.

"We'll have a powwow tomorrow. I'm about all in," was my answer. So we called it a day. For my part I would never forget that blue channel, and Bora-Bora standing up into the trade-wind clouds.

We had the powwow, the outcome of which was a general conviction that these unknown seas were to reveal staggering facts about game fish.

Only the natives had fished about the Leewards. And they used shell gigs for bonito. During the season when bonito are plentiful these natives never venture outside the reefs. They are in dread of the great *espadon*, some of which are the length of their canoes. I did not see a canoe in Raiatea that was less than twenty feet in length. I recalled to mind what the fisherman of Bora-Bora told us—in good English—that as many as five *espadon* had followed him in his sailboat while he fished for bonito.

On Sunday we planned to motor to a village some miles around the island, and there procure guides and climb Raiatea mountain to see the marvelous and rare flower that was reported to grow on the summit.

I doubt if I ever would have attempted the trip had I had the faintest idea of what lay before us. We left the road at about nine o'clock, and took to a trail through cocoanut groves into the jungle. It was a fascinating walk. The scarlet hibiscus bloomed wild everywhere, and I saw white blossoms high on trees. Ferns and vines and moss grew with a profusion I had not observed elsewhere. After several miles we began to go uphill, gradually at first. I had caught a glimpse of a mountain wall ahead, and I said to myself, "If we have to climb that—good night!"

We got into a canyon, where a roaring brook tumbled down over huge boulders, like any other mountain brook. The foliage of the prevailing tree here, a large tree with fluted trunk, the color of a birch, appeared to be a shining slate green. The shade was deep, dark, and cool.

Presently we left the brook and started straight uphill. The trail was old and poor, full of roots and rocks, and the slipperiest wet mud I had ever tried to walk in. The jungle gloomed overhead, so that seldom could we see the sky. We had to rest every few steps. We labored under considerable thrill and excitement, which no doubt spurred us on. We stretched out along that trail for a mile. Romer and Bob, with Peter and Reuben and one of the guides, soon were far in the lead. We could hear them whooping.

One of the mountain slopes we edged bore a thick jungle of green bamboo, so thick that it was impenetrable, so dense I could not see far through. The bamboos were about forty to fifty feet high, and not to be compared with clumps of golden bamboo we had seen before—upwards of seventy feet, as thick at the base as a man's thigh. I reveled in this green bamboo jungle. As a boy in Zanesville, Ohio, I used to buy a bamboo fishing-pole from a bundle, and I romanced about where the cane had come from and how they grew. It was wonderful for me finally to see a forest of bamboo fishing-poles.

At twelve o'clock we were up at the edge of timber line. We had to climb a knife-edge ridge, above which began a slope of ferns, and beyond that wet rock. Two of the six native girls who had chosen to accompany us turned back. Then presently Sid, purple in the face, vowed he could go no farther. Later two others of my party found it expedient to halt where they were. But the rest of us went on. When I got to the head of the fern slope I caught a glimpse of R. C. and Romer, a mile above me on the rocks.

At two o'clock, five hours later than the start, we were up on the summit of Raiatea. The view was grand. We looked down on the lesser Raiatea, and the many islands adjacent, and the encompassing reef. These coral reefs are the most astonishing and beautiful features of the South Seas. We could see a hundred miles of white crawling surf, and hear its bellow and boom. Lagoons of deep dark azure, and every shade of green, bewildered our gaze. I could have looked for hours. But time pressed.

A little after two we descended a short distance, through a fragrant and colorful furze or heather-like brush, to the swale where the tiare apatai bloomed. The flowers were worth such a strenuous effort.

These blossoms grow on a rather large bush, with branches ending in a bunch of long, dark-green, slim leaves, in the center of which blooms half of the tiare apatai. The other half is closed. Besides its rare loveliness, that is the striking characteristic. The flower in bloom is a delicate white, and has a faint perfume. It looks like half of a ten-petaled flower that has been split down the middle. The other half is a closed bud, which will bloom on the morrow. The natives said it would open with a pop.

We rested and photographed, the native girls gathering blossoms and making wreaths.

Then we started to retrace our steps. I, for one, old mountain-climber that I am, was pretty tired. I had on rubber-soled shoes that were more slippery than ice. My first slide was down thirty feet of fern trail. Did I scoot? I surely did. And when I got up there was a howl of glee behind me, for I had torn the seat of my pants.

We could not help making fast time, because we either slid down or fell down. Soon we reached the jungle, the muddy trail, almost straight down. There the most devilish descent began. It was hot in the jungle. I was as wet as if I had fallen in the sea. And soon I was black from head to toe. I tore the whole seat out of my golf trousers, and I was so sore, so weary, that I did not care how I looked. I fell at least a hundred times. I slid most of the way. I wore out my skin. My feet hurt so I could hardly stand it. It was impossible to go slowly. The brush, the roots, the vines, the ferns, the banana stalks, all but the hard woods, broke with us, and treacherously let us slide. Fortunately there was no serious danger. Outside of a sprain or bruise or scratch we did not risk much. But the strenuousness and infernal nature of that descent beat anything I ever experienced, even lassoing lions with Buffalo Jones and the Mormans.

We descended three thousand feet in two hours, and I was willing to bet that I fell most of it. We had worn white clothes. What was left of them was black. But at last we reached the foot of that terrible mountain. The wild-orange trees grew high, seventy feet or more, and the oranges from them were exceedingly luscious. And the brook of cold water! Who could appreciate oranges or water so well as we who had been parched for hours? The most wonderful sights and sensations come from the most tremendous efforts.

We arranged a native fish drive. Across the bay from Raiatea the reef makes a long curve and joins a large island in such a way as to form a perfect fish trap. Here we went in the morning to find several hundred natives waiting for us. About thirty canoes went out to the reef, approximately two miles down, and forming a line they proceeded toward the apex of the triangle, beating the water with paddles and casting huge stones to which ropes were attached. They worked fairly fast.

The natural trap ended in a built corral, which had a gateway into a smaller one. Then, women and children, after singing and having a prayer from their chief, waded in, and spread in V-shaped formation from the traps outward. The long line of men extended in a curve out on the reef. The day was cloudy and stormy. Rain was falling, and a heavy surf broke over the reef, flooding it at times to the depth of a foot or more, all of which we were instructed made for a poor fishing day.

The scene was noisy, colorful, primitive, and singularly thrilling to me. Probably this fish drive, a custom now fallen to disuse, had been a strong factor in the lives of the early Polynesians. It held something epic for me, long before the climax. There was much hilarity. But as the canoes with their beaters approached, the natives began to grow excited. A leader splashed up and down the middle of the lane on the reef, exhorting the assemblage in loud voice. The rain ceased and the sky grew lighter. The great rollers boomed on the coral; the wind waved the palms; and the shrill cries of the women chimed with the hoarse shouts of the men.

I waded out on the reef and took my place in the line farthest out. I had a stick with which I beat the water when the natives did so with their spears, and when they crouched I did likewise. The canoes closed up the gaps between them; the beaters jumped overboard, and began to wade, pounding the water with wide paddles.

This was the climax, and the fun began. Yet it seemed powerfully earnest, too. How they yelled! The women laughed and sang. Soon I saw a ripple in the green water and I knew fish were coming. This was what had excited the natives. Presently in the water before me I saw a school of fish moving up, green and gray and purple. I saw one big black-backed fish, and long slim fish, and flashing silver fish. Another school came on. This second one milled around, but finally went on. When the surge came over I perceived ridges on the water where the faster fish escaped between the natives. The beaters came crashing up, and then the V-shaped line closed in, and all drove the fish into the first corral, from which they ran through the gateway into the second and smaller one.

I hurried over to find it full of fish, large and small, and of many colors. The purple-finned crevalle struck my eye. But there were red and yellow fish, blue fish, and less brilliantly hued fish. The pond was surrounded by the several hundred natives, and evidently a gala event was to be enacted. I now found out what it was. I, for whom the drive had been given, was expected to enter the pond with the spear given me, and capture the fish I wanted, after which I was to present the rest to the natives. I could hit the fish most every time, but the spear would not stick. Finally I got hold of a big gray pig-snouted fish, to the delight of the onlookers, and lifted it wriggling out of the corral. Then the others of my party were instructed to take spears and wade in to follow my example. Mrs. Mitchell and Millicent Smith promptly complied, and they certainly furnished excitement and amusement for that crowd. Mrs. M. speared a big fish, and trying to hold it, she fell, almost going under, yet valiantly holding to her prize. Millicent splashed all over the pond and after many attempts secured her prize. Then Captain Mitchell and the boys took their turn with the spears, which to say the least was tragic for the luckless fish.

When all were speared and lifted out I selected a few small crevalle for bait, and presented the rest to the chief, who in turn gave me a beautiful wreath of flowers. That ended the ceremony of the fish drive, which we all agreed was a splendid and unique spectacle. I rather regretted the massacre of the poor fish at the end, but we could not escape any more than could the fish.

The French Administrator, who was with us, told me that some of these fish were poisonous and the fact that fatalities occurred did not deter them from going on eating them. A child-like, primitive, fatalistic race! Some of the young girls had tragic, brooding faces. The chant before the drive was interesting, and beautiful in places, especially the long monotonous wail at the end.

In the afternoon we had a race of the pirogues. These were native canoes, long and slim, with outriggers and huge sails. There were thirty-five pirogues—the most ever assembled for a race at Raiatea—and the sight was enthralling. A stiff trade-wind was blowing, and to see these half-naked native sailors manœuvre for positions, to tack back and forth, to stand far out on the outriggers, to steer with the huge paddles, and luff their sails, and then, after circling the flag boat, to come back with the wind, white sails on a blue sea, exceedingly graceful and swift, was one of the most beautiful sights I ever saw.

The race was won by a trim blue canoe with a monster white sail. The name was *Tehenaaro*, and the crew consisted of five young natives in *pareus*, a fine-looking quintet of sailors who came over the *Fisherman's* side wet and shining and gay as larks. I presented the prize—250 francs—to them, and a flag; and also 50 francs to all the canoes that had entered. This last appeared to please them mightily.

At sunset this fleet, like a flock of white gulls, sailed away across the bay, and that to me seemed the most colorful and lovely scene of a wonderful day.

CHAPTER FIVE

THE fire-walkers of Raiatea performed their ancient and picturesque rite for us.

There were ten men and ten women, all young, except the leader and medicine-man, who was very old. They wore short grass skirts and wreaths of purple bougainvillæa.

The fire-stones, I should hasten to explain, were arranged in a long flat pile. These had been laid on a high cordage of wood, which when burned out let the stones down. Under the top layer the stones were red hot. Rain fell at intervals, and it caused the rocks to steam. A sacred plant with long oval green leaves had been imbedded in the ground close to the fire. The most remarkable feature of all was the fact that this plant did not shrivel or change color.

The leader addressed the gods, presumably, and exhorted them to permit their passage in their bare feet over these hot rocks. He beat on the ground with leaves of this sacred plant, and all of his walkers carried a bundle of similar leaves. They marched two by two, following the leaders, straight over the fire. It was an extraordinary action. I had expected some sort of trick, but there seemed to be none. They turned and walked back again, and then they crossed from side to side, waving their long leaves, and they shouted a wild huzzah.

After the procession had ended we were informed through the interpreter that we could walk safely across the stones. We did so, and I can testify that the soles of my shoes grew uncomfortably warm. Then wood was thrown on the stone again, and in very short order it was blazing. There was entirely no doubt about the presence of heat. I observed that the stones were of slate. In olden times, we were told, blocks of lava were used, and these retained their heat.

I had read considerable about this fire-walker spectacle, and the articles were conflicting. Some of them drew largely upon a rather vivid and unreliable imagination. The writers are not few who have exploited the South Seas. They wrote fascinatingly about the natives, and their environment, and their life and legends. But I found these writers unsafe to follow.

I did not find anything supernatural in the feat of the fire-walkers, or in their *feet*, either. An observer will see that these natives have broad, heavy, thick feet, with spatulate toes. They have gone barefoot all their lives. The soles of their feet are as tough as leather. I saw natives run over sharp coral that would have crippled a white man.

This fact, and a singular and child-like faith, accounted to me for the fire-walkers. Nevertheless, that in no way detracted from the charm and beauty and simplicity of the ceremony. It added to my liking for the natives.

Upon our return, scarcely had we boarded the *Fisherman* when a terrific gale swooped down. Our anchorage was none too good. We began to drag, and for a while I was not any too sanguine. It took some work to get three cables fast to the buoy and one to the wharf. Then, by sending the launches in, and thereby relieving the drag on the boom, we felt safe.

Presently a large tree drifted across the cables and stuck fast. A heavy sea was running and threatened to break the ropes or saw through them. One of our Tahitian sailors, a magnificent specimen, dove off the ship and swam against sea and gale. He reached the tree and freed it from the ropes. Then it drifted right toward the launches. But the native managed somehow to tow it out of line. The whole achievement stirred me to keen enthusiasm and appreciation, and I vowed I would not forget that Tahitian.

This brought again to mind the efficiency and character of our native crew. Both former trips on the *Fisherman* were made in spite of lousy, drunken, good-for-nothing white sailors at an enormous wage, and with skippers as bad and worse. I never quite got over their conduct. The contrast offered by these Tahitians was remarkable. They utterly spoiled me for any other kind of crew. And if I am ever insane enough again to attempt another sea voyage I shall employ natives from mess boy to engineers.

The squally weather ended in a real southeaster, a black storm. Next day the wind began to shift toward the northeast. We had only old bait, but foolishly we went out anyhow. A big swell was running on the leeward side of the island, otherwise it was not so bad.

I raised a pretty fine swordfish that came alongside my crevalle, and just when I thought he would take it for sure he sheered off and left us.

That sent us inside the reef to try to catch fresh bait. It appeared useless. So we ran up on the inside toward the schooner. Presently I had a smashing strike and a long run. Something fast and heavy! We caught up with it, and I worked carefully on the light tackle, to bring up eventually my first barracuda in the South Seas. He was four feet long and weighed $43\frac{1}{2}$ pounds, a fine sample of this species.

Blue skies again, scudding white clouds, rippling seas, shining and beautiful shore line.

While two of the launches were out to try for bait I stayed on the *Fisherman* to write. At noon they returned without one single fish. Nevertheless, we ran out to try again, and to use stale bait if we could not get fresh. We had some mullet that would have given any swordfish nostalgia, or anything else.

In the pass we had a strike. Lost. Then Reuben hooked a nice bait which was stolen by a shark. We tried again, and this turn around the coral reef we got a crevalle. Whereupon we ran out to sea. The great swell was gone, and the sea appeared lumpy, yet fishable. We trolled several hours. About four o'clock Captain Mitchell hooked on, and we raced to see what it was. When the fish stuck out its head both Francis and I said, "Small marlin." Eventually, however, when it stood up on its tail we not only saw our error, but we saw a splendid sailfish. Romer went out on the bow with his camera, while I stayed in the stern with mine. He snapped seven leaps and I five, some of which were spectacular in the extreme.

When Cappy landed this sailfish I knew for sure my world record had gone by the board. Shortly after that we ran back to the schooner. The sailfish was eleven feet seven inches in length and weighed 163 pounds. It appeared to be in poor condition and had probably just spawned. The broad tail took my eye. No wonder those sailfish can race and leap and crack their sails like whips.

R. C. reported raising a fine sailfish, to get a good run and jump out of him before he departed. In this connection R. C. made a pertinent remark worthy of recording.

"Fishy out there! I'll bet if we were here at the right season we'd have our tackle taken away from us!"

The fish drive had proved so fascinating in its possibilities for pictures that we arranged to have it again, with three hundred natives, all in *pareus*. The weather turned out good and we were treated to a spectacle that for color, action, beauty, and thrill could hardly be surpassed. Anything, of course, that had to do with primitive natives and the pursuit of fish would be bound to captivate me. But this drive would have delighted any one. The setting was so marvelous—golden coral reef running in a curve to meet a palm-fringed islet—outside the dark-blue heaving sea, rolling in to swell in great white-crested breakers, to boom and crash, and slide in a flat millrace of foam in over the reefs, the singing natives, half naked, their beautiful brown bodies shining in the sun—the wheeling gulls and boobies, and a few curious frigate birds—the mountains beyond the blue channel, towering to the level trade-wind clouds, and lastly, dominating all, the changing, incessant, mournful and melodious sound of the sea.

In the afternoon, with some fresh bait—crevalle—we ran down to the lee side, and trolled for hours. Three boats, covering miles and miles, failed to raise a single fish.

Next day we trolled from Raiatea to Huahine, the most northern of the Leewards. It lay to windward, and therefore we had rough sledding until we got in the lee again. I dragged a bait for twenty miles, up and down roaring hollows of blue water. And it was no fun. About mid-channel we raised a dolphin (coryphene). He slashed at the starboard teaser, then at my bait, which was a mullet. He missed it. Then Bob let out a feather gig. The dolphin took it on the run, leaped to show the leader in his mouth. With a fling he sent it flying.

Huahine was not impressive from a distance, compared with the other islands of the group. But as we drew near it developed quite swiftly a loveliness I had not seen before in the South Seas. It appeared a fresh green-gold, with two high mountains, one at each end, and between them slopes and ridges running down to deep indented bays. The shore line was a blazing white beach and a fringe of cocoanuts. A deep-blue channel cut the reef, and inside the colors of coral showed from dark green to bottle green, aquamarine, pale yellow-green, and hues too exquisite for definition. Flowering trees gave contrast to the palms, and along the line of thatched huts the hibiscus shone bright and red. These were the details. But they failed to do justice to the beauty of Huahine.

We went ashore to wait for the *Fisherman*. The natives crowded to the little dock to inspect our launches. They did not appear very friendly. Only a few greeted us. The village was picturesque, clean, and neat.

Two striking incidents I recorded. I saw two natives with elephantiasis. One's legs were widened to the size of an elephant's, clear down to his feet, yet he actually walked. The repulsive nature of this disease cannot be described in words. The natives have superstitious ideas about it. One claimed that he got it by carrying a very heavy load and then drinking too much water. They call it *fee-fee*.

The other incident was funny. When we tied up alongside the wharf, Peter threw a dead crevalle into the water. It sank to the bottom, fully twelve feet. Now a number of ragged brown urchins lined the dock, and one of them, a mere tot, dove down and got that crevalle. I was dumfounded. He came up like a porpoise, climbed out, carrying his prize, and trudged away.

Captain Mitchell interviewed the natives about fish. November and December, when the bonito came in, there were swordfish about. Twenty feet in length were common. So again we heard the astonishing claim about these great *espadon*.

During late September and through October flying-fish came into the bay to spawn, and they could be seen in countless numbers standing up in shallow water with their noses in the sand. This seemed remarkable to me. But I have seen so many wonderful facts in nature—truth is stranger than fiction—that I am susceptible to stories of any kind, and the stranger they are the more I am apt to put credence in them.

The night we ran from Huahine to Papeete, the launches, with two boatmen and two natives in each, left the *Fisherman* and went on ahead. They encountered bad weather and had a severely rough time getting in. At that they beat us by twenty hours. This decided me not to attempt the long run to Rangaroa with the small boats. A heavy sea would swamp these thirty-four-foot launches, and I could not let the men incur such risk. We left the Paumotus for some other more favorable time, and we arrived back at Flower Point, my camp at Vairao, on September 12.

The weather conditions had altered in the month of our absence. Little rain had fallen; the wind had shifted farther toward the north; and it was perceptibly warmer.

On September 14 we went out to look around, as Cappy said. I ran east to the end of the island, finding it rough out there. On the way back we sighted more birds than I had ever seen at Vairao. Bonito, however, appeared scarce. Jimmy, one of my natives, saw a sailfish jump. I trolled a twenty-pound tuna for four hours, and never raised a fin. Captain M. caught a barracuda and a crevalle. He raised a thousand-pound swordfish, and when he told about it I shared his excitement, enthusiasm, and disappointment. The big marlin would not look at the crevalle bait. He was interested in the teasers. Captain said his dorsal stood up, and his tail likewise, far out of the water. No doubt this bird would have taken a fresh bait.

Altogether I considered the signs more favorable than I had expected, at least until October. It was my conviction that the schools of bonito were migratory, and the big fish followed them.

Next morning was still, cool, sweet, and clear—a most glorious tropic dawn.

We ran to the east end of the island, some ten miles or more. The reef breaks there and several miles of open sea run in to the steep green bluff. Shallow green water! The coral bottom, green, white, blue, amber, could be plainly seen. Huge swells piled up and all but broke. We trolled up and down with various lures. No strike!

Then we ran on out to sea on the return trip. Soon we sighted birds and bonito. We allowed the first flock and school to go by. But the next, farther on, we ran after. Thousands of black-and-white birds—terns—whirled and darted over the white patches on the water. We had never seen either so many birds or so many bonito. Our native fishermen, Jimmy and Charley, put out their pearl gigs, and the fun began. We had never caught any bonito from my launch, at least more than one or two, and we did not expect to do more here.

The native tackle consists of a long, thick, stiff bamboo pole, a stout line the same length, and a pearl gig. This gig is a clever job. It consists of a slender piece of pearl shell with a barbless hook made out of a copper nail bound on the inside or convex side. Two little whiskers of bristles stick out from the blunt end of the shell. This lure is skittered over the water, and slid to and fro. It rides like a little boat. The whiskers flutter back. In fact, it is a very delicate and extraordinary artificial bait. I do not see how it can be taken for a small minnow. But this day it was a killer.

Jimmy and Charley began to horse bonito into the boat. The method was most interesting. The boat kept moving fairly fast. When a bonito struck at the pearl gig he made no bones about it. He smashed the water. If he got the hook he would fight down. The thing was to lift and keep him from getting his head. As a result many holds were pulled loose. But when a bonito came out he did it with a vengeance—a solid, heavy, swinging six or eight pounds of fish right into the boat. They came hard and fast. Francis was struck four times. The natives tried to catch the bonito under their arms, and sometimes succeeded.

We caught half a dozen before the school went down. Then we followed the birds. Soon the water grew white again, and silvery bonito leaped everywhere. We had to run full speed to head them off. Then the carnage began again. This time the bonito flew aboard like hailstones. And at that the natives lost two, to one that they hooked. Peter and I trolled all through this mêlée. Once I was trying to get a fresh bait out of the flapping, bloody mess on the cockpit floor, and Jimmy swung one aboard that hit me in the back of the neck and knocked me down, my head going through the aperture of our canvas chair. How those men howled! Once Charley swung one over that hit him plumb in the stomach and knocked him down. He sat down in a bucket and we yelled with glee.

This sort of thing continued for at least half a dozen times when we caught up with one of these fleet schools of bonito. I never heard such a battering as those bonito made on the floor or saw so much blood and slime. We could not stand up. The bonito vomited quantities of small silver minnows, about three inches long, resembling anchovies. These were feed for them, and for the birds also. We had a wonderful time and caught four boxes full of bonito. And all during this circus we kept out two baits.

I had a try at it, and though I prepared myself for a lusty stout fish, I was indeed surprised. My first one nearly jerked me in. But I lifted and lifted, and when I got him up in the air he came like a bullet right at Peter. He yelled and ducked, but he got a thump on the back. My bonito flew off and went sliddering and thumping about. Francis climbed up in the jitney to escape this rough-house treatment. I had ten more strikes and caught ten more bonito. This elated me so that I let well enough alone. R. C. had never caught any, and Captain M. only one. I could now enlarge upon the proper method of taking this wonderful bait upon a native rig.

Swordfish evidently were not in this day, or surely we would have raised one. We ran in at sunset. And I watched a rose and gold glory on the heights of mountain and cloud, thrilling anew at a beauty beyond description.

On Sunday, September 16, I saw the most wonderful fish that my eyes had ever beheld.

The afternoon was cool, with a fine mist blowing. Edge of gray clouds overhead, but sun shining out at sea. Fair breeze and ripple.

We were trolling a mile or more outside the reef, Francis, Peter, and I, in the boat. We had out two bonito and two teasers, the large Z. G. gold teasers. Suddenly we heard the water crack. About one hundred feet to the left a big splash flew up and a fish leaped. Then we were treated to a magnificent spectacle.

After it was over we talked and reduced the details down to the nearest it was possible to fact. Francis is keen-eyed and practical; Peter is an old whaler; and I have most likely seen more fish jump than any other angler in the world. So much for veracity and observation!

This strange fish leaped four times, the last two leaps exceeding fifty feet. He leaped on his side, his belly only exposed to us. His velocity was incredible. He covered over one hundred yards in the four leaps, and when he ended one leap he was out again before the splash had subsided. The leaps were greyhound, long and low. He resembled a cannon shell ricocheting over the water. He was pale yellow in color, about eleven or twelve feet long, round and thick all the way to the tail, and over four hundred pounds weight. He had a short broadbill, apparently the same color, and on the under jaw. Peter said his head resembled a duck's. I looked for his mouth, but could not see any, and that strengthened my conviction that the bill or sword was underneath. We did not see any fins.

All of us were struck alike by the fish's speed, power, ferocity. Either the launch had scared him or there was an enemy after him. He might have been a broadbill with his bill broken off about half. But the color of any broadbill in any sea is a purple-bronze on back, and white underneath. This fish tallied closely to the *espadon* we learned about in the Paumotus, from natives, and an Armenian who lived at Rangaroa. The short bill, the yellow color, the tremendous speed, all combined to make me sure I had finally seen one of these rare unclassified fish, and fired my ambition anew.

It also led to more consideration of the fact that we might raise an unknown and wonderful fish at any moment. That I had always believed. But now we knew. This is a decided stimulus to fishing, when the days are endless, the good luck so little and far between, and the great mysterious sea seems empty of fish.

CHAPTER SIX

THE necessity of fresh bait was never more exemplified than on the following afternoon. We had eight bonito caught the day before and put on ice. They had a little shine, but were pretty soft. After trolling one for half an hour it would burst and go to pieces.

Finally we raised two beautiful marlin, one about 400 and the other, that hung back, around 300 pounds. The large one weaved back of my bait, swift, but not as if he were mad or scared. Then he sheered out, turned, and rushed my bonito, shoving his head out to take it. Maybe that was not a pretty sight! He went off fine and easy. I signaled to R. C.'s boat, close at hand. All was activity at the possibility of pictures. Then the marlin ejected my bait, and both of them came to the boat. They were hungry. It certainly made me use language. I wound in my bonito to find it a rotten mess, all squashed up.

We made up our minds that we would have to solve the bait problem in some way, if we could find it possible. To that end we put our heads together.

The water had a temperature of eighty-one degrees. And very likely as summer came on it would rise higher. This fact, and the sun shining down hot on a trolled bait, would spoil a perfectly fresh bait in short order. On cloudy days a bonito would last longer. Thus a very great obstacle to successful fishing stood in our way. Not many anglers could consistently fish these waters, at least when bait and fish were scarce, as they were in July, August, and September. I had yet to experience October and November. But even so, not many fishermen would stand the hot sun—which burned a hole through a helmet and burned a straw hat up—let alone the long drill to raise a fish. The extreme difficulty, however, did not pall me on this fishing, for the simple reason that these unknown waters contained the most magnificent game fish I had ever got any data on. Nothing thrilled me so much as virgin fishing.

Inside the reef we sighted a humpback whale—a cow—and a calf. We gave chase and soon were upon them. The water was fairly shallow, so they could not sound, and restricted to rather narrow confines, so that they could not mill around much. The mother whale had to accommodate her pace to that of her baby. The little one had to blow often, and presently got frightened, when we ran over it, and came up with a great flurry, almost all the way out. I had a fine view of a baby whale, about twenty feet long, thick and plump, dark chocolate color, with a pronounced hump, and a hog-like head covered with knots. The mother had these identical features magnified. It was too late in the day to photograph, so we chased them back to the passage, and had a lot of fun out of it.

R. C. raised one of the big marlins the next day—one of the long heavy gazabos that looked yellow on the back. But it would not strike at the strip bait he was trolling. R. C. said he believed this swordfish had come along under his bait, had sized it up, and was dropping back when discovered.

The day was certainly beautiful, fine and cool in spots, hot now and then, breezy, then calm—all the same Zihautenejo weather. It was not exactly a joy to troll leagues across the blue sea, but if there had been a fish hooked once or so, no more could have been asked.

Toward sundown a slight wind sprang up from the southwest, and birds and bonito appeared. We chased one school for miles, and catching up with them, we soon had the cockpit a bloody mess again. Jimmy snaked bonito out of the ocean as fast as he could haul them out and cast his pearl gig back. It was a treat to see him. He would weave the gig over the surface, and when a bonito struck he would lift and swing it in low and hard. A number of them actually left the barbless hook before they were in the boat. I dodged a number, swung right in at me, and I got plentifully spotted by blood.

After a while I let down a live bonito, three, four hundred feet. Something took it, moved off. When I hooked it I thought maybe I might have a swordfish. But he came to the surface—a long six-yard green-and-silver shark, entirely new to me. It was tangled up in the leader. I began to drag it toward the boat, when it rolled over, freed itself, and dove.

I had on a strong drag. It was nothing. That shark made the line melt off—one hundred yards—two—three, until five hundred were off—fifteen hundred feet straight down in a few seconds. Then I stopped him, or he decided to stop himself, most likely the latter. I could not budge him one inch. We threw in the clutch, and I held the line with both gloved hands, and we dragged him a hundred yards or more. Then we backed the launch, while I pumped and reeled in line. In this way I got back half of it, when the strain slackened. Off! I thought the line had broken. But it turned out he had bitten through the leader. There was a new specimen of shark that I wanted.

August 20 was a day to remember. But not for fish or birds or bait! We had a hot, clear, almost windless day, absolutely barren of clouds. Not until about two o'clock, after trolling for hours, did I realize I was dizzy and weak. I got back under cover, which helped somewhat, though my head continued to ache. One by one my boatmen and the natives and Romer and Bob showed the effect of the heat and the monotony. Romer held one of my rods for nearly four hours—a very commendable feat for him, considering his youth, restlessness, and infernal energy. He had vastly improved in a year.

When we got in to the passage we were surprised to find a mountainous swell running in. The grand green-and-white curling breakers were awe-inspiring, and beautiful in the extreme. This northwest corner always gave me a thrill, but I had never seen it so majestically turbulent, so furious in its break, so frothing in its maelstrom of spent wave against its barrier, the coral. The swell would begin far out at sea, half a mile or more, and move in with wonderful rapidity, to rise along a horseshoe front, swell and mount to change from blue to green, and with gathering momentum lift high and higher, in a stately and colossal power, to curl its spindrift crest into a long green whorl, like the wheels of thousands of chariots, and then, falling in terrible thundering roll and boom, burst into white chaos over the reef, like white horses of the gods.

The *Fisherman* was anchored broadside as close to the coral as possible, which in this case was perhaps thirty feet. We had a dock made of native wood and a gangway, so that we could go on and off easily.

The coral band extended perhaps a hundred yards out from the shore, white marl with bunches of live coral, shallow water with about a foot difference in low and high tide.

This reef fell away into deep water very quickly, but when it was calm and smooth the white and streaked coral could be seen under the ship. I was therefore able to see many and various kinds of fish and marine creatures. Starfish as large as a melon, with stars scarcely discernible, so round was this creature, often dotted the bottom, deep down. Many-colored little fish showed along the edge of the coral. I made note of one, a ten-inch fish that looked like a piece of gray-and-black coral, until it moved. Here was perfect protective coloration. Once I saw a queer fish, about a foot or more long, gray and slightly flecked, with the shape of a sucker. He had two long feelers, and he rooted in the coral like a carp in the mud. I saw mullet with black pectoral fins, and a black band around the body, between dorsal and tail.

One very still morning I made a discovery. Back by the stern of the schooner, and somewhat outside, stood up a huge coral head, as large as a house and shaped like a rose. It was not less than fifteen feet under the surface at its highest point, and on ordinary days, when the water was even the least ruffled, could not be seen clearly. But through the exquisitely transparent water on this morning it might as well have been out in the light, so vividly did every detail show. The colors were subdued, gray and bronze. Its surface resembled that of a sponge, and it was the home of myriads of fish. No aquarium I had ever beheld could be named in the same breath with this one.

I hung over the rail for a marvelous hour and missed my breakfast. When I realized that I could not record a hundredth part of what I saw I was in despair. A school of angel-fish floated out, swimming in order, as if on parade. They were of one species, and varied in size from the size of a hand to nearly a foot in length. Pale yellow in color, with black bands around the body, and a long yellow streamer floating back from the dorsal fin, they were surely striking. Deeper down, big fish showed dimly, seldom coming up far enough to describe. I saw a number of purple turbot. Then a two-foot gray fish, built something like a snapper, with a spur standing out from the head just below the eyes. This was surely a weapon, and the fish acted pugnacious. But I did not observe one of a dozen of this species, or any other species round this coral head, make one threatening move toward any other fish. Black angel-fish with gold tails were visible now and then, but deep and hard to study. I saw green parrot fish, and a blue fish like a bream, with electric spots and streamers from both lobes of the tail.

Twice during this vigil I was treated to an exceedingly beautiful spectacle. And both times it chanced when the larger fish had gone down. A thousand tiny little angel-fish came out of the myriad holes in the coral head and like a shower of colored sparks came upward, within a few feet of the surface, near enough for the sun rays to strike them and for me to see distinctly. Such lovely forms seemed unreal, delicate creatures of the imagination, floating petals of roses, intensely vivid bits of sea shell endowed with life.

The first time this phenomenon occurred I was too thrilled and dazzled to define anything. The second, lasting longer, afforded me opportunity for details, in some faint degree. I saw a flock of tiny pale-blue marine fish, like swallows, flitting in the sunlight, and purple ones with golden tails, and little black fish-like dainty things, spotted white, and a school of goldfish with blue eyes. These few I noted absolutely and remembered. The rest, vastly in majority, moved there in the aquamarine medium, lovely, tranquil, bright-winged, it seemed, beyond any classification or capture. It was just a glimpse into the mystery of the coral sea.

On September 25, the equinoctial upset culminated in a tremendous rainstorm. It began in the night, but did not reach a climax until about 7.30. Then the clouds opened to let down a flood. Hills and sea were shrouded in a pall of obscurity. The rain beat through the windows of my cottage, through the weather stripping, through all but the roof. In fact there are three roofs, and they at least defied the deluge.

It poured for two hours, then cleared, and the sun shone hot, the jungle steamed, the water poured down the trails and paths and flooded the gullies. I walked down to the ship and back, by which time the blue sky grayed over, and again the rain fell, but not torrentially now.

I wrote all day, finding the bungalow above the sea an inspiring place. The reef boomed above the nearer wash of the surf. About five o'clock the sun burst through the clouds again and shone on the misty rain falling on the shore. And a high-arched rainbow appeared—the loveliest phenomenon of nature, and here in tropic Tahiti so rare, so pure, so vivid, that the beauty of it made my soul ache. It began in the canyon just back of our cottages, and curved far aloft, with a background of mauve cloud, to bend down to the next and deeper canyon east. I stood out in the rain and watched, and while I watched a golden lightning suffused the western sky, clouds, and sea. Caught between two evanescent and exquisite spectacles, I lost the best of each by being drawn from one to the other.

Later, I found that the sublime scenery of the Tahitian skyline and shore line, the glory of the wandering reef, the shell-pearl and golden dominating hues of the gorgeous trade-wind clouds, had been so constantly before my gaze, in all the mystery of change, that only phenomena such as I have described above could get my attention. I was shocked to discover this, and vowed I would correct it.

When the afterglow of sunset was on the sea I went out on my porch to look. It faded swiftly. Dark clouds obscured the mountain range, and the shadows lay on the sea. Low boom and crash floated in on the damp salt-laden air. Then a cloud shifted, and I saw a star of such brilliance and magnitude that I gazed spellbound. It shone above in the black sky, like a white lantern, and it had four points. Whether Venus or Jupiter I was not astronomer enough to know, but it was the evening star, "fair as a star when only one is shining in the sky." I thought of Bethlehem and the Wise Men who saw a star, and talked and went their way.

Ruskin wrote that men of any serious turn of mind had a natural love for fair scenery, and those men who loved nature most had most belief in God. It is something to think of in these swift, ruthless, modern days, whether one is fishing, or watching the skies, or toiling at his humdrum daily task.

The storm passed and we went back to fishing, finding a slight improvement in conditions. My continued bad luck showed no sign of changing. One instance only I will record. Jimmy, the native, snagged a cocoanut branch while trolling, and as he could not reel it in the launch had to be stopped. Just as the teasers came to a standstill, a long, purple, waving shape loomed out of the depths. A sailfish—the largest I had seen. He swooped up and by, and disappeared. A few seconds before he would have come for the teasers, and most likely my bait.

The sea continued rough, with birds and bait almost impossible to follow. R. C. hooked a small marlin that went straight down six hundred feet and stayed until he was pulled up—163 pounds. Next day R. C. raised a marlin that would not look at the poor bait. Captain Mitchell raised another right on the reef, but had no bait at all. The following day, however, while trolling a ten-pound tuna, two swordfish rose, one large and the other small. The big one grew excited, but refused the bait. The little one charged it five times, finally got it, and ran nearly all of seven hundred yards off the reel before stopping. Then he made a surface fight. Weight 167 pounds.

This day four marlin rose to follow the boats, a most encouraging sign. But if we were compelled to chase bait half a day or more, and then not get any, this Tahitian fishing would be impossible on any consistent lines. It was growing to be a tremendous strain.

One morning, as usual, we had no bait on starting out, and could not catch any in ten miles of reef fishing. So we ran out to look for birds. At last I espied a flock, moving fast. We gave chase. After a few yards we saw we were not gaining. The boobies and terns would circle and work over the bait, then when it went down they would fly like the wind. Bait and bonito, and of course birds, traveled against sea and wind so we had to buck it. The swells ran high. We risked going faster, and then it was tremendous, even frightful, the way we splashed and bounced. But we could not catch up with that school of bait. Sometimes we gained, when the

Captain Mitchell with Sailfish Caught on Feather Gig, 109 Pounds

World-record Marlin of This Species, 464 Pounds, Caught by Zane Grey at Tahiti

birds worked over the bait. But before we got near they were off again. We ran fully fifteen miles offshore—all in vain.

But on the way in R. C. raised a marlin on cut bait, hooked and caught it. Upon getting back to the ship I found that his fish (152 pounds) had a curiously bent bill. It had been broken and had healed.

Later we chased another school, in calm water, and they actually ran away from us—with the boat making fourteen miles an hour. The bait problem seemed to grow more serious.

At the end of September I had a string of eight blank days in a row, which was the worst spell yet. Altogether, I had thirty blank days out of less than six weeks fishing; and by blank days, I should have explained, I meant days when I raised no fish. This probably caps my record for bad luck during a pioneer fishing trip.

R. C. said: "It's the hardest game we *ever* tackled, even harder than broadbill swordfishing. And as for chasing those flocks of boobies and schools of bait—that is the limit—the d——est job I ever undertook. I chased a bunch today, and got madder and madder, until I took to running the boat myself. Believe me we touched only the tops of the swells! But we caught up with them—after ten miles—and I snaked out one bonito!"

The irony of the Tahitian game of swordfish angling was exemplified that day by Captain Mitchell, who had fine fresh bait, and raised two marlin, separately, neither one of which would so much as look at the bonito.

Yet we had to stick. I do not know what Cappy and R. C. called me, but I have long since autographed my fishing books to them thus: "——Old Sticker——"

The great game fish were out there somewhere, and cost what it might, we were going to get some of them, if it were possible to do so by endurance, skill, experience, and the finest tackle yet manufactured.

How many other things to write about! Along the road from camp to our dock, where the *Fisherman* lay, were thousands of crab holes, and whenever I walked by I watched them. They were a species of sand crab—ghost crab, we called them in Florida—but here they were certainly neither ghostly nor beautiful. The Florida crab is transparent, a pale color, and he is covered with a hair or fuzz. The Tahitian beach crab had the same shape, but was dirty and dark and altogether disreputable. Everywhere along the road they would be out, and upon espying me they scurried to their holes, paused a moment to look—then slipped out of sight. I saw leaves, sticks, and pieces of cocoanut fiber that these crabs had partly pulled into their holes. I decided they were vegetarians. On Tahiti they could hardly be anything else. The Florida ghost crab feeds mostly on the Portuguese man-of-war, which blows ashore on the tide.

I caught a moray in the coral, using small hook and fish bait. It was a pale gray and speckled, dark, a perfect imitation of the coral bottom. We had a tussle with a two-foot octopus, but he escaped. Then Reuben caught one of the many angel-fish called *shatoya*, or something like that, M. Herve, who was with us, said. It was a marvelously beautiful creature, round except for a sharp snout and fan-shaped tail. It had a black bar round the head across the eye, which was also black. Silver belly and sides over three-quarters, with blue stripes running diagonally in opposite directions. Lines of yellow spots between the dorsal fin had a streamer of gold, and a prolongating blue edge all around, and in the center a large black spot, on a background of intensely vivid gold. The tail was gold, and the under part, the end, had a pale-yellow bar and a narrow black one. These were the details. How poor and meager to the quivering realities when the fish was alive! It was an exquisite blazing shield of striped silver or pearl, with the upper and back third fiery gold.

Days passed. Blank days! When I got to ten days without raising a fish I realized that I had come to a familiar sad pass. How many times that has happened! Seventeen days without seeing a fin had been my record. It looked to be a sure thing that I would beat that record at Tahiti.

Crowning this unparalleled dearth of game fish was information received that the bonito, tuna, and swordfish did not come in any great numbers until along in December. We had staked all on October, November, December. The natives we had fished with in 1927, Charley, Arurie, and the others, had vowed so sincerely and earnestly that October, November, and December were the months for us to come. We had come before October so as to get ready, and we had fished our fool heads off, all the time relying on the good season soon to come! I had made arrangements to go on to New Zealand on the December boat. And here we were stuck. Upon being taken to task, the natives claimed they had meant the fish *began* to come in in October. But they frankly admitted that from mid-December on to March was the full season. Bonito and tuna sold in Papeete market for twenty francs in October, ten in November, and in December, January, February, March, one franc. That told the tale. If the simple-minded fellows had only given us that information last year! Some of the natives were not any too honest, but I acquitted these particular bonito fishermen of an attempt to deceive us.

I had been confronted with many problems in the fishing game —with many hard decisions to make. But this was a staggerer. To stick it out or not? That was the question. It was not a question of gameness or endurance on our part—I was satisfied of that. But it was a risk. Six more weeks of such fishing as we had just had would very likely make Tahiti pall on us. And we wanted to come back. We *knew* the magnificent game fish were there—larger and stranger than any that had ever been caught anywhere. No anglers but us had fished these waters. The urge, the fascination, the certainty were mighty strong. Yet on the other hand day after day trying to catch bait, and then long hours trolling without raising a fish—would surely grow deadly. It took the starch out of even an old angler used to fishing new waters—just to think of six weeks more of blank days! Hot sun, glaring seas, wind, rough water, rain and rain and rain, the seared eyeballs, the ache from rocking boat, the pangs of sitting all day long, the necessity of being always alert and ready—these after any large number of unrewarded days lost their zest and charm, lost all but the terrible sameness, and could become insupportable. This I knew, and as always, the cardinal decisions I had to make. I had never had a harder one. Cappy and R. C. would stick till hell froze over, but in this tropic South Sea we could not get even that. I had to take a few days to ponder over this predicament.

The *Fisherman* was practically sold to Father Rougier, one of the famous residents of Tahiti and owner of Christmas Island. We had our beautiful camp almost finished. We had supplies, boats, fuel. R. C. said, "Let's hang on till our hair blows out!" And Captain Mitchell's English chin bulged as he said, "I haven't lost hope yet!" But it was up to me and I was up a tree.

CHAPTER SEVEN

A NATIVE of Manihiki, an old experienced fisherman, told Mr. Nordhoff, the American author living in Tahiti, of the *ihe taviri*, a rare fish of great ferocity and strength, growing to huge size, and almost impossible to catch. This fish was yellow in color and had a short blunt oval bill protruding from the under jaw.

Unquestionably, this is the strange fish my boatman and I saw leap four times, covering one hundred yards with incredible rapidity, and which I described as well as possible in a foregoing chapter.

Mr. Nordhoff, who is something of a scientist and keenly interested in all forms of Polynesian fishing, and I discussed the *ihe taviri*. It is certainly unknown to ichthyology, and would be a startling discovery to the natural-history world. I doubt if this fish is the huge swordfish with bill underneath about which we learned in the Paumotus. One of our native fishermen, Jimmy, who has spent years on the reef, told me of a black swordfish with sword underneath. There are surely some rare and wonderful fish swimming around unclassified.

Funny things happened, even at a time when glum anglers could not crack a smile.

Cappy's native boatmen, and Arearea in particular, thinking to make more comfort for their master, conscientiously and thoroughly greased his swivel chair. Of all the things for boatmen to do! A fishing-chair should be stiff and turn hard. And, lo! Cappy's whirled round like a whirling dervish. I defied anyone to make me laugh those days. Still, this was funny.

However, not near or half so funny as another disaster of

Cappy's. With bonito scarcer than the proverbial hen's teeth, and no kind of other bait procurable, a fresh bonito was precious. Cappy caught a fine one, just the right size, late in the afternoon on the way back to camp. Carefully he put it on ice. Next morning when he went himself to secure it he found it had been cut in half. The blamed Chink cook or some one else had stolen half and no doubt cooked it. Cappy was wild. How seldom did he give way to irritation or anger! But this time he almost hopped up and down. I surely felt the tragedy of that loss, but I had to laugh. I had one laugh left!

On October 10 a high wind from the east whipped round the end of the island, and the sea became a world of blue mountains with white crests.

We went out only because the day before we had caught ten bonito, the first for days. Birds and bait had been seen more often lately. R. C. caught a fifty-five-pound *crevalle* on light tackle—an achievement—and Cappy was cleaned out by a tuna.

Before noon I raised a marlin—a long, dark fish, wary and swift, that refused to come near the bait. But I was happy. After all, I was not to break my record of seventeen days without seeing a fish. Not long after that Captain M. ran down on us and hailed through his megaphone. "Raised swordfish big as that one I had on last year!" he yelled.

"No!" I yelled back.

"Yes. He whacked the bait, but wouldn't take it. My heart was in my throat."

Not long afterward we saw R. C. raise a fish that wouldn't strike. Things were looking up.

In the afternoon we ran in because all our bait was so rotten it would not stay on the hooks. A flock of boobies, noddies, and terns, sailing round in the bay, lured us to a chase. And for two hours we ran after them, now full speed, now slowing down to skitter our pearl-shell gigs over the water. But we never caught a bonito.

Captain Mitchell was the last in, and he reported raising another marlin, a small one 160 or 180 pounds. The fish appeared hungry, but did not care for Cappy's dirty old bonito.

Taking the day altogether, we gathered hope again. Unquenchable is the fisherman's optimism. Tomorrow may be a good day! It is not an illusion.

But next day it stormed. Black clouds and rain. Deluge! But we went up the island inside the reef and fished for bait. I had sport, and considering that I could not stop the rain I let it rain. It was pleasant to feel the cold wet on my bare flesh—I forgot to mention that we removed shirts and undershirts and let the sun and wind and rain have their will.

At noon the rain lulled and we ran outside, to find a magnificent sea rolling. When you can see green light through the crest of the combers, then you know it's rough. But the swells were long and my launch, *Tahiti*, rode them easily, so that I did not have to hold to the chair to stay in it. I trolled a ten-pound tuna five miles out, where we had to turn back, and five miles in. Sometimes I would be lifted high, higher, to the very sky, it seemed, and could look down on a thousand blue gulfs and white ridges. R. C.'s boat, the *Moorea*, half a mile away, looked like a piece of driftwood, and then as I went down he disappeared. Down, down, till I looked up at a roaring hill of blue water. It was frightful, although the danger was negligible. If, however, I had hooked a big fish—then I would have been in a serious predicament. But I did not.

We ran in to the lee, and found comparatively calm water in the bay, where birds were working over bonito. We chased them, and found them milling around, here and there. First I caught one on my rod. Then Jimmy and Charlie, my native experts, got busy with their pearl gigs. Jimmy caught three, while Charlie lost the same number. Two he swung outside the boat, and the other he missed. So I put up my tackle and took Charlie's long bamboo. Meanwhile I had to dodge the bonito Jimmy was hauling in, and at that one hit me a resounding smack on the thigh. It was not easy to stand erect, owing to the choppy sea, but I braced myself, stuck the end of the bamboo pole in the socket of my rod belt, and began to dance the pearl gig skitteringly over the water. When a bonito hits one of their gigs, you think you have snagged a trolley car going the other way. I missed three. Then watching carefully, as I played the delicate lure zigzag across the water in the boiling wake of the boat—of course we were moving, and pretty fast—I saw one dart like a brown streak. Smash! I had him. It was all I could do to pull him up, and once free of the water he swung at me like a bullet. I ducked and he shot over my head into Peter's lap. We all roared.

I caught five, one after another, and I was panting as if I had climbed a steep hill. Another caught me unawares and, hooking himself, jerked the pole down. I heaved. But he would not budge. My comrades had a most hilarious time. They yelled and I heaved with all my might. I got the bonito coming—got him to the surface, and then he struggled for a moment, until by dint of my last ounce of strength I lifted him in. And that was enough for me. It was sport and fun, and no child's play, and certainly thrilled me.

Peter put the bonito on my hook alive and let it down. He took line like a swordfish, and when he was down three hundred feet I stopped him. Peter did likewise with another live bonito, and we drifted for an hour with birds and bonito all around us. I hoped a stray swordfish might find my bait, and failing that, I hoped a mean old shark would run across it. But all that happened was a black squall bearing down on us, enveloping us in a gray pall and shrieking wind.

We could not see fifty feet. We rode it out, and when it passed we made for camp. R. C. reported having a big hammerhead shark behind the teasers, affording a fine target for sixty feet of motion-picture film. Captain M. could not catch any bait, and finally he raised a marlin on a feather gig. The fish followed him a goodly distance, curious about that gig, but would not strike it.

Somewhere back in this narrative I mentioned rain. But I was in error. That was not rain. That was only mist. This day it *rained*. You could not see a boat length; the roar was deafening; the drops of water filled a bucket in jig time.

But all the same, likewise nevertheless, my brother R. C. and Captain Mitchell and I patiently fished. I chased bait all the morning, sometimes through a rain squall. We got after a school of skipjack and hooked several, all too big to hold. Finally we caught a couple of ten-pounders. Jimmy hooked one on his shell gig, and to see him lift that fish out was a spectacle. With these two fresh bait—for whales—we started to troll; and halfway up the island we found a lee, and sighted R. C. and Cappy outside.

Gradually the weather improved and the sky cleared enough to let the sun shine. It was fine to sit in the sun and dry out. We raised two sharks, one of which snapped at my bait and got the hook. The other shark kept tearing round the hooked one, and at last took the skipjack off the leader. I hauled away like a man in need of exercise and soon had this 400-pound shark up for the boys to massacre.

R. C. ran up on us and asked for bait. "Marlin tore off two rotten baits, and then tried to climb on the boat," he called. "I just couldn't hook him."

We furnished one fresh and one stale bait, and followed R. C. around for an hour. But nothing happened. We ran in. All around the sky was obscured again by gray clouds. The mountain peaks were lost. White clouds like sails moved out of the great canyons. The scene was gloomy, yet wonderful.

Captain M. had beaten us in. He had waited to tell us his report. He had raised an enormous tuna, which struck at a teaser. It had a tail two feet across. This, however, was nothing to the marlin he had enticed out of the depths. Sixteen feet long, as big around as a horse! This monster rushed Cappy's needlefish bait, excited, apparently hungry, yet would not take it. Cappy tried a fresh bonito, which likewise was refused. He said, "By Jove! I nearly expired!"

We saw in all seven schools of bait with birds over them, and three of these at one time. We gathered hope. Conditions had changed. And if the weather cleared we believed we might make up for seven blank weeks of intolerable fishing.

Here are a couple of stumpers for the naturalists.

One evening after dusk, R. C. called me to the door, and when I went he showed me, by the aid of his flashlight, a gigantic hermit crab in the path. It was gray in color, as large and round as my fist, that is the stolen shell that this cunning species of crab lives in. Hermit crabs had for many years been pet studies of mine, and I have been told that the most beautiful paragraph I ever wrote was about the lovely hermit crab of Long Key.

I picked this one up and carried it inside, but quickly dropped it. This Tahitian hermit was a surprise. He let out a strange sound.

A kind of yowl, and if it did not have a note of anger, I was badly mistaken. We stood there amazed. The hermit kept it up, with the sound growing louder. Then I knelt and touched him. Whereupon he yowled louder and stuck out a massive claw fully thrice as large as my thumb. He looked nasty. I gave him a tap, and he caught hold of the edge of my rug. He could not be dislodged. I pulled till he tore the rug, and refused to let go. Then I gave him a hard rap with a stick. It knocked him loose, not from the rug, but from his shell. He appeared a huge, hairy, grisly object. Then quickly he let go of the rug and backed with a snap into his shell. Once safe, again he began that yowling. I put him outdoors on the sand, and still he kept it up.

The other stumper is concerned with wasps. We were three miles out at sea, in the warm sunlight, when we began to note the presence of wasps. The boys had been stung before this and resented it. They began an onslaught. I heard them beating with hats and cushions, until I thought the launch was overrun with wasps. So I complained. Francis said, "That bloomin' flag of yours is covered with them, and more comin'."

I could vouch for the approach of more wasps, from every direction, it appeared, though I was sure they all came from the land. It began to puzzle and interest me. When Charlie got stung we had a good laugh. He was funny. Then Francis, batting at an incoming wasp, got stung on the nose. He yelled bloody murder, and soon committed it upon that offender. Wasps began to alight on Peter and on me, which last was not so funny. Then while I brushed one off another stung me on the cheek. I surely grew hot. That Tahitian wasp could have stung rings around an Arizona yellow-jacket or Ohio hornet. When I got through swearing the pain appeared somewhat relieved, but the boys still yelled, and kept on slapping wasps.

R. C. ran over in his boat and called through his megaphone: "What the hell's wrong with you guys? Are you going bughouse?"

Then I told him. He replied that that seemed strange. He had been close to us for hours and had not noticed any wasps. It was then I associated the wasps with my red flag which blew at the masthead. Without doubt this had attracted them. Why? How far did they see it? What were they doing so far out on the water? Why did red attract them when no other color did so?

On Sunday, October 14, we hoped the almanac would not lie. It stormed and rained torrents up until three o'clock. Then the wind changed to north, the clouds broke, the sun shone, and the air grew wonderfully cool and invigorating, like early fall at home. Sunset was a gorgeous spectacle. Rose-pink and salmon-gold trade-wind clouds lined the horizon like a range of turreted peaks. The afterglow out-colored the sunset, and for long the west, and clouds far to south and east, burned with opal and pearl and porphyry.

How one day can be more beautiful and wonderful than another is magically exemplified at Tahiti.

October 16 was the most perfect day to fish or to be on the ocean that I ever saw. We ran ten miles off east end. Ripply, dark blue, sunny sea and patches—leagues long—of glassy water. The light west wind and the warm sun felt good. We trolled west ten miles. No sign of fish! Finally we caught some bonito and I put down a live bait. While waiting for a possible (?) strike I gazed about me, and suddenly realized that there had to be something startling to make me note it at all.

The grand Pacific was gently heaving, in slow, endless swells, and the water was dark purple toward the island—which was hidden in a vast gray pall—and toward the west a shimmering silver. Storms were all about us, except the central west, where some sky showed pale blue. A thunderhead mass of cloud, black as ink, whorled and columnar, with a funnel-shape dragging, occasioned us alarm. But it passed on out to sea. Other storm centers let down lines of wavering rain that trailed along. All the grays and blacks prevailed.

As we ran on in toward where the island ought to be, these conditions of light and shade and storm were magnified, until I seemed on neither land nor sea, but in some region of magnificent dark lowering light.

We entered the zone of rainstorm where a soft, seething, silky roar of raindrops fell, gray as steel, and sweetly fresh to the face and hands. We ran out of the storm, and there loomed Tahiti, vast and black and splendid, a mountain range of sharp lines, peaks, ridges, with not a curve in sight, and not a bare spot of earth or rock. All verdant green, dark in the absence of sunlight.

White clouds, like smoke, drifted in broken sections through all the canyons, low and high, lodging on a slope, pouring over a notch to resemble, a waterfall, even touching the tops of the palms on the shore line.

Then we ran into a flock of boobies screaming over a school of tuna. We gave chase, and by running full speed we caught up with them. The tuna were breaking water, and when they began to leap, twenty- and thirty-pounders, and often one much larger, to shoot high in the air and quiver momentarily and dive like a plummet, I was reminded of the great schools of blue-fin tuna I had chased.

Peter hooked one and lost it. We were running full speed. Then I hooked one. Quick to relieve the drag I saved this fast fish, and after a long sounding run he stopped, and we had it out to his defeat.

It was a very beautiful fish. One of the mackerel family, more albacore than tuna, beautifully built like a bullet, huge dark eyes, small sharp nose, black round back, then splashed with gold and amber and stripes of opal, down to the iridescent side of mother-of-pearl, of such scintillating brilliance that it seemed incredible. It had pectoral fins considerably longer than those of a tuna, though not so long as the true saber-finned albacore.

Again we caught up with the school, and this time, as if to dazzle us, they engaged in pyrotechnics that brought long yells of acclaim from us. A dozen would crack out of the water at once. One leaped quite close, a beautiful parabolic curve, during which we saw every detail of his graceful fish form, instinct with life, and the ferocity of nature. The same beauty, the same life, the same death that have always appalled and fascinated and mystified me!

By way of a change, on October 17, just forty-seven days since I last had a strike from a swordfish, I raised a fine marlin, about 400 pounds, that shot in close between the teasers and almost got the right one. My stentorian yell sent the whole crew tumbling. In just the nick of time the teaser was jerked out. Like a big bird with purple wings the swordfish dropped back, his motions just like flying. I had drawn in my bait until it trolled on the surface about forty feet behind the boat. Suddenly he saw it. He shot out to the right, turned with incredible swiftness, darted under it, and then sheered again to charge it, swift as a bullet. What a hole he made in the water! He ripped off the line, and before he had a hundred feet off the reel he broke on the surface. I knew he had felt the hook and was coming up to throw it. So I jammed on the drag and tried to hook him. But he leaped and came back, getting slack just as he threw out the bait. The hook did not catch. Free, he leaped clear out, showing a thick, broad back, a dark-colored fish, with no stripes showing.

Gone! Our native fishermen, Jimmy and Charlie, made characteristic exclamations. Francis and Peter swore—mildly. I sat there watching the limp line, and made no move to wind it in. What a great game this sea fishing was!

CHAPTER EIGHT

MY BOATMEN told me of an Englishman who had fished two seasons in New Zealand waters. He used a large outfit, of unknown make, and as crude as the contraption, with a three-foot lever under the reel and a brake to match. His method of fishing was unique, not to use another word. After the manner of the majority of anglers, before we introduced American fishing methods in New Zealand, he did not hook his fish, but let it run off and swallow the triangle gang hook. The boatman ran his launch after the fish. How many times did I see a boat run to sea out of sight!

This angler in question held his rod up straight and stiff before his eyes, and he never moved it. Above the reel he had a wrist watch strapped on the rod, and presumably this engaged his attention until the fish died of strangulation or exhaustion.

To us Americans who had long experience of deep-sea fishing, this was about the funniest thing we had heard of. It was more than funny, however; it revealed much. It absolutely proved that this watch-watching fisherman did not fight his fish and had not the remotest idea of the truth, which was that the boatman caught the fish.

It is doubtful if a man of that type will ever see the light. He does not realize that the thing with him is to get the fish and not be concerned with how it is caught. Anglers of this kind fall under one class—they are the merest novices at the game, and have no realization whatever of this grandest of sport.

One afternoon at sunset, a dark pearl sunset with no color, I ran along the reef toward camp. It was high tide and the great swells were heaving in, a mile long and as high as a hill. When they piled up on the coral the sight and sound were tremendous.

My boatman ran the launch perhaps a hundred yards out from the reef, just at the place where the mounds of green water rose as if by magic, to lift the boat high and higher, and sometimes so very high that I shouted out in excitement and joy, not unmixed with fear. Boom and hollow thunder! Another green curving billow swept on, slow and majestic, to rise and curl away from me, so that I could not see the white—to crash in muffled roar on the reef.

We passed that shallow shelf where the swells lifted out of the ocean. I could see the pearly coral bottom at a hundred feet, a varigated mosaic of white and black. Giant needlefish, nearly a fathom long, darted away from the boat, like arrows. Now and then one shot up out of the water, to skitter along on his tail, and then to leap incredibly. Schools of flying-fish scattered like bees, and I noticed a new one to the reef—a large, heavily bodied fish, pale in color, with pink wings. Large round fish which must go nameless sported on the surface.

But for all this, fish were scarce here where there should have been myriads of them. Perhaps there were, and the crystal-clear sea water gave them warning of our approach long before we could see them. But I doubted greatly that there were many fish at this season.

I had heard a great deal, even before I visited Tahiti, about the nature men, and I confess I was not much intrigued. Back-to-nature men, or "gone native" men, somehow seemed synonymous with fakirs.

These nature men of Tahiti evidently do not rely on tourists for a living. I saw one. He was a husky brute and should have been ploughing corn. He wore only a loin cloth, and his naked body was a reddish brown covered with spots. He had long blond hair and a black beard. He was striding along the road out to the end of the island, where, the natives told us, three nature men lived. A day after this meeting we ran in our launches round the extreme bold end of Tahiti, and I saw the coral strand and cocoanut grove, in the mouth of a grand canyon, where these nature men lived. We ran close, but could see no more than a thatched hut.

The place was lonely. It could only be reached by a five-mile trail around and over the bluffs of the wild and rugged east end. A wide gap in the reef opened there, letting the surf in to beat upon the shore. I wondered about these men. What men think is even more fascinating—and terrible—than what they do. Our native fishermen said the nature men lived on bananas, cocoanuts, pawpaw, and breadfruit. They did not use fire. We were told that the manager of a cocoanut plantation offered them a job. "What will the work be?" they asked. And were told that there was very little work—only to gather the cocoanuts and keep the natives from stealing them. "But we couldn't do that," they replied. "The natives have more right to them than you have."

That retort hit me hard, for I agreed with them. Still, I could not find excuse for the so-called nature man. If a white man had consumption and hoped to cure it by going naked in the sun and living solely on fruit—which very probably would cure him—then it was well and good. But these nature men were as healthy as any other men.

What was in their minds? What did they do with the hours? Tennyson's lotus-eaters could not have been nature men such as these. Dreamers do not necessarily have twists in their minds or a disgust for contact with humanity or a hatred of achievement. Thoreau was perhaps the most aloof of the naturalists, but then his life was farthest removed from idle.

These nature men of Tahiti let the world slide. Far indeed from the maddening crowd! They could be worse men, surely, and they did no harm, but they enriched nothing, not even a spiritual growth upon earth. It was hard to understand them, probably impossible. And what I could not understand I dared not condemn. I envied them that solitude, where the surf beat its many-toned music on the shore and the waterfall fell from the purple notch of the great mountain slopes. The world is too much with most people. How impossible for them to see remote Tahiti! I passed over by that lonely strip of coral beach where the palms leaned away from the wind, and I was perplexed and saddened.

Most all of the rivers of Tahiti are swift, cold streams, fed from mountain springs. Some, however, are subject to daily rain storms and go dry with a week of dry weather. The little rivulet

The "Fisherman" at Raiatea

Captain Mitchell's 163-pound World-record Sailfish, Caught at Raiatea

that runs through my camp belongs to this last class. One evening it will be dry and the next morning a roaring brook.

The *nato* does not run up any but the spring-fed streams, and the *nato*, I should explain, is a most beautiful and interesting little fish. He lives in the sea and runs up the rivers, and he will take a fly just like a trout.

Tautari River, across the mountain from Vairao, and emptying into the sea on the north shore, is one of the largest streams on Tahiti, and perhaps the best for *nato*.

The natives catch the fish in nets. We were indebted to Mr. Allister Macdonald, an English artist residing in Papeete, for knowledge about *nato* and that it affords capital sport on very light tackle. I went fishing one evening with Romer and Mr. Macdonald, and liked it so well that I spent the next day on the Tautari.

I had a two-and-a-half ounce Leonard rod and some fine line, very light leaders, and tiny flies—a delicate rig aptly suited to a delicate but game little fish. I raised several before I hooked my first one. Then I was treated to a surprise. For a fish only a few inches long this *nato* certainly did put up a battle. But finding I could not tire him out, I most unconcernedly jerked him out. That was the first I ever saw. He had the shape of a bass, in fact he was a bass, a brilliant mother-of-pearl, dotted with black spots. I caught two more, and then fastened to a good one, which took an extraordinary lot of skill and work to land. Six inches long and as wide as my hand!

Next day we went again, and I had time to see the wonderful scenery, as well as enjoy the fishing. Tautari comes down out of a magnificent canyon, and is a wide swift stream of crystal water with a slight greenish tinge. Palms and breadfruit trees, hibiscus and water hyacinth, lined the green banks. Just below the long riffle where I fished the whole day, the sea broke with boom and roar on the sandy beach.

It rained on and off. Soon we were soaking wet. But you do not mind rain at Tahiti. The dark sky and fine mist brought the *nato* up in schools. I could see them turn and shine like silver. I think they fed mostly on the bottom, though occasionally one rose to something on the surface. They would bite greedily at times and at others could not be tempted. I was several hours, really, in learning how to fish for them. Eventually I got the hang of it, and had such sport as I had not had for many a day. It brought back Dillon's Falls and Joe's Run—where as a boy I learned to fish. We used to fish with long, slim, light, stiff reed poles, very fine silk thread, and tiny hook and bit of helgramite tail for bait. The method was to cast into swift, shallow riffles and work the bait with the current, to entice shiners and chubs. I became a past master at this art. And here on the Tautari it came back to me—absolutely the first time since I was a boy. The fishing was identical, except the *nato* were larger, and of course very much gamer than shiners or chubs.

I fished with a short line and trolled my fly with success, and then cast a long line quartering down stream in deep water, with like result. After some heavy rains the water grew dark in color, and then the *nato* shone gold instead of silver. If anything, they bit better in the roily water than the clear. In all, I caught about forty *nato*, the largest being about six inches. But I had hold of a couple of whales. The little rod wagged like a buggy whip. Both these *nato* pulled loose, when I imagined I was handling them very deftly. They were amazingly strong and quick. As always for me, the big ones got away!

What a far cry of difference between *nato* and the great *espadon* of the Pacific. The one a dainty little bit of silver, big-eyed and speckled, the other a grand, purple monster with a sword. But there is no telling the fascination of fishing. I loved it as a boy, and now no less as a man. And to tell what I owe to fishing would take a better book than I have written.

The Tautari, sliding down from the mighty cliffs, where the waterfalls gleamed like white lace, and the luxuriant flowered jungle grew to the peaks, was another beautiful river to add to the treasure store of an angler. Along its banks I waded knee deep in green moss and amber lilies and lilac hyacinths, and gazed up at tropic slopes. And always and ever in my ears sounded the trumpet call of the sea, the thundering surge, the boom and hollow roar, and the scream of the pebbles in the undertow.

Storm! Another blow, and rain like buckets of water turned upside down. The afternoon of the second day we went out, nevertheless. In vain! Huge seas!

On October 25, R. C. broke his streak of thirteen blank—I had almost written blankety-blank—days by raising a 600-pound marlin that refused the bait, then leaped close to the boat, no doubt to look it over. Broadbill swordfish have a trick of doing this. A little later I raised a small marlin, that flashed like a purple meteor and vanished.

October 26 was what we call a perfect fishing day, part sun and cloud, cool breeze, rippled dark sea. We ran ten miles up inside the reef, trying to catch bait. No use! Then we ran out with bait caught the day before—very large bonito. We hoped to find a flock of birds over a school of bonito, but our hopes were futile.

R. C. raised a fish. We could tell by the excitement on board, the pulling in of the teasers, all standing up, etc. That fish followed R. C. for more than a mile. Later he told me that he thought the bonito was too large. Soon I saw the darting of a purple fish past our teasers. I yelled as always, "There he is!" And there was a scramble. This marlin flashed like light, and charged my bait, to miss it.

We were thankful for that much. To such sad pass had we been reduced that even sight of a swordfish was elevating. The time was 12.30. At 3.30 I saw a purple mass loom up and shoot forward with the speed of a projectile. It was another marlin, a big one, very broad across the shoulders, a 500-pound fish, very probably. He dropped back, came ahead again, then dropped back farther. I was too slow in letting my bait back and did not believe he saw it. Then at 5.30, on the way in, almost inside the bay, I raised what I thought to be a good-sized sailfish. He came straight and fast from behind, then disappeared. If it were not a sailfish it had to be a marlin.

That was three for us, and we were much encouraged. But the fish were not striking. R. C. reported, besides the marlin mentioned above, a huge dolphin (*coryphene*) that sighted the teasers at four hundred feet, and came so fast he made a long bulge on the water. One look at the teasers and away he went.

Captain Mitchell fished to Papeete and back, taking two days. He lost a rod on a tuna, caught some bonito, raised one sailfish. He reported that several days past Mr. Nordhoff saw tuna and birds all the way from Point Venus to Papeete. The first day he saw a swordfish over twenty feet long; the second day he sighted six swordfish. The tuna were feeding on some small stuff and both birds and fish were crazy over it. This bunch of fish went out to sea. He sent us word that we might expect such a wave of bait to come in any day.

Then a most wonderful story came by schooner from the Marquesas, and Captain M. said the source was reliable. Two boats and a number of men harpooned a marlin and killed it. The fish was thirty-three feet long, and could only be dragged in shoal water and cut up. The bill or spear was curved, and five feet long.

We had heard so much about these giant spearfish that we really would not be surprised when we saw one. R. C. said, "I'll be satisfied just to *see* one!" Captain M. said, "Excuse *me!*" And I said, "Just show me one and I'll take him on!"

Three fine days in succession, during which swordfish were raised, enlivened our hopes. Somehow the hopes of fishermen spring eternal. On October 29 I lost Captain Mitchell and R. C., who had started out ahead of me. When I got outside the reef I sighted a small flock of white and black terns hovering over bait, and I followed them a couple of hours. I had a blank day.

On the way in I sighted R. C.'s boat with a swordfish flag up. Did we whoop? We straightway took the whooping-yells! What was more, when we neared camp we sighted Captain Mitchell's boat already in, and it had a flag flying. I nearly fell overboard, and Francis ran the wheels off the boat.

R. C.'s marlin weighed 237 pounds, a fine fish. "Some jumper!" he said. "I'd sure have liked to see Romer and Bob try to take photos of this bird."

He said he followed a flock of boobies and terns (noddies) all day, trolling a bait, and just before sunset raised this fish.

Cappy said he could not get a fresh bait, though he worked schools of bonito for hours. He was not dragging teasers when one of the natives yelled and pointed down. There were two swordfish right under the boat, one of which was a hunker. Cappy dropped his bait rod and threw his bonito overboard. It was rotten and broken, but he threw it over, anyway. "By Jove! Would you believe it? They charged my bait," declared Captain. "And of course the small one reached it first. I soaked him good and hard, and landed him pretty quick. . . . You should have seen these marlin under the boat. Only about ten feet. They shone bright lilac. The big fellow had his pectorals spread, and they sure looked great. We were chasing a school of bonito at the time, and you can bet some of them had taken refuge under the boat. Now wouldn't that jar you? Think of the swordfish lately that wouldn't look at even a fresh bait!"

It did jar me. I had been jarred so much that I had spinal meningitis. R. C. forgot, it seemed, to report that he let down a live bonito about two hundred feet, and presently it jerked hard, ran off a yard or so line, and stopped. He reeled in. Bonito gone! It did not occur to him that that bait had been knocked off the hook by a swordfish.

The following day, the sixth fine day, by way of a welcome change, R. C. chased a school of bonito at good speed (about twelve miles an hour) all the way up to the east end, and halfway back. He was trying to catch a fresh bait. Nevertheless, he kept trolling the bait he had, with the rod stuck in the rod-socket and teasers out.

Lo and behold! he raised a skyrocket marlin, that made two flashes and then took the bonito, old as it was. When hooked he came up and at the boat, and they had a few moments of excitement getting away from him. Nobody on the cameras! This fish gave a grand exhibition, then sounded. While he was down R. C. saw another batting round among the bonito—a much larger fish.

It took an hour to lift the swordfish, after he went down, and it proved to be a black marlin, closely resembling the New Zealand species, with short bill, short dorsal, and no stripes. Weight 367 pounds. R. C. said these Tahitian swordfish were very much faster and fiercer than the Californian and Mexican coast species. I had noted this last year, and gave the cause.

Captain M. raised one marlin that refused a poor bait. Birds were plentiful, but traveling too swiftly for us.

In the afternoon I was trolling the only bait I had, a ten-pound bonito. Raised a fish that shot to and fro behind the bait, then rushed the teasers. He got one, then the other, and it took hard pulling to recover them. Then he dropped back to charge my big bait. He missed it. What a treat to see him sweep out, turn round, and flash all purple and bronze, and try again. Three more times he had a go at my bait, yet never actually took it. I felt him hit it, but for some reason he would not or could not take it in his mouth. Then he faded out of sight.

The weather grew better and the wind less strong, mostly from the southeast these days. We expected a storm around full moon. The glass was high, but the storm did not materialize at full moon or a day later. No doubt it could miss us. But conditions on the whole appeared encouraging.

But the storm did not materialize.

R. C. came in one evening with that intent bright beam in his eye. "Well, Z. G.," he said, "I've seen one of your big swordfish."

"Good Lord! I'm glad, but don't call them *mine*," I replied. "Never do I expect to get one unless the ocean goes dry."

"This fellow came at us like a flash," went on R. C. "I saw him first riding down a swell. You know how you can see through this clear water. He looked three feet across the shoulders. His purple pectorals stuck out like the outriggers on an albacore boat at Avalon. I just gulped. He was *not* slow, as you told us to expect these big marlin. He came like a streak for my bait, and if it had not been an old rotten thing he sure would have taken it. At that he struck at it. Then he sailed for the right teaser, looked that over, and then turned to cross to the left. Here was where I saw his length and depth. Of course I was hypnotized. But he *was* all of sixteen feet in length and four in depth. A marvelous fish, all silver and purple, and as swift as a trout. He looked that teaser over and then left us. Thad estimated him to weigh ten hundred to twelve hundred pounds. The native on my boat did not appear to think it was *very* big. I just sat down in my chair, weak in the knees, and tried to imagine what the fast swordfish would have done had he been hooked. . . . You had better look out, Old Top. Here you have not caught a fish for nearly seventy days. Something terrible is coming to you!"

The flu struck Papeete, prostrating most all of the natives and many of the white people. My camp at Vairao was hit hard. On November 1, Captain Mitchell was ill in bed, Peter in the hospital,

Francis running the boat while sick as a dog, Jimmy down and out, Arearea the same, and the rest of us sniffing and sneezing. It was not malignant, though natives were dying with it, but very mean and infectious. Some years ago a deadly type of the disease hit the island and killed nine thousand natives. They are very susceptible, and like the American Indian, succumb easily. It is fatalism with them.

Tahiti ordinarily appeared to be a very healthy place, outside of Papeete. Flies did not bother us; mosquitoes not enough to be concerned about; fleas were bad, and a nuisance. They came on the rats and their bites were something to conjure with. Household ammonia relieved me, but did R. C. no good whatever. He used poison-oak remedy. Ants were plentiful, sometimes, and occasionally would bite. Half a dozen kinds of lizards took up their abode with us, under the pandanus roofs of our cottages. At first they annoyed me, but I soon got to like them, and knew several. Early in the evening they came out to catch insects. I wished I could catch swordfish like these lizards catch bugs. A rather large, fat, gray lizard emitted a very queer sound. I heard it often before I connected it with a lizard. The noise resembled somewhat the grating squeal of a rat. In fact, I thought it was made by the rats. But one evening I satisfied myself that the lizard accounted for it.

Land birds were scarce. The *mina* birds, imported from India to clean up the wasps, have been more of a scourge than were the rats. It was a rather pretty bird, brown and gray, with white marks. Early in the mornings the *mina* sings a little, not unmelodiously. I also saw a small dove and a gray kingfisher, up the brook that ran through our camp. Mauu, the native chief who was friendly with us, told me that the common rooster went wild on Tahiti and became a bird of gorgeous plumage. Mr. Guild, an American resident who maintains an aviary, frees pheasants that grow very wild. I saw several dull drab and yellow little birds flitting across the road. But any visitor to Tahiti will observe the marked scarcity of land birds.

One day on the way in to the reef, I sighted a large ray—a giant ray, or devilfish, as they are called in Florida. This was the first we saw in Tahitian waters, or anywhere in the South Seas. I had seen larger ones, but this ray was eighteen or twenty feet across his back. When the boat was nearly over him he dove, and the white of his under side shone like a great triangular shield, burnished to silver, then paling to blue and fading into the depths.

CHAPTER NINE

ANOTHER day we ran into a school of bottle-nose blackfish, which were accompanied or followed by a bunch of sharks—the common long-finned sand shark. The biggest we saw would go to 400 pounds. They had no fear of the boat whatever. We teased them with baits, right up to the stern, against which they bumped their ugly heads, and bent the wheels of our propellers. I certainly would not have wanted to fall overboard. The more I see of sharks —*mauu*, the natives call them—the less use I have for them, and the more I realize how very wide of the mark Mr. Beebe and Mr. Heilner are in their scientific assertions that sharks will not attack human beings.

That same day I sighted several of the long, slim, yellow fish with the short spiked dorsal fin—the same strange fish we had seen before in that same place. They were fifteen or twenty feet long, and somewhat resembled baby whales. The natives have a name for them, which in our language means maiden-fish, so called because of their habit of playing and frolicking like maidens.

Captain Mitchell watched two white terns from his cottage porch. They were always sailing and darting over the water before our camp. I had seen them often myself. But he observed them catching fish, and flying up to a large vine-covered breadfruit tree, just on a level with our cottage porches. With the aid of his glass he found the nest of the terns and that they had one little gray baby tern, which they were feeding. Upon my return from the sea, Captain M. gave me the glass and told me where to look, and I had the extreme pleasure of seeing these shy wild sea terns with their little one, nesting in a tree top. So much for the naturalists' claim that sea birds nest on rocks and coral.

Mrs. Mitchell saw two of the *mina* birds with a little one, which they were teaching to fly, and their notes were nearly identical with that of robins with their young.

And I made further inquiry into the sound emitted by the gray lizards that live in the pandanus roof of my cottage and come out at dark to catch insects. It is certainly a chatter and almost a chuckle.

To look on a calendar one would not take November 3 for an unlucky day, any more than any other date. But for me it was terrible.

The day dawned clear, yet dark, with misty rain. We found birds at once, and took to chasing them, at the same time trolling a bonito caught the day before. We ran all over the ocean after these birds, and by noon had five bonito. Meanwhile we were twelve miles offshore. Arearea caught another bonito, which I put on my hook and let down. It pulled off two hundred feet of line, then stopped. Something struck it. I waited. No go! I wound up my line to find the bonito cut off in the middle. A cleaver could not have made a cleaner job. There was a deep cut on one side, that looked as if it had been made with the point of a sharp weapon. Some kind of a flat-sharp-sworded fish cut that bonito in two pieces. Why did he not take the piece left on the hook?

I put on another bonito, dead of course, and let that down. Almost at once I had a tremendous strike. Elated and tingling, I let him run. He stopped. Again I waited. No go! I wound up to find my last bait gone.

We went back to trolling and following the birds. If anything, they increased in numbers. Bonito came up oftener and all over the ocean. We saw a swordfish strike at R. C.'s bait. Later R. C. told us this swordfish shot under the boat. He was chasing bonito. R. C. said hundreds came right under the boat, so close that the propeller hit several. The marlin darted to and fro underneath, like a purple flash. Presently he saw R. C.'s bait, attacked it, and committed suicide.

It was now about three o'clock. The sky became partly overcast with cumulus clouds, those in the west being particularly impressive. The birds were working inshore. Presently I espied Captain

Mitchell's boat and was surprised, for he had been laid up with influenza for several days and the launch the same for repairs. But there was the Captain all right. He bore down on us, and hailing us he yelled that the sea inshore was alive with bonito and bait. He had caught forty-six, all by himself. Said he had just come out to try the engines. But all the same he put a bait overboard and began to troll.

When we ran off perhaps a third of a mile all of a sudden Arearea and Sid, who were substituting for Francis, Peter, Jimmy, and Charlie, all down with the flu, let out loud yells. I turned in time to see big splashes behind Captain M.'s boat. Then I saw a huge swordfish batting at the bait, following and batting. Captain Mitchell did not see this because he was forward, with his back turned. And neither of the natives on board saw it. I shrieked and waved like a madman.

We did not see the swordfish again, and imagined he had dropped back. What vain assumption! He might as well have been tied to Captain's boat. Anyway, Captain M. came back to the cockpit and his rod, and pretty soon we made sure he had sighted the swordfish we had seen, or another. He turned the boat, and I lost track of him for a moment. Presently Arearea called out that the Captain was hooked on.

I ran over to photograph him, and slowed down for that purpose. He was pumping hard. When we got close I saw the Captain had on a heavy fish and from my judgment was working on too strong a drag. Afterward he said not. But the swordfish made a sudden run and instantly Captain M. was in difficulty. Sid and I thought from the violent motions of his rod that he could not lose the drag. Captain M. fumbled over the reel—then threw up his hands. The fish had broken off.

We ran close. "That d—— Hardy-Alma reel jammed. Broke me off," he shouted, hoarsely, his face red with anger. He slammed rod and reel down. "It's no good! . . . No d—— good! . . . Did you see that swordfish? He had a short black bill as big as my leg!"

I was too upset by the misfortune to offer any condolence. And I went on trolling. In this connection, after we were back in camp R. C. asked me if I had seen Captain's fish jump. I said "No."

R. C. had a funny grim look. "Never saw such a swordfish. He was as thick as a door—his tail spread six feet!"

The sea had become dark and calm. Birds were not now so thick. They had gorged themselves. And bonito were everywhere as far as eye could see, breaking the surface in white patches.

I raised two marlin at once, one of which was a whopper. I yelled. But Sid and Arearea were not quick enough to haul in the teasers, and the swordfish nailed them. I thought the one on the right side never would let go. The teaser had to be pulled out of its mouth. These marlin both followed us, but after that would not bite.

All the way in bonito followed us, jumping in the wake of the boat and splashing on each side. The light was not good by this time, and when another swordfish came up, I did not see him before he lunged at the teaser. He got to it before either of the boatmen, and broke it off and ejected it.

And that was my day as far as fishing was concerned.

But the sunset was mine, and no words could measure its worth. Heavy banks of purple clouds hung low over the west, down to a broad bar of gold that extended along the horizon. The sun was hidden. The grand mountain of Tahiti stood up with its sharp peaks in smoky sulphurous cloud. The canyons were full of smoke. And as the sun began to get below the under rim of the cloudbank, the golden lightning flared out all over the ocean. Above the purple bank another mass of cloud caught fire and burned rose and red. And soon such a glorious light as could never be given a name spread over the world of waters. I gazed spellbound. The sea was aflame, the sun was sinking white-gold, and the clouds changed color as if by some enchantment.

The effect was not evanescent. It lasted long. Then the sun sank, and the afterglow seemed vastly different, yet equally beautiful. And when all the trade-wind ships of the sky had turned dark there was still a band of gold low down along the horizon, and across on a bright place R. C.'s boat passed, silhouetted black and strange against that background.

By November 6 we had pretty good assurance that fish and bait were coming in strong. I fell victim to flu and never had I been any sicker. It appeared to be a contagious and violent type of the disease. So I could not fish during these days. On November 6 R. C. saw schools of tuna, some of them over 100-pound fish, scores of flocks of birds and patches of bait, and many bonito. He raised two marlin. Captain Mitchell caught one—160 pounds.

The Captain made a most interesting and valuable scientific observation.

Very frequently we had noted wounds and scars on the backs of bonito we had caught. Captain happened to ask the natives what caused them, and was astounded to learn that the diving boobies made those wounds. They cross their wings and shoot down like a plummet, and go clear out of sight. Often as I had watched this performance at close range, I had never seen a boobie come up with a little fish in his bill. It is a wonder that did not lead me upon the very discovery Captain made. Because at the time I considered it strange, and wondered if these birds were diving at the tiny minnows the bonito feed on. They do feed upon them, but only when the schools of bait are very thick on the surface, and then the boobies alight on the water and stick their beaks under. I have seen a large black patch of boobies all with their heads under—a funny sight.

This boobie is the only fowl of this species that wounds fish in such a manner. The gannet of New Zealand is a wonderful diver, sailing high, and plunging down with great speed. And when he comes up he usually has a luckless little fish—a piper—in his bill. The owl-eyed, blue-footed boobie of the Galapagos Islands is perhaps the most magnificent diver of all. But he sits on a ledge and solemnly watches till he sees a fish. Then he falls like a thunderbolt. The small brown boobie of the white Friars on the Mexican coast is a skillful diver, and generally comes up with something.

But this large gray-and-white boobie of these Tahitian waters is the only sea bird I have observed that sinks his bill in large fish he could have no notion of killing. Bonito are very full-blooded and soft-fleshed. The boobie has a large powerful bill, and there is no doubt that he gets a certain amount of sustenance in this way.

I was very ill with flu for ten days. It was the first attack for me of this pernicious disease and I was completely knocked out. I did not remember ever suffering such pain in the head, such restlessness and aching. The fever left me with such a racking cough and miserable weakness.

Peter returned after three weeks in the Papeete hospital, and he looked pretty bad. Francis dragged out a recovery. My natives, Charlie and Jimmy, lost about a week. All the rest of our native help had the thing from a few days to weeks. Thad Williams, R. C.'s boatman from Florida, went down and out. But up to November 13, when I went back to fishing—that is I made a bluff at it—R. C. had been immune. Romer and Bob also escaped, and I sent them on to New Zealand to take a trout-fishing trip on the South Island. They were a couple of wildly happy boys.

Only one swordfish was reported during these days, and that by Captain Mitchell. It was enough, however, to make up for the barren stretch. He had been following bonito and trying to catch some. There were small patches of white water around his boat, and he was fishing near one of them, when an enormous swordfish stuck his head out, holding in his bill a kicking bonito. Captain said the size and beauty of the monster paralyzed him. His natives, however, yelled bloody murder. Captain said the fish came out only to his shoulders, and that was five feet or more. He had a short thick bill and a massive head, with eyes as large as plates. When the fish slid back into the sea Captain M. came to and dragged a fresh bait all around the patch of bonito, to no avail.

Notwithstanding an occasional sight of one of these great fish, I must go on record by saying that Tahitian waters, during the months of August, September, October, and half of November, offer the poorest sport of any waters I have ever fished. We were there in the off season, to be sure, and that was the only circumstance to make us consider any possible return to Tahiti.

One of the hardest trials of this hardest fishing trip I ever had was to see R. C. and Captain M., my faithful allies, stagger along the road, and up the hill to the cottages—every day, rain or shine, wind or calm, for four months. R. C. took an occasional Sunday off to rest his eyes and nerve; Captain M. had five days off on account of flu. For the rest they toiled over that rotten southeast trade-wind belt from the east end to the isthmus; and for the most part it was hankless toil. During that siege I had eleven days out for flu, and when I went back I was as weak as a cat. Time and again I swore the thing to do was quit—quit while we had one little iota of fish sense left—quit until another and better season. But there was always the chance—the one thousand to one chance—of hooking into one of those big swordfish. And so we endured it.

My long and unparalleled streak of blankety-blank days was broken on November 14. I had caught my last fish around August 22. Here was a stretch of eighty-three days without catching a fish. I know quite well it cannot be beaten. There is a record that will stand.

But about noon on November 14, while we were chasing bonito and birds, and I was dragging a huge bait—more from habit than anything else—I raised a swordfish. He was down pretty deep, so I could not judge his size correctly. He went under the boat. We kept running, and saw at once that he had chased some bonito to the boat. He would drop back a few yards, then shoot forward again. Peter said about 250 pounds. I guessed more. Francis said, "Pretty fair fish." Anyway, he paid no attention to my bait. We kept on moving, so that we might have a better light. Finally he dropped back farther, and then he espied my bait. Whew! Talk about cyclones! He smashed a hole in the water and was off like a rocket. I had to thumb the reel hard. Almost before he started he came up to crash on the surface and to throw the bait. But I was too quick. I hooked him. Then he came out—a splendid big marlin—looking to us poor fishermen enormous in size. I never heard such yelling on a boat. He took four hundred yards of line as swift as lightning. Then he began to leap and thresh. He ended one succession of lunges by a jump of surpassing beauty. Then he settled down, and I had my work cut out for me. The sea was rough. I was still a sick man, and believe me when that strain came on my back I knew it. Nevertheless, I labored on, and despite my fears I bested him in one hour and forty-five minutes. We were elated. The men, four of them, had all they could do to haul him on board. I found it convenient to lie down out of the wind. I saw the fish was big, but at the time I did not realize how big.

When we arrived at our dock we pulled the swordfish ashore and strung him up. He was a superb specimen of the ordinary striped marlin spearfish, 11 feet 5 inches long, 4 feet 8 inches round, and he weighed 464 pounds—being the largest we ever recorded. This beat my own world record of 450 pounds, made in New Zealand in 1926. The congratulations and the unmistakable delight of R. C. and Captain Mitchell and everyone else, really made the occasion more significant for me than the actual taking of the fish. I felt that I would have to catch one of the eighteen-footers ever to reconcile myself to this job.

Three days later I had a relapse and had to go to bed again. It was bitterly sickening. This flu was said not to be malignant, or fatal except in a few cases, but it was the worst malady that ever attacked me. I had no patience with illness. I had been too healthy, too fortunate. A patient continuance is necessary to the living of life. As Fosdick says, it *has* to be lived. Of course if one gives up and dies that is another question.

While I lay on my bed, in the cottage high above the sounding reef, where the wind swished and murmured through the bamboos, the palms, and breadfruit trees, my indefatigable and unquenchable comrades stayed on the job. The superiority of white men over all other living creatures is exemplified in this spirit. Take Ahab, and his resistless will to live on and kill the great white whale that had maimed him! Even in death he was unconquerable.

Perhaps any worthy object is excuse for men to keep on trying. But sometimes I began to doubt the worthiness of this big-game fishing. It could become an obsession. Too much time and strength and spirit could be sacrificed. But as I lay there, feeling the slow boil of my blood, the dragging ache of bone and muscle, sometimes I would have an illuminating flash of thought. Presently I would be well again, and on my way to New Zealand, or back home at Altadena, and the perspective would gradually change. Of what avail to make judgments when I was sick, moody, weak? The call of the sea would come back, even to its sweet salt scent; the boundless blue expanse would shine with that bright alluring horizon; the great waves would rise and swell and mount, and move on with stately majesty, to curl and fall in thundering might on the reef; the crystal depths would gleam with their myriad of coral formations and their millions of mysterious fishes; I would hear

The Fish Drive

The Fish Drive

Note the Wave of Fish Entering the Trap

the boobies and terns squalling as they flecked and whirled over a school of luckless little fish; and the great purple swordfish would rise as if by magic out of the deep.

Always these things and this trenchant call will have to be met. And the time will come when I shall see and hear them while sitting beside a shady river or wading a rapid trout stream, and perhaps even beyond the beyond.

CHAPTER TEN

OUR snowy terns raised their single fledgling and departed from Flower Point.

Often during the weeks of my illness I watched them from the porch of my cottage. It stands on the extreme point, high and far out over the water. I could look back and somewhat down to the broad-leafed tree where they had their nest, and with the aid of a glass could see it and the young tern.

Just a few days before they flew off on his first flight of life it was very interesting to watch them. At this time only one of the parent terns would go out in search of food. Where the other was we could not determine, but the probabilities were that he stayed close at home to keep watch over the obstreperous youngster. Very little gray color was left on the young tern at this stage, and he was fully as large as his father or mother. He would not stay in the nest, but perched or walked on a branch near by. When one of the faithful old birds hovered and sailed around over the tree he would strut pompously and let out most imperious cries.

One day, in fact the last on which we observed this interesting family, we were all seated on Captain Mitchell's porch, which was far back from mine, and within two hundred feet of the nest. Presently we espied what we took for the mother tern coming in from the sea. She sailed quite high round and round, but the young one saw her and let out piercing notes.

With the aid of a glass we made out that she had a little fish in her bill. She sailed around several times, and then gradually dropped to a lower level, until finally we could see the little fish with naked eyes. I believed the young tern saw it, too, for what a squalling he made! He at least had no concern about us. But it grew evident that the mother did not trust us. I made certain of that when she sailed along the ridge of the point, out over the water and back again, just above a level of the cottages. And when she passed us she was so close that I could see the tiny, black, gleaming eye.

She circled the thick-foliaged trees so many times that I marveled at her patience. Gradually she drew away from our side, and narrowed down the circle, until at length she darted down behind the trees and came around so low we could hardly see her, and fluttered under the leaves to her impatient offspring. I saw him gobble that little fish, and clamor for more. It was not long, then, until she flew out toward the reef, and we never saw her again.

I wondered why those snowy terns built their nest in a lonely vine-covered tree, and then exercised such extreme caution while rearing the young one. As far as I could tell there was not one enemy to be feared. No gulls, no sea hawks, no snakes, no gunners! To be sure, rats live in the cocoanut palms, but it is doubtful if they climb other trees. It is likely that the watchful terns feared us, and misconstrued our attention. Out at sea where these snowy terns are plentiful they are tame and come close to the boats. But something made this couple extremely wild while nesting.

Captain Mitchell broke his spell of bad luck—three weeks—by raising two fish on November 24. In fact, however, he did not raise them, for he had neither teasers nor bait out and was chasing bonito at the time. Bonito taking refuge under the boat really raised the two swordfish. One was about 300 pounds, the other more than twice as large, around 700. Captain was frantic. No bait! Just then one of the natives hauled in a bonito. Captain put it on and threw it overboard. Quick as a flash the smaller swordfish had it. He ran off. When Captain struck to hook him there was slack line. The fish had doubled back. Then he leaped. The hook, minus the bait, was swinging clear. When the swordfish switched his head he got free of hook and leader.

R. C. had gone more than three weeks without even raising a swordfish. Most of this time the sea was rough, and particularly the last week. This date, November 24, both anglers reported many flocks of birds and schools of bait, mostly far offshore.

Days passed, and it so happened that the one on which I resumed fishing was the best day for weeks. I fondly took it as an augury that the weather gods were going to reward me for all my bad luck. A fisherman can believe anything.

The sea was dark and ripply, the wind slight, the sun obscured, the misty rain pleasant, the flocks of wheeling, screaming gulls followed the schools of bonito all over the ocean. About noon I came down upon Captain Mitchell to find him hauling a marlin aboard. The reason it had not jumped or otherwise attracted my attention was because it had been hooked in the tail. I trolled a good bait for five hours among these scattered schools of bonito, all the while tense and watchful for a purple flash to loom up. But it did not. Nevertheless, I had a fine day, that passed swiftly. Not until we got to the dock and I essayed the walk to camp did I feel any exhaustion.

The next day dawned with lowering cloud curtain over the mountain. The glass said 29.60, and that looked bad. But we ran out to find a sunny blue sea and no wind at all. The worst of it was we had no fresh bait at all, and presently I raised a fine 350 marlin. He flashed by and was gone.

I saw Captain M. raise a fish, but I could not get close enough to ask him about it. Later he told me that he raised two marlin, neither of which would take his rotten bait.

We got ten miles offshore. All the while a short chop had been rising from the west, and presently it brought a breeze. We turned about and ran east for a while. Finally we saw a flock of boobies wheeling and diving, and in our eagerness to catch up with them we forgot to pay attention to wind and sea—until they forced themselves upon us.

A heavy short swell was running, with a kind of twist, and vicious, green combers. To get in we had to buck this sea, which grew worse all the time. R. C. was half a mile back of me, the Captain still farther on, and outside. To see their boats toss and jerk and fall was positively frightful. We headed for the opening in the reef, and I never want such a ride again. I feared the whole bottom would drop out of my boat, or that one of the twisters would flop us over. Once it very nearly happened—how I did not see, as I was lying down on the seat. The shock threw me into the middle of the cockpit, where I was deluged with water—a fine thing for a man convalescing from flu. After that I sat shivering in a chair, clutching the handles, and every huge, roaring, engulfing wave gave me the horrors. But by careful steering, dodging the big waves, and some good luck we made the pass. It was a narrow white caldron, but we ran it, on into the smooth green water behind the reef. No one can appreciate the meaning of a harbor until he has had this experience.

Once inside we hove to and watched R. C.'s boat pitch up and down, now high on a great swell, and again completely out of sight. We could not even see his flag. It seemed ages to me before his boat reached the pass and made the turn safely. How she rode those swells! It was thrilling. Then we had to watch for the Captain. At last we espied him, and were glad indeed that he had been able to get a better slant in than we had. He had been more to the southward. He made the pass, buried in spray, and then we ran on down inside the reef to camp. I was a nervous wreck; R. C. was grim and sick, and Captain M. had been shaken and knocked about until he could hardly walk.

I recalled no worse experience. We were careless, of course, but it all came about very quickly, and illustrated how treacherous the sea really is. The boats were strong, thirty-four foot, with two powerful engines, but surely not intended for such rough water as that. In five months' fishing we had never encountered a west wind until this one. We did not want any more west winds.

That night the glass dropped to 29.56 and the wind increased. The tumult from the reef was deafening—a thundering, pounding attack of mountains of water flung upon the coral. There were no adequate names for the sounds. But the might of the Pacific made chills creep over me and my hair rise on my head.

The full moon did not bring us luck, nor good weather, and that was our last hope. We had one fishable day. The rest were unsatisfactory, for some reason or another. And we drew on into December.

R. C. reached thirty days without seeing a fish or getting a strike. Captain M. caught a fine wahoo, the first we had seen at Vairao since August. He said he hooked a still larger one that shook the hook. There were indications of fish coming. The next day we sighted a big sailfish on the surface. He would not take my bait, nor could we drive him down. R. C., however, came over and got fast to him, and he turned out to be a splendid specimen, 120 pounds.

The rainy season set in. Did it rain? Oh no! There is no adequate epithet for what it did. You could not see whether it was rain or the ocean pouring over the land. You could not stand on your feet. I fell down three times in the path on the way to the dining-cabin. Slippery? It rained slippery-elm!

Then every little while it would stop raining and the sun would shine. Very beautiful, and hot. This rainy season was what we had needed to make the fishing good. There had been no rainy season for two years. The mountain rivers had to fill up and give the white-bait a chance to come in from the sea. The tuna and bonito followed the white bait in shore, and the swordfish followed the tuna and bonito. The season had just held off for us. November should have seen the beginning of the rains. But it did not.

This five-month stretch, as my notebook tells, was a scorcher in more ways than one. We failed again—the second trip—to land an enormous marlin or one of the several new species we knew inhabited these waters. And the strain of those blank days had told on all of us. We could not stand Tahiti any longer, even if we had not been booked for January, February, and March in New Zealand. We had food for reflection and much to discuss. There was not much liability of leisure hours dragging. We had to come back to Tahiti. We had to fish the Paumotus and the Marquesas. And we had not even proved the possibilities of the Society Islands and the Leewards. The difficulties all together were almost insurmountable. Yet they had an irresistible lure. I had to choke down my bitter regret over blunders, my intense disappointment, and try to forget them in talk at least of other attempts. It was always a relief to talk to R. C. or Captain Mitchell. "Come back?" echoed the Captain. "By gad! I'll say we'll come back!"

"We stick till our hair blows out," added R. C. with the old baseball slogan of college days.

And there we were. Stranded between this trip and one in the future, and then more, in order to get what seemed possible. I would wake out of a dream and wonder at my obsession. But the incomparable greatness of the game might be proved. Dugmore, Carl Akeley, Martin Johnson, and Stewart Edward White, and Burbridge, not to mention others, had proved the wonder of African game trails, with story and with film. Other parts of the world were being exploited.

But no one else had tackled the great game of the sea. In fact, no one dreamed of 1,000-pound swordfish until we photographed and caught them. We have it all to ourselves. And I will say it is a handful. Motion pictures on land are easy—even if you have to wait for weeks, and then to stand a charge of some huge wild beast. But when taking pictures of leaping fish you have the unstable sea under you. And you have all the land difficulties besides. Nevertheless, here is man's grand prerogative—to seek, to strive, to find and not to yield.

WEATHER AND FISH IN PAEA, TAHITI

From

Notes of Carrie-Finn and Ham-Fish

This report has to do mostly with Paea and is underestimated, rather than over. That is to say, we have tried to be truthful. There has been much *"parau parau"* about swordfish and sailfish and the bonito, and you will see some have been caught.

December 7, 1928—January 5, 1929.

Dec. 7—Good weather; report in Paea; bonito 200, tuna 6, caught by natives.
" 8—Good weather—no report.
" 9—Good weather—Sunday—no fish.
" 10—Good weather—bonito and tuna plentiful, unable to get actual number caught.
" 11—Good weather, bonito plentiful but not feeding. We caught 3 medium-sized dog-tooth tuna.
" 12—Good weather, slight wind. Tuna reported in district.
" 13—Good weather, some wind. Tuna reported in district.
" 14—Good weather, no wind. Bonito and tuna caught in district.
" 15—Good weather, some rain. 300 tuna, 14 bonito. We caught 4 large crevalle (*picheri*).
" 16—*Sunday*—no fish.
" 17—Fine fishing day. Eight native boats in Paea (four power) fishing for bonito. Caught hundreds and 10 tuna. Our man, George, said he saw a swordfish longer than the sea sled (13 ft.).
" 18—Good weather, little rain. Many boats after bonito and tuna. Big catch.
" 19—Good weather, light wind. Many bonito.
" 20—Good weather. We caught 17 bonito—6 very large. Saw 5 sharks. Many tuna caught in Paea.

Dec. 21—Fair, but high winds. A very large yellow-fin tuna on sale in market—couldn't find out where it came from.
" 22—Good weather, 300 bonito, 7 tuna.
" 23—*Sunday*—A sailfish, weighing 60 kilos in the market—came from district between Arue and Papenoo, the other side of Papeete.
" 24—Fine weather. 500 small bonito in Papeete from Moorea. Plenty of bonito and 10 tuna caught in Paea.
" 25—Christmas. No fishing.
" 26—Good weather. Many bonito in Papeete from Moorea. We caught dog-tooth tuna, 15 kilos, with spoon. Natives in Paea saw large swordfish when they were fishing for tuna. They gaffed him but he escaped.
" 27—Many bonito from Moorea. Good weather.
" 28—Good weather. 300 bonito, 11 tuna caught in Paea.
" 29—Good weather. Bonito and tuna reported in district.
" 30—*Sunday*. High wind.
" 31—Good weather.

January 1, 1929.
Jan. 1—Good weather—tuna and bonito plentiful.
" 2—Good weather.
" 3—Good weather. Many boats out for bonito. Big catch.
" 4—Good weather.

About December 15 two big swordfish were caught in the Puamotus near the island "Fangatau." The heads were on sale in Papeete and George said the fish must have been about 15 ft. long. Devilfish was used for bait.

Since the *Loren G.*, renamed *Te Anuanua III*, slipped into the water, on January 21, our interest has been so intense in our own activities—that is to say—what we can, or *cannot* do with our rods and reels, that we are quite unable to give any intelligent information to the fishers of big fish. The fact that we had six strikes on the first day out, lost our two best feather gigs (contributed by Mr. R. C. Grey), and didn't land a fish, is much more important to our present state of mind than to have forty-nine giant swordfish follow the boat for forty-nine miles! Mr. Zane Grey was correct in his prophecies, to the smallest detail: first, we are so keen for the sport that we not only fish all day, every day, but all night (E. Guild has had to give up coffee and drink Ovaltine, so he can sleep); second, we have lost a large percentage of fish *and* leaders; third, the first day out started with polite conversation as follows, "Now, you want to hold it this way and do it that way." "No, dear, let me show you how, et cetera," and ended in a knock-down, draw, or throw-out fight in the family.

An experienced fisherman would have been highly amused at the actual landing of the first fish. To begin with, when the line ran out and the clicker announced to the world that there was a fish on the hook, some one, in the excitement, threw the gaff overboard; then, with nine people telling me what to do in three different languages, I pumped so hard that I pulled the screws of the fishing-chair right out of the floor boards, and went over backward in a heap, all bound up with line, reel, and rod and Tom finally flopped into the cockpit, on top of me a *crevalle*, weighing about eight pounds! We were far from home, no way of repairing the chair, and determined to fish; so we stuck the handle between two cushions, sat on the top one, and continued our fishing. In spite of this handicap, I managed to land three more *crevalle*, the largest weighing about twenty-five pounds and Ham-fish pulled in a good-sized barracuda.

We have not attempted any big fish yet and won't until we have practiced on all the unsuspecting creatures lurking along the edge of the reef; but I don't think that Z. G. landing a half-tone Marlin gets any more thrill out of it than we do when our line runs out with maybe a small crevalle on the hook.

But, of course, all of this "baby-fish-talk" isn't very helpful—it just proves that the world contains two more ardent fishermen. On the whole, the weather here in Paea has been *very* good, this month, and the bonito running fast and furiously. One of the natives, near us, who owns a small launch has been out practically every day and brought in hundreds of bonito. Of course he has not caught any swordfish, but he has reported many and even speared two. Naturally, they escaped; but he said that one was two fathoms and the other, three fathoms long.

February 3—28, 1929.

Feb. 3—*Sunday*—no fishing.
" 4—Good weather for fishing, many bonito, but we couldn't go out—working on boat.
" 9—Good weather, but boat still not ready.
" 10—*Sunday*—no fishing. Good weather.

Feb. 11—Fished all day, but not a strike—very high sea. 400 bonito reported caught in Mateia—*inside lagoon!*

" 13—Very rough—couldn't go out through pass.

" 16—Very high wind—no fishing.

" 17—*Sunday*—no fishing but bonito in quantities just outside pass.

" 18—Took Governor and Am. Consul fishing, but had to come back—too rough.

" 23—Out all day—had first experience with big fish! C. was trolling with light tackle and feather gig and got a strike. It proved to be a bonito, at least it was when it took the hook, but only half of it remained when it was pulled in. Our first thought was sharks., but on looking over the stern we saw two *beautiful* wahoo and a third big fish, unknown. We put the half bonito back in the water, just as it was, on the feather gig—one of the wahoo grabbed it and ran. C. handed the rod and reel to Ham (being too excited to handle it herself), and he (being equally excited) tried to bring the wahoo in before he was ready—result—one more feather gig gone and about 100 yards of C.'s line. These were the first big fish we had seen and we were furious because we had not put the bonito on to the heavy line, instead of risking the light one. But we learned a lesson, which is just as good as getting a fish. After that we tried for two or three hours to get another bonito, to put on the big tackle, but didn't have any luck. So we trolled along the reef, with a feather gig on the big tackle, to have experience with it and C. caught a 17-pound barracuda and Ham a 12-pound *utu*. The big tackle seems awkward and hard to handle after C.'s light rod and reel. (This Z. G. outfit is perfect!)

" 24—*Sunday.*

" 28—Fine weather—started at 7.30, with two bonito for bait and teasers in action. Everybody very nervous, as that was our first attempt for a big fish. After trolling for two hours, raised two swordfish. They came up close to bait; we could see them just under surface, but they didn't touch it. We hung around and circled around for an hour, but nothing doing. Tom said perhaps bonito were too old, having been caught day before. Trolled a while more with teasers and bonito. Then saw big disturbance ahead which boatmen said was school of tuna. Took in bonito and teasers and put out light tackle with feather gig. C. had tremendous strike. Took out most of line and went straight down. Same old story! Too much brake and line broke—there goes another feather gig! Ham put out heavy tackle with gig—big strike; same kind, played it very well for twenty minutes, then with a mighty jerk, something happened—pulled in line and it was intact, feather gig, leader all right, but *hook* had broken. There we were right in the middle of hundreds of leaping, small yellowtails, and violently pursued by two huge sharks. We wouldn't risk our lines overboard with those hungry sharks, so we let Tom try and catch some with bonito pole. For every one he landed, the sharks took four, right off his hook. Great excitement—sea alive and bloody with activity. We let them catch seven and then, much against their wishes, made them stop and take us to the reef where we could troll again, and try and land a fish of some sort, with our *one* remaining feather gig; but the fishing was over for the day.

We returned at sunset, tired and sunburnt, but full of conversation, and reread pages in *Fishing Virgin Seas* and *The Angler's Eldorado*, especially the parts that describe lines broken and fish lost! And felt slightly consoled for our bad luck.

March 3—March 30, 1929.
" 4—Good fishing weather, but we did not go out; mail day.
" 6—Good weather—birds and bonito. Fished for swordfish with bonito and teasers all day. Raised nothing.
" 16—Good weather. Mr. Robinson hooked a large fish in pass; had a hot box in *his* reel (not ours, thank goodness) broke his rod, pulled in by hand and finally broke leader!
" 17—*Sunday*—no fishing.
" 18—Good weather—small *pihiri* and barracuda on feather gig.
" 27—Red-letter day—C. hooked and landed first wahoo! Ham put line out and within half an hour hooked and landed another one. Decided very early in the morning best time to fish. Both C. and H. used light tackle and fifteen-thread line, and our last feather gig (a terrible old thing). C. thought she had a tuna, because it took out so much line, and so fast and so deep and when she had it near the surface, down it went again. Great thrill!

March 28—Went out again, at 4.30 in the morning to same tuna hole as yesterday. C. hooked another wahoo, got him alongside; boatman slow with the gaff and lost him. Then H. hooked one and brought him safely in. Then C. took the rod and trolled awhile; then our empty stomachs said it was breakfast-time, "let's go home."

Just then a tremendous strike; out flashed the line, yards of it; finally when it stopped C. started to pump it in, thinking it was another wahoo, and *couldn't lift the rod!* Then a splash and away far from the boat, a magnificent marlin threw himself out of the water. C., in her excitement, yelled, "Never mind my wahoo; let him go and let's put out a line for that swordfish." Whereupon H. and the crew shrieked, "You've got him hooked yourself, you darn fool!" C. hollered like a wild Indian with excitement and then became cold with apprehension when she realized she had hooked a swordfish, on a *feather gig*, small DOUBLE HOOK, and No. 15 line!! Down! Down! he went taking all but the last few inches (it seemed) of line. Then, as he relaxed, she pumped him up, slowly, her rod bending until the tip was in the water. He leaped twice at the beginning and then never showed again for two and a half hours, when he made two more gleaming leaps, 50 ft. from the stern of the boat. Then he went right down again and broke the faithful but fragile line!

" 29—Of course after yesterday's experience we were out again at 4.30, with our heaviest line, a huge hook and a feather gig we borrowed from Nordhoff, but naturally no swordfish was interested in us this day. Caught one wahoo and he didn't put up much of a fight—the huge hook, meant for a swordfish, came right through the top of his head and completely paralyzed him. We eat, talk, and sleep nothing but yesterday's marlin.

" 30—Fished all morning—not even a strike. On the whole the weather has been favorable for fishing this month and bonito most plentiful—the market has been absolutely flooded with them. Our local tuna fishermen have been very successful, bringing in from five to twenty tuna nearly every day. We have been slightly handicapped by lack of gig heads (all white roosters in Paea are plucked bald-headed in the tail. We have decided to keep White Leghorns instead of Rhode Island Reds, to have feathers for the gigs). We ordered a gross of gigs from McRae, but he never sent them—said we didn't need that many, so he didn't send *any*.

But having had the feel of a swordfish, we will never be happy until we have landed some—can get the bonito with bamboo pole and native hooks. All the old "salts" swear that April is *the* fish month and we are certainly going to find out for ourselves. We are convinced that the big fish come to the surface *very early* in the morning, and we will go out every morning at 4.30, prepared for the day with a marlin on the other end of the line. C. couldn't move out of her bed the next day after her two-and-a-half-hour battle, she was so lame, back, arms, neck, legs, etc. But it was worth it and she would probably be sitting there yet if the line hadn't broken, subsisting on bully beef, sandwiches, and bananas!

April—1929.

April 1—Fine weather—started out at 5.00 to meet the "Greys"—caught one wahoo and one barracuda, *en route*. Captain Mitchell came back with us—caught a bonito, put him over, with the teasers out and had a strike, about halfway home. Fish took out a lot of line and then when the Captain began to pump him, line parted—old line! Moral—mustn't use a line too long!

" 2—Fine weather—went out right after lunch, and E. hooked big tuna (98 lbs.) in tuna hole, on feather gig. Broke butt of big rod and had to hand-line it in.

" 3—Fine weather. C. got a wahoo in tuna hole—then we went after bonito and as soon as we got one, remembered Captain Mitchell's advice and put him right on alive, with the boat standing still. He was right—we got a bite *immediately*, a fine, big shark! And what he did to the line! I suspect Captain Mitchell *expected* that this would happen to us!!

" 10—Fine weather. Many bonito. Put one on hook and let it down, trying Captain Mitchell's suggestion once more and once more caught a shark—who once more broke butt of rod and then leader. Decided *not* to do this again, with any of OUR tackle.

" 11—Fine weather. Pretty mad at sharks, so we put over a bonito on a huge rope, with bronze cable leader—caught him, shot him, drowned him, hit him, cut him, kicked him, and now feel better about the other two that damaged our tackle! (Still have it in for Zane Grey and Captain Mitchell.)

April 12—Very rough.
" 13—Fair weather. Fished all afternoon—no strikes.
" 14—*Sunday*—no fishing.
" 15—H. out in morning, caught nothing. In afternoon small tuna and some bonito—very plentiful.
" 16—Good weather—saw big swordfish come out of water but couldn't hook him.
" 17—Good weather—didn't fish.
" 18—Good weather—had a strike near reef—fish went under a rock, nearly pulled us on the reef—had to cut line.
" 19—Good weather—didn't fish.
" 20—Good weather—Went out early and H. caught record wahoo (record for us) 63 pounds. Trolled all day for marlin—no strike. Natives said two marlin and one sailfish at Punaira.
" 21—*Sunday*—no fishing.
" 22—Good weather—plenty bonito. Big swordfish in market. 13 bonito caught beyond Papenoo.
" 23—H. hooked swordfish, line not carefully put on reel— caught some way and parted when fish was still going out (feather gig). Afterwards caught wahoo and bonito.
" 24—Fished early in morning. C. hooked swordfish on feather gig and lost him—hook straightened right out! H. took boat to town to put it up for the few months we are away. The market has been absolutely flooded with bonito this month. We have seen them every time we have been out—some days, although they were plentiful, they did not seem to be feeding and would not bite native hook or feather gig. But on the whole, bait has been very plentiful this month. We have not trolled as often as we wished to for swordfish, because we had only one good line left and wanted to have some fun with it before losing it all—and we certainly have had fun. Now we are in a good mood to buy all the tackle we can possibly afford and go back and "lick the big ones"!

May 1—July 20, 1929.

May 1—Robinson, who was taking care of our place for us, reported that during the month of May the weather was so bad that fishing was practically impossible. The sea was so high that it covered our pier with a foot of water; outside the lagoon, storms of wind and rain prevailed, preventing even the natives from fishing. Mr. Grey's man at Flower Point Camp said that no bonito were reported in that district during the month. Apparently June was a better month as far as weather was concerned, with more bonito running in Paea and Moorea. Several swordfish were reported as having been seen especially off Taapuna Pass, in Punavia. Also, there were two or three caught by natives and sold in the market. We asked Phillips, a bonito fisherman who lives in Moorea, to keep a record of any swordfish he might see while out bonito fishing, and although his notes cover a span of time mostly previous to the time we were away, here it is:

Swordfish seen:

Nov. 17—(1)	1	mile off Motuta at 4.30 P.M.
" 20—(1)	3	miles off Motuta at 2.00 P.M.
Jan. 9—(2)	2	miles off pass at Taapuna 2.00 P.M.
" 19—(3)	1½	miles off pass at Taapuna 3.30 P.M.
" 29—(1)	2	miles off Paea
Feb. 1—(1)	1	mile off at Terapa at 3
" 2—(1)	1	mile off Terapa at 3
" 14—(1)		Between Moorea and Tahiti 2-3
" 22—(1)		Between Papeete and Vairao 2.30
Mar. 4—(1)		Between Papeete and Moorea 2.30
" 9—(1)		3 miles off point Temae at Moorea, 3.00 P.M. This was the largest fish seen this season.
" 21—(1)		Off pass at Vairao, 2.00 P.M.
Apr. 12—(1)		Off pass at Tavona, 2.30 P.M.
" 18—(1)		Off pass at Tavona, 2-3

He says that he did not go out in December, but his cousin, who was out every day, reported that on many days the bonito fishing was spoiled by the swordfish.

July 20—Sept. 16, 1929.

We returned from America, full of enthusiasm, new tackle and good advice! Arrived here the 20th of July, but couldn't get the boat in the water until August 10th. We put in new driving-shafts, went all over the wiring and painted and varnished her inside and out to have her in good condition for the strenuous season ahead.

Aug. 10—Weather fair, went out early in the morning for our first trip and came back with nothing but one small

The Belle of the Drive

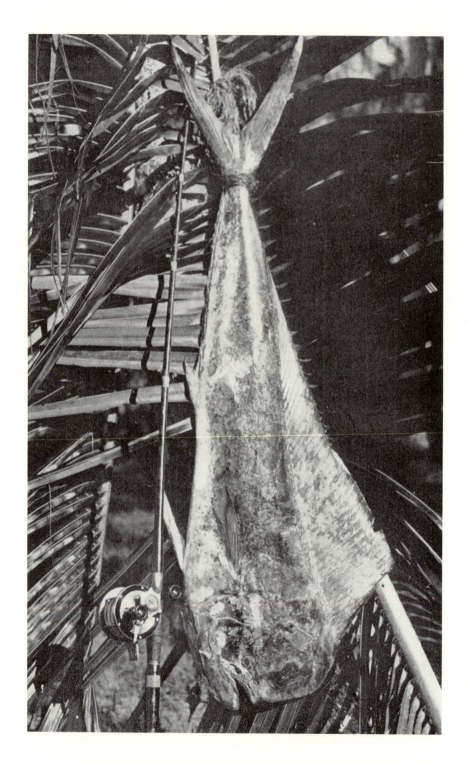

World-record Dolphin, 63 Pounds, Zane Grey

pihiri. Went out again in afternoon and got another small *pihiri* and a small *evau* (dog-toothed tuna). This is evidently the season for *evau*.

Aug. 15—The pass here has been so bad we couldn't go out these previous days. Went out early this morning and got one *evau*—11½ pounds.

" 22—One big *evau*—40 lbs.

" 23—Beautiful day. Started out early and caught a nice-sized *otava* (something like bonito). Put him right over on heavy tackle and started toward town. At Punavia, about where Cappy had his strike that day with us, Carrie, who was fishing, saw a Marlin just near her bait. She let it out a little farther and he grabbed it and made a beautiful run. She struck him, but evidently not hard enough, for he made one grand leap into the air and threw the bait and hook out of his mouth. Tough luck—she had a cable all sent to Mr. Grey, mentally! Put out a feather gig in same place, having no more bait, and caught a nice wahoo—about 45 lbs. He put up the best scrap of any wahoo we have caught.

" 24—Caught another *otava* in morning and put him on the heavy line—trolled all day, but raised nothing. Caught 2 *pihiri* in pass coming home—late and dark. Natives reported swordfish in our tuna hole.

" 27—Wahoo.

" 28—Up to now we have seen very few birds, and whenever we have gone through small schools of bonito have caught nothing. But today we ran into a fine school of bonito off Paea about two miles. We caught them with feather gig and native shell hooks. Put them on the ice for tomorrow morning.

" 29—Went out early well prepared with bait, etc., hoping to land a fine marlin. Trolled all day, but didn't raise a thing or see a *fin*! Late in afternoon trolled over with feather gig. Ham had a couple of good strikes, probably wahoo, but didn't hook them.

Sept. 3—Tuna in district and plenty of birds just outside pass. We went out then and saw hudreds of *small* bonito jumping, but they wouldn't take a hook of any kind.

" 4—*Fine Weather*. Ham hooked an *otava*, but lost it in the propeller. Later saw tuna jumping ahead, so we went over with feather gig, No. 21 line, and new Atlapac. Ham hooked one—a beauty—must have been over 100 pounds. Took out about 300 yards of line. Ham got it half back when it sounded again, took out so much line that Ham got scared and jammed on finger drag too hard and snapped line. How we *jumped* on him! George had that tuna all in the frying-pan and was starving (mentally) when Ham lost it. Ham says he doesn't take a hundred-pound tuna seriously, because he has his mind so full of 600- 700- 800-lb. fish, after reading *Angler's Eldorado, Virgin Seas*, etc.

Sept. 10—Fine day. Started out about 9. Saw birds all going in direction of Mataia, so we went out that way and located bonito. They were plentiful and biting well, but *so big*. We tried and tried to get some smaller ones and failed. So we chose the smallest of the ones we caught and put it out. About ten miles out to sea, raised a fine marlin. He looked at the bait, stayed near it for three or four minutes, hit it with his sword and disappeared. I think it was too large for him. He wouldn't touch it. We tried again to get a smaller bonito, since there were birds all about us, but this time they wouldn't bite our hooks at all, so we finally had to come in, once more taunted and teased by a marlin and we defeated!

" 11—Wonderful day. Ham had to take car to town, so Carrie went in by boat, planning to get some bait to troll for marlin on way home. Just outside pass tuna were leaping, a wonderful sight. We made straight for them, and Carrie got a strike at once, feather gig, No. 21 line on Atlapac reel. Remembering Ham's experience of breaking the line with too much drag, she handled him very carefully. Out and down he went then stopped, and Carrie got back a little line. Down again—this time a little more line, etc., until after about thirty-five minutes of hard work the double leader came out of the water and the battle was nearly over. He weighed 68 pounds and was the biggest fish Carrie has landed so far. Carrie very proud because she didn't lose him! There seemed to be great activity on the water this morning. Birds all about—put line out for another tuna and landed a *huge* bonito—33 pounds. He will hardly do for bait! But, again, could get no small ones. So we had no chance to troll for marlin on this day. No more fishing until after mail day because some little part of steering-gear is broken and a new part must be made in town. It is too bad that Mr. Grey will not be here for November, December, and January, because it seems certain that bait will be very plentiful. Just these last few days we have seen more birds and bonito—it looks as if they were beginning to run early, this year.

Sept. 15—In town Saturday Nordhoff told Carrie that he had hooked a marlin Friday and that it weighed 350 pounds, but it got away. Why, certainly! He was out after bonito, and since they wouldn't bite a shell hook, he put out a feather gig on the thirty-nine line, and a heavy reel. Just as he put it out, in the school of bonito, a marlin grabbed it and immediately jumped ten feet in the air, and broke the leader, which was piano wire. The marlin jumped again five or six times, just from pure joy at being free again.

P.S.—Ham says that, anyway, Carrie has saved a lot of money on cables by not landing a marlin or two.

Sept. 16—Oct. 14, 1929

" 16—Town today with our mail; saw Nordhoff and he said he saw another marlin Saturday in a school of bonito. Having hooked and lost one on Friday and seen one on Saturday, he has become keenly interested in swordfishing.

" 17—Didn't go out—photographer here.

" 18—Out all day. Caught some bait, trolled but raised nothing—bait too large. Ham caught one small wahoo in tuna hole, with feather gig.

" 19—Got some bonito from passing trucks from Taravao and went right out. Started toward town and raised marlin just off Paea. He was interested in teasers, swam around bait, but refused it (probably not fresh enough). Finally disappeared. Then we saw some birds toward Moorea—just a few—and hastened over there, hoping to get fresh bait, but they wouldn't take the hook. Just as we were about to give up and put out the teasers again, Carrie had a strike—just a jerk, like a wave catching the line. She saw the fish strike and thought it was a tuna. But instead of sounding, this fish stayed near the surface and came toward the boat, finally breaking water about fifty feet away. Lo and behold—a golden dolphin! Then he went down again, up again— another blue and gold and silver leap in the air, much twisting and turning and down again. Finally we had him right up where we could watch him and thought the end was near. But out of sight he went again, just a steady pull when suddenly, with one terrific jerk, the line parted (No. 15 on Pfleugar Templar). You can imagine our expressions—we were *crushed* with disappointment, never having hooked or seen a dolphin before. There was nothing left to do but try and hook another, so we put on another red-eye feather gig (we lost four that day). But no more dolphin in our kettle of fish, so we put out the poor water-soaked bonito once more and found an appreciative friend—a shark! He came right after the bait and only by the boat—men yelling lustily to Carrie was she able to avoid hooking him. He followed for half an hour, so we decided that *perhaps* it was he that snapped the line by taking Mr. Dolphin for the fish course of his midday meal. Home late and no fish but one of our most *thrilling* days.

Sept. 20—Barracuda and bonito—bonito too big for bait.

" 21—Took out nieces of Princess from Hawaii—Carrie tried to show them how to catch a marlin, but no marlin appeared.

In afternoon we saw birds and hundreds of fish jumping, but they wouldn't bite. Trolled over tuna hole with feather gig for tuna *or* wahoo *or* dolphin (always thinking of that dophin), but caught nothing. Came in late, bathed in rosy glow of a beautiful sunset.

" 22—*Sunday.*

" 23—Went out in morning for bait—few bonito jumping in tuna hole, but no bites. Wanted a fish for lunch, so caught a *crevalle* along reef with red-and-white spoon. Ham went out along in afternoon and *said* he saw a marlin in the tuna hole. Hooked an *otava*, but too big for bait. Natives in the district fishing commercially for flying-fish now, so we will get some every day and use them for bait, instead of bonito.

" 24—Went out early with flying-fish after that marlin Ham said he saw yesterday afternoon in the tuna hole—only that marlin turned out to be a shark. Fortunately we avoided hooking him on our marlin tackle. We tried to get him on a shark hook, but he wouldn't bite. The natives said he was a "missionary" shark—had been taught it was wrong to bite. Caught a barracuda on way home. They are very plentiful now. Few bonito, but they wouldn't bite. Lots of flying-fish in the market now, but practically no tuna or bonito. Prices very high.

Sept. 25—Blankety—blank—blank—BLANK! (All fishermen understand *that* language.) Carrie just lost her second dolphin. Hooked him in the tuna hole, on a feather gig, and he made four magnificent, twisting leaps into the air and shook the hook on the fourth, before she woke up. This makes ten different kinds of fish we have hooked, on a feather gig in our tuna hole. 1—yellow-fin tuna, 2—dog-toothed tuna, 3—albacore, 4—bonito, 5—*otava*, 6—barracuda, 7—wahoo, 8—marlin, 9—dolphin, 10—green shark. Caught 2 *crevalle* along reef on way home. Wonderful fishing weather. No birds, though—some bonito jumping in and around tuna hole.

" 26—Went out at five o'clock in the morning to surprise those dolphins in the tuna hole, but we got the surprise, in the shape of a big wind and heavy sea, and we had to rush back, in order to make the pass while it was still navigable. Carrie had a chill, went to bed with a high fever, and Dr. Cassieu came and pronounced it tonsilitis. Ham says it is "dolphinitis," having lost two in a week.

" 27—No fishing—rough weather and Carrie in bed.

" 28—Ditto. Ham in town, met an ex-British naval officer named Branson or Bransome, who fishes. He had some tackle with him but no boat.

" 29—Still rough.

Oct. 2—Went out with flying-fish for bait, raised nothing. Saw few bonito and tuna jumping—no bites. Caught 2 *crevalle* along reef on way home.

" 3—Fine fishing weather. Ham out in morning—Saw few birds diving and one tuna jumped, but no bites. Caught 1 *crevalle* in pass.

" 4—Out with flying-fish for bait. Trolled almost to Moorea—raised nothing. Big sea came up and we had to go in near reef. Caught 1 *crevalle* and 1 *otava*, just right for bait, but it was too rough and too late to troll any more.

" 11—*Friday*. First day this week we could go out. Mr. and Mrs. Gifford Pinchot (here on their boat) out for lunch and we took them fishing in afternoon. It was too rough to go out far, so we let him troll with the Atlapac No. 24 line, over tuna hole, hoping we might get a tuna or wahoo; *and if he didn't hook and land a mar-*

lin! Carrie and Ham could have cried! They have trolled over that hole hours and hours and hours and then he comes along and lands a marlin—a small one, yes, but a fine fighter. He made twenty-four leaps out of the water. Mr. Pinchot was extremely pleased with our Z. G. launch, tackle, enthusiasm, etc., and sent his captain out to take measurements of launch, exact position of chair, etc. Of course we were delighted to put on such a perfect show for the benefit of our guests, but *why* couldn't one of us have landed the first marlin in that boat! We are getting to be the butt of all jokes—the swordfishers that never get a swordfish. Never mind, we are getting a lot of valuable experiences and if we ever *do* get fast to a big one, Heaven help him!

Information from Nordhoff.

"About the 8th of October, three or four miles off the Taunoa passage, a large fish made a rush at a pearl bonito hook, and on same being hastily hauled in, the fish stationed himself just aft of the propeller, about two feet under the surface, and stayed there for about forty-five minutes. I had an excellent chance to observe this fish, which was quite new to me. It was about eight feet long and fairly slender in build. The top view showed its entire body the color of newly burnished gold. The tail, very large and wide from tip to tip, was of an extraordinary vivid electric blue."

Oct. 15—Nov. 10, 1929

On the whole there is nothing of importance to report this month. There have been very few bonito running and no swordfish reported. This is just about the time, I think, that Mr. Grey made his record last year—record of fishing more days without catching anything than anyone else in the world. 83 days! Mercy! We have been out practically every day that the weather permitted and have had some great thrills, but of course we get a thrill out of anything over a three-pound *crevalle*.

" 16—Saw tuna again. Ham had a wonderful strike from a wahoo—he jumped straight out of water about ten feet and turned in air—put up a good fight—weighed 44 pounds.

" 17—Ham out in morning. Saw bonito jumping, but they

wouldn't bite. Caught *otava*—pretty large for bait, but put out teasers—raised nothing. Caught 78-pound tuna in afternoon.

Oct. 18—Very rough—out after lunch but too rough for fishing. Saw a few birds, but none feeding. Caught a barracuda in tuna hole.

" 22—Still rough—but we went out. No strikes.

" 24—Weather fine. Having no bait, we bought a flying-fish from a native fishing in tuna hole—Put out teasers and this flying-fish but raised nothing. Mr. Branson, an Englishman, was with us, with his New Zealand tackle, so we let him drift with the bait—being curious to see this style of fishing. Of course we hoped he'd get a shark (the same as we did when we followed *certain advice* and let down the bait), but he didn't have a strike—only succeeded in getting all tangled up with a native's line, down for tuna.

" 29—Fine day. Started out early. Got a flying-fish from a native and started out toward the peninsula. Ran into very heavy sea, so headed back for Moorea. Ham had strike, without any fish showing—hauled in bait, but there was nothing left but the head—then we saw a shark astern—he had ruined our only bait. Birds ahead, so we went through them with a feather gig. Ham had a strike, then a leap into the air followed by a wild cry, "Dolphin!" (Our boatman calls them "doll-fish!") Sure enough, at last we had hooked another dolphin. Ham played him like a master, keeping a tight line, so the fish couldn't shake the hook. He came out of the water ten times and we all yelled like lunatics from sheer joy and wonder. We were wild with excitement, and so anxious to land this fish that we have read and heard so much about. He finally got him in the boat and we spent the next fifteen minutes admiring his colors and shape. Then it was Carrie's turn to troll and try to hook another, but the birds had scattered and there was "nothing doing," so we came in. Out again in afternoon and ran into a fine flock of birds and fish near Moorea. Bonito and tuna jumping. Carrie hooked a tuna, but broke the line—too much brake. She lost three more in quick succession and passed the rod to Ham in deep disgust. He caught some bonito and then Carrie got some and a small tuna. Saved smallest of the bonito for bait.

Nov. 1—Ran into school of bonito—biting fine, but *very* large. Caught one small one and saved him for next day (it being late in the afternoon).

" 2—Out right after breakfast, teasers out—bonito for bait. Saw nothing all day. Chased two schools of fish for fresher bait—they wouldn't take gig or shell hook.

" 6—Trolled several hours over tuna hole. No birds and no bites, so Carrie fished along reef—hooking a big needlefish—4½—first one we ever caught on spoon. He was great sport, stayed on the surface all the time and jumped like a dolphin. He was hooked in the under jaw, from the *outside*—never took the hook in his mouth. 70 bonito were reported caught in Mataiea, and there seem to be a few in market every day, now. Our boatman says "December."

Dec. 12—Ham out early in the morning, ran over tuna hole a few times, but raised nothing. The birds all seemed to be going in direction of peninsula, so Ham headed out a bit and toward Mataiea. Couldn't locate any big flock, but followed a few white ones that were feeding and hooked a dolphin. The fish struck like a rock, jumped only once, and came in heavily, without much action. The boatman lost him after he had hold of leader. Put out gig again and hooked another dolphin, which jumped out of water just once and didn't put up much of a battle. Perhaps Coxe reel and No. 24 line are too heavy for these fish. Miss Atlapac and lighter line for this fishing. He weighed 36 pounds and was 4 feet 11 inches long. The larger dolphin don't seem to put up the fight that the smaller ones do, nor are they so beautiful in color. Z. G. says there are two kinds of dolphin, or "*coryphene*," here; the larger size seem to have a different shaped head, much deeper and squarer. Ham had to go to town in afternoon, so Carrie went out alone. Headed out to sea, looking for a fight with a dolphin or tuna. Didn't see any signs of life and as it was very rough came back along the reef and had a great time with the Pfleugar Oceanic, catching two big *crevalle* and a barracuda and incidentally knocked her right hand black and blue on the rapidly revolving handle of this surf casting reel! Miss the Pfleugar Templar, which is a favorite of Z. G.'s.

" 13—Ham out early in the morning and caught an *otava* in tuna hole. Then he hooked another, but before he got it in a wahoo grabbed it, hooked himself with a splash, and then just as quickly unhooked himself, taking *otava* along, too. Put the feather gig out, *hooked* another wahoo, which got off near the boat. Caught another *otava*, just right for bait, put it over, with teasers out, and trolled all rest of morning but saw not a FIN!

Dec. 16—Went out in afternoon, taking Mrs. Stergius and Mrs. Jewett as AUDIENCE (no chance of anyone *fishing* in our boat, any more), and these two ladies were better than any dead rabbit's foot ever carried along for luck! Went out five or six miles without seeing anything, and then ran into the biggest flock of birds we have seen this year, with fish of all kinds jumping on every side. Hooked a bonito and put him right over, on the heavy tackle, with teasers out, hoping and expecting to raise a marlin in this paradise of fish. Didn't see a sign of one, so after a while we decided to run through the birds again with a feather gig and see what we could get. The fish were biting well and we caught four small tuna and many bonito, but not a suspicion of a marlin. It was late and we were far from home, but the moon appeared and we had a delightful ride back, more or less pleased with quantity, if not quality—and more sore hands, having caught these fish on the Pfleugar Oceanic.

" 17—Went out right after lunch, taking Mrs. S. and Mrs. J. with us again, since they proved such satisfactory shriekers! Started off in same direction as yesterday to try and locate the birds and get the marlin that surely *must* be with that school of bait. Rode and rode and rode and saw nothing. We were all more or less asleep when Ham yelled, feeling a slight *tap* on his line, then feeling nothing more ordered the boat ahead again. The next instant he let out an unearthly yell and BANG—WHIZ—out went the line like a greased pig and immediately we saw a marlin come right out of the water and *stay* there, it seemed. Ham struck him so hard, using only his thumb to break the line, that he burnt the skin off his right thumb. Such excitement and screaming and rushing for the big gaff, ropes, harness, etc., etc. He jumped fourteen times, lovely graceful sorties from the calm surface of the Pacific. Then he sounded. The suspense was terrible! But the outfit was good—Coxe 90, new No. 24 line, 12 airplane wire leader, and 9-0 Sobey hook (and Hom). Ham yelled "Take off my hat!" "Take off my glasses!" His shirt was filled with the breeze and sweat dripped from the end of his nose like Niagara Falls. Tom, the witness of our many battles, kept murmuring and muttering, "Take it easy," while Carrie and Tihoti hovered over his chair, looking *simple* with anxiety. Carrie, anxious for him to land it, for the honor of the family, but always consoling herself with the thought, "If he *does* lose it, how I can *laugh* at him, and still have a chance to land the first one!" At the end of twenty-five minutes give and take, he came up again, made three more leaps, and landed rather feebly on his side—a welcome sight and a tired fish. In ten minutes more Ham had him up to the boat, and the boys gaffed him dexterously, and after putting rope around his tail hauled him on board with much slipping, sliding, and swearing, and Ham beamed like a young mother with her first child. Of course we rushed right home to measure and photograph this most wonderful fish and to send a cable to Mr. Grey. Carrie tried to make Ham sign just his name to the cable, but Ham generously and nobly said, "No, this is *our* fish." He weighed 162 pounds and was 8 feet 4 inches long, and we were just as happy as though it were a big one. Ham handled him beautifully and was the hero of the day, as he rightly deserved to be.

Dec. 18—Carrie, fired with ambition and determined to get a bigger one, even if only *one* pound bigger, started out at 5 o'clock in the morning and trolled for hours, without a strike, until she was forced to come in on account of high seas in the pass.

And that is all, because we decided that the engines should be overhauled—one of them was not working very well and we want them to be in fine shape to keep up with the Grey fleet of greyhounds. And it is a good thing we took them out because we discovered that the intake water pipe was corroded and held together in one small place only. It came right off like a stick of candy and this could have happened at sea. In a rough sea we would have filled so rapidly with water that we would have all sunk quickly to the bottom of the ocean.

But, of course, in the meantime, reports of marlin came in from every side (from commercial fishermen). One was caught by a native near Mauu's, weighing over 200 kilos. Many have been seen near Moorea by Phillips. There has been a monster playing around the tuna hole, bigger than Jimmy's 200-kilo catch. On Tuesday next our boat will be in commission again, and if Z. G. doesn't get a cable signed "Carrie" before he gets this book, he will know there is a pretty miserable girl in Tahiti.

Bonito plentiful—market full of them. Of course, this is the beginning of the season, all right. Only hope it keeps up until you get here.

June 24—July 19, 1930.

Once again the sun rises over the green hills and shines on the backs of the lazy porpoises, playing in the lagoon; the waves crash in green and white grandeur on the reef; there is a slight swell in the pass, as the *Te Anuanua* heads for the open sea—we are going fishing!

June 24—Ham and Martha out in the morning. Fine weather, especially good day for dolphin, but had trouble with one engine, so had to come in. Caught nothing.

" 25—Good weather, but couldn't go out—working on engine.

" 26—Good weather. Ham and Martha out in afternoon. Martha trolled in lagoon—had a strike, but didn't hook him. Went outside and ran into birds and bonito—caught one.

" 27—Good weather. Ham and Martha out early—ran into bonito and Martha hooked and landed her first fish—a 10¾-pound bonito. She was using a light tuna rod, Pfleugar Templar reel, No. 15 line (the same outfit with which Carrie and Ham had made their first catch). The fish ran out on her four times, putting up a grand fight, but she handled it very well and was proud as Punch when Tom pulled it into the boat. Ham went out in the lagoon later with light tackle—had two strikes and brought one *pihiri* up to the boat, for Tom to lose.

" 28—Ham out in the morning—saw a bunch of white birds and expected to get a dolphin, but didn't.

" 29—*Sunday*—Sold the *Moorea* to Clymer Brook.

June 30—Fine day, but couldn't go out—in town all day.
July 1—Carrie out with Ham for the first time. Didn't fish—just watched. Ran through few birds, caught one large bonito. Too late to troll—fine day.
" 2—Ham out at 5 o'clock, with fresh bait. Ran over toward Moorea, raised nothing. On way home ran into flock of birds and tried for fresh bait. Hooked a big tuna on light rod and No. 15 line,—took out a lot of line and broke off. Put a gig on heavier tackle, with No. 24 line and caught a 30-lb. bonito. Put gig over again and hooked what he thought was a tuna, but it turned out to be a small marlin—not over a hundred pounds. He shook the hook on the fourth jump. Ham saw far out at sea what is called here a "puffin." These rare birds are usually only out at night and live in a hole, and this one seemed quite blind and lost. Fine weather.
" 3—Ham out at 5.30. Trolled over tuna hole with feather gig and had magnificent strike from wahoo. He seemed to come right up from the bottom and leaped 8-10 feet in the air. He took out one red eye and half the feathers from the gig, but didn't get hooked. Some small bonito were jumping in tuna hole, but they wouldn't bite. Caught a good wahoo. Went on out to sea for bait and a marlin tapped gig twice and then took the hook. Ham struck him so hard he pulled the hook out of his mouth. Went on trolling and had another marlin strike, but didn't hook him. Ran into birds and caught a 30-lb. bonito. These big bonito are the wise ones that escaped Z. G. and Cappy and are grown up. Trolled through white "fairy terns" feeding and caught two dolphin and a barracuda. Fine weather, five fish and lots of fun.
" 4—Ham and Martha out at 5.30. Martha trolled with spoon to tuna hole—no strikes, so she changed to feather gig. Just as she was letting out her line, a wahoo took the gig and gave her a good battle. She got him up to the boat twice, then got a little bit lazy, rested the rod on the gunwale, and when she started to pump him again—he had gone! She was crushed with disappointment but learned a lesson. Put over feather gig again and caught a nice sized bonito for bait. Ham trolled all the morning but raised nothing. On the way home Martha was trolling a gig again and hooked

and landed, all by herself, a 34-lb. bonito. The boat came in with all flags flying!! Rather rough weather.

July 5—Bad weather.

" 6—*Sunday.* Bad weather. Drove out to "Flower Point." Admired elegant new sign which has inspired the *bougainvillæa*—it is as high as the sign and in bloom. Everything looked fine out there, but LONESOME. Sat on Z. G.'s new veranda and talked about him!

" 7—Bad weather—high wind. Worked on tackle in morning. Went out in lagoon after lunch with new very light tackle—the smallest Pfleugar Templar and No. 9 thread line. Trolled with red-headed "pal o' boy" bait casting lure—had one strike but missed it. Then put on blue enamel "last word wobbler." Hooked a small *pihiri* but lost it. 6 oz. tip.

" 8—Bad weather—wind and rain.

" 9—Bad weather—no rain but high wind.

" 10—Bad weather.

" 11—Weather better. Ham, Martha, and Carrie out right after breakfast with some bonito we bought. Fished all morning but didn't see a thing. Still pretty choppy, with quite a bit of wind. Out in lagoon in afternoon, one strike, but missed it.

" 12—Ham and Martha took Dr. Wagner, of Pasadena, out at 5 o'clock. Martha trolled over tuna hole with feather gig and caught *evau* or dog-toothed tuna, 12½ pounds. Bonita jumping, but they wouldn't bite at first. Finally Martha caught one on a feather gig and Tom and Dr. Wagner each got one on a native hook. Trolled about three hours for marlin, but raised nothing. Saw "fairy tern" feeding, so Ham went after a dolphin and caught one weighing about 25 pounds. He got 13 jumps out of it.

" 13—*Sunday*—no fishing, of course! Ham and Martha cleaned tackle after they came home from church.

" 14—Took Martha in town to the celebration.

" 15—Very rough outside. Ham trolled in lagoon with light tackle, and in pass, but had no strike. We have no small red-headed Knowles automatic strikers, and they are what get the fish inside the lagoon.

" 16—Ham and Martha out at 6.30. Saw several flocks of birds and few bonito jumping, but they were all traveling fast and wouldn't stop to bite. Took Clymer

Brook out in afternoon for a demonstration. Just fished along the reef, no strikes. Our new pupil!

July 17—Good day, but couldn't go out.

" 18—Ham out at 7.30—fine day. Couldn't get any bait, so started for home. Hooked a small bonito, right in front of our pass, but shark grabbed it and got hooked—just a baby shark. High wind in afternoon.

On the whole, bait is scarce and hard to catch just now, and we are having high winds nearly every day from the southeast. The natives are getting tuna, down deep in the tuna hole every day—they are all down there for the winter, I guess. There won't be anything really thrilling to write about until Carrie begins to fish, because when she is fishing, if nothing happens she *invents* something.

HOME-COMING, TAHITI—1930

The alembic of the tropic sky
   Distills a magic of the night
Of gold and silver is the blend
   Fused in the diamond's crystal light.

Dissolving all the little stars
   While Venus sulks, her glory gone—
The vanishing celestial spheres
   Await the dawn.

A silent ship glides slowly on
   Towards shadows rising from the sea—
The lapping murmur at the prow
   Intensifies the mystery.

                         F. B.

January 9—1930.

Jan. 9—At last the engines are back in the boat and we went out this morning, just in the lagoon, so the mechanic could make any necessary adjustments. Carrie trolled with a small spoon and caught one *crevalle*. Right after lunch we started out, "loaded for bear." We had the new Atlapac which Mr. Grey sent, a new thirty-thread line on the Coxe (for Carrie's marlin), new hooks, gigs, and leaders, and new ambition. After we had been out about half an hour, expecting to stay long and late and come in by moonlight if necessary, the mechanic informed us that we had better go back, because it wasn't wise to run the newly assembled engines any longer that day. Of course we could do nothing but go back, but we could easily have killed him. Furthermore, I don't think there was anything wrong with the engines, but with the mechanic—it was quite rough and I think he was seasick, or afraid he was going to be. Fortunately he is not part of our regular crew. On the way home, Carrie, with a line out, under *any* circumstances, hooked a *crevalle*, in the lagoon, on a small spoon and light piano-wire leader. The leader snapped just as she had him up to the boat, ending very disappointingly our first day's fishing after this long wait.

Jan. 10—Carrier trolled the *whole day long* without a strike or a sign of a fish! We saw flocks of birds flying toward the peninsula and started in that direction, but the sea was so rough we had to turn and go back toward Moorea. In general it is much rougher out toward "Flower Point" than between our place and Moorea.

" 11—What a morning! I must write about it at once, before I forget any details. Not discouraged by yesterday's fruitless efforts, we were out at 5.30 this morning. Trolled over tuna hole to pick up an early bonito, and Ham hadn't finished letting out his feather gig before he had a strike. We saw a dark swirl and a big splash on the water and the fish sounded with more speed and power than a bonito. Then he seemed light again and Ham brought him quickly and easily to the boat. It was a bonito, but he had a huge bite taken out of one side of him. There was much discussion as to what kind of a fish had attacked him. George said "sorefish" (swordfish), Tom said "wahoo" and Carrie said nothing. Anyway, there were fish in the tuna hole, so we trolled around a few more times, but had no more strikes. This chewed-up bonito was no good for bait, so we went out to sea and soon located a big flock of birds diving madly into a sea boiling with bonito. Carrie immediately hooked what she supposed was a bonito and started to reel him in, when out went the line fast, but firmly, like a marlin takes it—then the fish sounded and took more line, in jerks like a tuna. She worked and pumped with glee and pleasure and perspiration until the boys looked over the edge and announced the presence, on her hook, of a twelve-foot shark. He had taken the bonito and hooked himself. She worked him awhile longer and then handed him over to Ham, not wanting to wear herself all out, as this was her "marlin day." Ham finally got him alongside and George had the wire leader in his hand, when the shark gave a big jerk and broke away. So then Ham trolled for bait with very short line and Carrie tried her luck with bamboo pole and shell hook. Ham caught several bonito and a small tuna. Carrie hooked a bonito, but a shark grabbed it and broke off hook. By this time we had sufficient bait, so we moved on, out of this shark-infested spot, and put on a bonito, with the teasers out. Within five minutes a marlin made a rush at the bait, nearly scared Carrie out of her chair, and disappeared. We took in the bait to have a look at it, and saw a hole where he had struck it with his sword. Put out another bait and within half an hour a second marlin grabbed the bait and ran. But he was gone when Carrie pulled herself together and struck him. We pulled in the line and only the head of bait was left—the body was snapped or broken right off—not bitten. Fortunately we had plenty of bait, so we put on a fresh one and within another half hour there was a third marlin, underwater right near the bait. He grabbed it and ran like lightning—then Tom yelled "Hook!" and at the same instant the fish jumped out of water, threw bonito and hook, and was away. Carrie struck him just as he jumped, but he had gone out so fast and she was so dazed that she had a back-lash in her line, and when she struck there was no pressure on the line at all—slack line. Three marlin before nine o'clock in the morning. It was simply too exciting for words. Of course it is needless to say that Carrie was an object of *derision* and *scorn* on board and called unrepeatable names. Nevertheless, she put over another bait and kept right on. Mr. Grey said in one of his books that you are lucky to get one in every ten—this makes seven she has raised or hooked, so she figures she has two more to lose before getting the one! About an hour and a half later we saw more birds, so we decided to get fresh bait for the afternoon. Ham put over a feather gig and got a strike right away. The fish acted like a small tuna, sounded with a lot of line. Then he began coming up rapidly and we all thought the lucky cuss had hooked another marlin, but it was a shark. He landed it in short time and the boys operated.

Beautiful Tahiti

They recovered the original fish that Ham hooked—a small tuna—then they did a little fancy carving and let him go. He was still wiggling, but couldn't last long, because a whole army of sharks was waiting greedily for his remains. By this time the birds had scattered and since we were just in front of our place and it was late, we went in for lunch. Carrie trolled on the way home and caught a four-foot barracuda, inside the lagoon, as she was taking her line in. We were so excited we couldn't eat much lunch, and now we are going right out again. The marlin this morning weren't very large—125-250 pounds—but *they were marlin*!

It is a good thing these notes were written this noon at the peak of our enthusiasm, because we didn't have a strike this afternoon. Went out at two o'clock and ran into birds just outside our pass—just a few—and couldn't catch a bait. Then we saw five or six canoes over toward Moorea and went over. No birds—couldn't even buy a bait from the natives—they had had no better luck than we had. One of them had a dolphin, so we continued trolling with a feather gig, hoping to hook one of these fighting beauties. Stayed out until six o'clock, then came in tired, but very well pleased with our twelve-hour day. The success of the morning more than made up for the disappointment of the afternoon, and it was the best day we have had so far.

Jan. 13—The sea is certainly full of fish *and* sharks. We went out at seven o'clock, straight out and toward peninsula, in search of bait. Ham had two vibrating taps on his feather gig, one right after the other, suspiciously like a marlin, but no strike. We located the birds, very far out, and hooked a bonito, only to have it grabbed at once by a shark. It took off yards of line, but broke off double leader at swivel. Then Tom caught our bait for us, on shell hook, and we immediately left this sharks' playground, and at what we considered a safe distance, put over one of the bonito. In a few minutes a monster of a shark made a rush for it—Ham pulled it away from him, however, and he angrily started for the teasers—but we got them in safely also. When he had disappeared we put our bait over again and raised one marlin, but he just looked at the bait and didn't take it. He was a small one. We had remarked in the boat that it was useless to troll for bait with so many sharks about, and in the future we would let the boys get our bait for us, with the native outfit. This news was evidently sent out over the "cocoanut wireless," because when we went down to go on board the launch after lunch, two expert bonito fishermen of the district, Tefa and Bene, were there, equipped with their pet lures and poles, begging to go along and catch our bait for us (and incidentally a few bonito for themselves). Bene has a famous hook called muma fire. He named it that because with it he catches many bonito which he brings home and puts on the "fire" to cook. We took them along, but, alas! couldn't locate the birds until late in the afternoon. We let them catch some bonito, but it was too late for us to troll with bait and take a chance of getting fast to a marlin, so we trolled on the way home with a feather gig. Ham had a big tuna strike, but he broke off on first run. Then, just as the sun was setting, he hooked a dolphin. What a sight that was! He leaped 24 times, between us and the flaming sunset, and his colors, catching the last rays of the sun, were even more vivid than the sunset. Ham handled him expertly on the Atlapac and twenty-one-thread line and brought him to gaff, a defeated fish. It took us an hour to get home, under a full moon on a calm and glistening sea. The moon disappeared behind a cloud just as we came through the pass—a fitting finale to another eventful day.

Jan. 14—Twelve hours at sea today and we are just as dirty as Romer Grey in *The Cruise of the Fisherman*, and equally as enthusiastic over fishing. Started at 5 o'clock and caught a bait at once, in the tuna hole. Had him over at 5.30 and trolled until 12 o'clock without raising anything. In for lunch and out again at 2 o'clock, looking for fresh air. Saw three motor-boats over near Moorea that looked as if they were fishing, so we went in that direction and found big flocks of birds. The boys couldn't catch any fish with the pearl hooks, so we put over a gig and immediately pulled in a 35-pound tuna. Then Ham hooked a dolphin that played on the surface in the usual spectacular way—he was apparently well hooked and came alongside without giving much trouble, then just beside the boat he made one tremendous leap, high out of the water and got away.

The hook must have pulled out, because it felt as though he broke the line—a quick jerk. Then Carrie hooked and landed her first dolphin. It seemed to be a big school of tuna, with a few dolphin and no bonito. We had a great time catching tuna on the Atlapac and twenty-one-thread line and caught 7, weighing from 35 to 50 pounds. Then we suddenly realized that we were about twenty miles from home and it was late, so we had to leave this playground and satisfy ourselves by recatching each fish, on the way home.

Jan. 15—Couldn't go out this morning—had to stay at home and work. Went out at 1.30—found birds quite far out. Ham was trolling with feather gig and before he got it in, to let natives catch us our bait, he hooked a bonito *and* a shark—which gave Ham a two-hour battle. He was a tremendous brute and would *not* come up. The rod (a medium weight hickory) was bent almost double all the time and the twenty-one-thread line whanged like a banjo string. When he had the shark near enough for the boys to see him, George declared that it was not a shark, but some strange fish, very bright and shiny. Of course, this announcement put new strength into Ham's tired arms and back and he quickly had it alongside. But, alas! it was just an ordinary shark, a very large one, weighing about 300 pounds, the boys said. The reason George thought it was some other kind of a fish was because the shark was all in and lying on its side and George saw the belly shining and white, deep down. They mutilated it in the usual fashion and found fifteen young ones, which went to a watery grave. By this time the birds had completely disappeared, so we started back. On the way we ran into a small school of bonito—the boys caught some and we put one over and trolled until dark, but didn't raise anything. The weather has been wonderful these last few days and bait, though far out, plentiful. Jimmy (who used to work for Mr. Grey), said that while fishing for bonito yesterday, he saw a marlin longer than his canoe; it came right alongside and his canoe is three fathoms long. So, the big ones are here all right. I only hope that we don't get fast to one like that, because it would only be a good fish gone wrong—we couldn't handle him— YET!

" 16—In town.

Jan. 17—Varnishing deck.

" 18—Beautiful day, so we started out at 8 o'clock, with our lunch on board, prepared for a good day's fishing and hoping for a marlin. Went straight out and located birds, about eight miles out, and what a flock! In a very few minutes the boys had two gasoline boxes full of bonito and we put one right over for bait. The sea was rolling in big swells, with a slight breeze roughing it up—an ideal day to hook a big one. We trolled for hours, but never raised a thing. While trolling we saw many flocks of birds, each one bigger than the other—the whole sea seemed to be alive with small fish. Since our bait was getting a little bit soft, we tried to catch fresh bait, but there were so many small fish for the bonito to feed on that they wouldn't take any kind of a hook. Finally, on our way home, late in the afternoon, we ran into a school of tuna. Carrie landed one (30 pounds) and Ham hooked one and lost it. Later he caught a dolphin (38 pounds). He was hooked right in the eye and jumped only once.

" 20—Ham out at 7 o'clock. Caught a *crevalle* on the way to tuna hole. Trolled over hole for bait, but caught nothing, so he started out to sea to look for birds. Went out far and wide, but couldn't locate any. Caught a barracuda, about six miles out, on the way home. Strange to find barracuda so far out—they are usually near the reef or in the lagoon.

" 21—Out right after breakfast. Located birds right away and Ham hooked a bonito, only to have it snatched by a shark. To pump in a shark is very good practice, no doubt, but in the meantime the birds and bait all disappear. By the time we got through with this nuisance, including twelve unborn sharks, the bonito had gone. Later we found them again, hooked some and put one right over. Trolled all the rest of the morning, but raised nothing.

" 22—Ham out early—got bait right away and trolled all morning, but raised nothing. Spies, who lives at Professor Harrison Smith's, stopped in to tell us that he hooked a marlin yesterday on a feather gig. He said it was a big one and must have weighed 200 kilos. He hooked him on a feather gig, twenty-four-thread line on a Pfleugar Adams reel. He had him on for about five and one-half hours, but was all in at the end of that time and broke the line and let him go. He had no swivel chair—only a leather belt—and he had no harness with him, so it was a tough job. We went out in late afternoon and trolled along reef for *crevalle*.

Carrie caught a needlefish on a Pfleugar record spoon. Tom wanted a fish to eat, so we let him troll with a hand line and a feather gig. Just in the pass he caught a 40-pound dog-toothed tuna. Carrie had a strike at the same time, probably another d.t.t. but he broke line. Tom's fish had a big tumor on one side of his head, and when we looked inside we found a hook, rigged up on a brass wire leader, such as we used last year when we went out in the sea sled before we were taken under Mr. Grey's guiding wing. The hook had been in there a long time—it was almost rusted through and we all decided that it was the very fish that Carrie hooked last year when she cut her hand so badly on a hand line. Revenge at last!

Jan. 23—Started out at 7 o'clock. Beautiful day. Located birds and bait, but they wouldn't bite. We tried and tried and couldn't get one, and finally had to come in without anything. The bonito were plentiful, but very, very small.

" 24—Out at 5 o'clock. Trolled as usual over tuna hole a few times, but picked up nothing, so went straight out and found plenty of bait. They wouldn't bite the pearl hooks, so we trolled with feather gig and very short line—to avoid sharks—and caught plenty of bonito and one small tuna. Put bait right over and trolled through birds—didn't raise anything. Ran into a school of very large tuna jumping, on the way home—put over a gig but couldn't hook one. Really expected to get a marlin today, it was so perfect, but didn't even see one.

" 25—Ham planned to go out at 5 o'clock this morning, but when he woke up it was raining and he thought his crew wouldn't be around. On the contrary, they were all ready and waiting and full of enthusiasm. They predicted plenty of fish on a day like this, and they were right. Not hooking any bait in the tuna hole, they started out after birds. They saw a few white birds feeding, indicating a school of dolphin. Ham could see one going after his hook, riding along the crest of a wave, and looking exactly as though he were swimming about in an aquarium. He hooked him and got him alongside, but broke the double leader as Tom started to haul him in. Ham made the remark that he must turn that line tomorrow, but tomorrow is always too late. They fixed a new double leader, put on another gig, and put it over. Soon he had a terrific strike, a big swirl on the water, out went the line 300 yards and broke again in double line. It must have been a marlin, although it didn't show, but Tom said he saw it. They couldn't fool with that outfit any more (Atlapac and twenty-one-thread line) so they put over a gig on the Coxe. Then they ran into the birds and Ham hooked a fine big tuna that made a great run and broke hook off wire leader. By this time the boys had caught enough bait, so Ham put one over on the Coxe and twenty-four-thread line (300 yds.). They started off toward the peninsula and the Grey fishing-grounds. Ham was sitting there, rather miserable over his bad luck, so far this morning—wishing he could raise a marlin (never having raised one with bait), and consoling himself with the thought that if he went out practically every day for a year, he would surely get one, some day—when suddenly one appeared between boat and bait. Tom yelled and Ham pulled bait in a little closer to the fish. Bang! he took it and off he went. Then Ham put into practice all the things he has read, been told, and been thinking about for the past six months. He jammed on the drag, hooked him right through the eye, released the drag and let him go. He took practically all the line off the reel and then came up miles away, it seemed, and way off to the left. While Ham was reeling in the big belly in the line he jumped sixteen times, clear out of water. Then he sounded and didn't show again. When he struck the bait, he broke the head off the bonito and that slid over the wire leader and up the line. The boys were afraid this would attract a shark and he would bite the line in two to get it. So Ham pumped frantically until he got the head up to the boat and they cut it off the line. The fish came in rather easily, apparently quite exhausted by his leaps. But when Ham got him up where they could see him, he was not *alone*! Two sharks were right along with him, calmly taking big mouthfuls out of his stomach and back. They were very brazen and had to be pushed in the head before the boys could haul what was left of the marlin aboard. Of course Ham wanted to bring the remains home to Carrie to show that he had really caught one, and it was a pathetic marlin that was lying on the deck when the launch came alongside the pier. He was about the same size as the other one Ham caught. He was much more pleased with this one than the one he caught trolling with a feather gig, because this one was hooked in proper fashion. It is the first time any of the boys ever heard of sharks attacking a marlin. Maybe, being hooked through the eye, he was bleeding and that attracted the sharks, or it might have been that half bonito. Everyone is laughing at Carrie now and say all she can catch is *crevalle*.

Jan. 27—Out at 5 o'clock—drizzling rain—fine weather for fishing. Trolled over tuna hole—Carrie had a strike but lost it. Then out for birds, located them and on way to them Carrie had a powerful strike—a big tuna. He went straight down—took 350 yards of twenty-one-thread line off the Atlapac, and *kept* it. Realizing it was a tuna, she threw off the drag when he struck and she couldn't stop him at all. He went down until the line was gone and then broke it off a few yards from the boat. Boys then caught some bait and we started to troll. A little after 9 a fine marlin came right up and grabbed the bait and started off with it. Carrie let him run a bit and then jammed on the brake to strike him. She struck him all right and set the hook, but he was going to San Francisco in a hurry, and before she released the drag he broke the line and that was the end of that. Put on another leader and hook and bait and trolled for hours more but never raised another one. She lost her chance that day, and was as mad as a wet hen.

" 28—Ham out at 5 o'clock until 12, but didn't get a thing. They didn't locate the birds until after 9 and then only caught one bonito. Trolled it all the morning but didn't raise anything. Saw some big tuna jumping —trolled with gig but couldn't hook one. They saw something strange that we had already heard about from a native fisherman in Taravao. Five or six black creatures, round like a big telephone pole and absolutely flat across the end (not pointed like a porpoise), rose straight out of the water, about six feet, and then slowly sank out of sight, like a drifting log, on end. One of them looked as if he blew some sort of a spray. Then they saw them swimming and their dorsal fins were very curved. They were far away and so they couldn't see them plainly and they have no idea what they could have been, unless some species of whale. Later Mr. Grey classified these as a rare species of blackfish.

Jan. 29—Out at 5 o'clock and didn't get any bait until 10, but got plenty then, about 18 miles out. While looking for bait ran through a school of tuna. Carrie hooked one—he went out and down with the usual power and speed. Then she laid right back in her harness and began to get back line. His second run was almost disastrous—when he stopped there were only about five yards of line left on the reel. But that run finished him and Carrie pumped him right up to the boat without much trouble. Just as George was about to take the leader Tom yelled, "Sharks!" and we all saw a big shark right behind him, so George grabbed the leader and jerked so hard to get the tuna away from the shark that the leader broke and the tuna lay on the surface, in a daze, not realizing that he was free. We almost got him with the gaff, but the shark got there first. These sharks are a darned nuisance. After we got one bait, we trolled four or five hours but didn't raise anything. We seem to raise all of our marlin before or around 9 o'clock in the morning and seldom see one later.

" 30—Carrie fished all the way to town today and arrived there, in the late afternoon, practically cleaned out of tackle and with no fish on board. She got plenty of bait just off Punavia and then, seeing a big school of tuna jumping, decided she would catch one before trolling for marlin, just to have something on board when she arrived in town. She hooked one right away, which broke the hook off the wire leader. To make a long and sad story short, she hooked and *lost* five big tuna in rapid succession and stopped this game only because she had lost all her feather gigs and most of her line. George and Tom said they had *never* seen such big tuna and there seemed to be hundreds of them. If you put on any drag they broke the line, and if you didn't

TALES OF TAHITIAN WATERS

they took it all and kept it—it was no place for an amateur. Having had such bad luck with the tuna, she was sure there must be an accommodating marlin waiting for her—trolled all the rest of the day with bait, but raised nothing. Ham had gone to town by car and was waiting for Carrie on the quay. She had smuggled the tuna and marlin flags on board and expected to sail proudly into the harbor with one or *both* of them flying, and *that* is probably why she didn't catch any more fish, although Ham says the reason she didn't catch any is because *he* wasn't there to tell her what to do. If he tells her what to do just *once* more, he will find a gaff handle growing out of his head with his hair! We can't fish any more this week on account of the mail, so we took advantage of these few busy days to have the boat hauled out and repaired on the stern where a shark bit some paint off.

Four more weeks of trying and then, WE LEARN TO FISH!

Some Native Names for Tahitian Fish

1—*Parata*—very large black shark.
2—*Rohoi*—shark with pointed nose or head—seen mostly in Paumotus.
3—*Mararu*—small yellow shark that sleeps under coral in reef.
4—*Aahi*—can get no information.
5—*Moemoeava*—very big, very bad.
6—*Ootea*—small gray or greenish shark, often seen inside lagoon.
7—*Mamaru*—?
8—*Ururoa*—ordinary round-nosed green, always seen in bonito and tuna schools.
9—*Tutui*—red shark, very rare.
10—*Taumata*—very small—eyes sunk in like under eyebrows.
11—*Mao Aahi*—?
12—*Ao*—?
13—*Arava*—?
14—*Uravena*—?
15—*Tiatiauri*—not a shark.
16—*Pararanti*—?

This information (that is the translations) came from an old native in the district and he didn't know these last ones by name.

17—*Mako*—I don't know if this is the same species of mako as Mr. Grey caught in N. Z. Naturally the natives living in this district know nothing about it.
18—*Haura*—marlin with sword on upper jaw.

19—*Aurepe*—swordfish with big dorsal fin (sailfish).
20—*Eieheraha*—sword on lower jaw. This is probably the great swordfish Mr. Grey discovered in the Paumotus.
21—*Hakua*—?
22—*Nini*—?

PART THREE

1930

CHAPTER ONE

THE enchantment of Tahiti never fully burst upon me until I returned to my camp at Flower Point, Vairao, early in March, 1930. This was our third visit. The marvelous growth of luxurious green and the blaze of color would have to be seen to be believed. I was quite beside myself with ecstasy, and could only inhale the fragrance of frangipani and stare at the gorgeous scarlet hibiscus and the exquisite yellow bisnonia and the white tiare Moorea as one who had ventured into another world. The cabins could hardly be seen in the foliage. To walk up and down the narrow sand-paths, under an arch of pawpaw and coleus, and to gaze out through the cocoanut palms and the breadfruit trees at the deep dark blue of sea, was to realize the magic of the tropics. In the year of absence Tahiti had unconsciously grown on me, and was now, after three years, acknowledged to be the loveliest land I ever saw.

The hot sun burned down one moment and the next was shrouded in white-rimmed, purple-massed clouds, from which poured a flood of silver rain to roar on the roofs and through the palms. Soon the sun blazed out again upon glistening leaves and wet flowers. The air was full of warm, sweet, intoxicating perfumes.

For two days I moved about as one in a trance, looking mostly, and feeling, walking to and fro, resting, unpacking my bags and trunks. Even the assembling of fishing-tackle could not long distract me from the magic beauty and glory of this place.

Our native boatmen, *Areireia, Peto, Punia, Eetuarii, Amuru*, were on hand to greet us, even before we landed from the steamer; and these big simple-hearted Polynesians were so delighted to see us that they almost wept. I had my New Zealand whaler, Peter Williams, and Reuben Moran and his mother, come on from New Zealand. Al, the caretaker at the camp, had run across a Swedish lad who had been stranded here at Tahiti, lured by flamboyant books about the beauty and ease of this Tahitian island. His name was Sverre, and he and his young wife, Margot, certainly must have had viking ancestors. A more strikingly handsome blond couple I never saw. My engineer, John Loef, from California, was also from Sweden, and he took an instant liking for the young couple.

Our guests for a time were Mr. and Mrs. Eastham Guild, who have a home near Papeete and who have manifested unusual signs of having gone mad over our fishing game. I do not often take any novices under my piscatorial wing—I should say fin—but these two were so eager, so sincere, so faithful in the year of our absence, during which they fished all the time, that I was completely won away from my rule not to attempt to train aspiring anglers any more. Their remarkable experiences and data I have used in part in this book, where they have appeared as Ham-Fish and Carrie-Fin. Captain Mitchell, his wife, and my secretary, Millicent Smith, completed our party. My brother R. C. and my son Romer, with his chum Bob, were to join us on the April steamer from San Francisco.

Early on the second afternoon, Cappy, as we call Mitchell, threw his tackle on the launch *Moorea*, and with his three natives went out to look around. I saw them run out through the reef, and later with the marine glass I located them some miles out, and at the time I remarked to Peter, "Looks like Cappy was hooked on!" I can usually tell, by watching a boat, what the occupants are doing. Then I forgot about Captain Mitchell until he came in. I knew the minute I laid eyes on him that he had hung a big fish of some kind and lost it. I put on a sympathetic look as he approached with that face of woe, but I was afraid that inwardly I was rather tickled. Here is what Cappy said: "By Jove! What do you think happened? Look at that." And he shoved a feather gig at me. The hook had been straightened out.

"Gee! How'd you ever snag bottom in that deep water?" I asked, innocently.

"Snag! It was a fish, a blooming tuna that the natives said would weigh two hundred kilos. That's four hundred pounds. But he'd have gone more than that. . . . We saw some boobies and we ran over. The natives said, 'bonito' so I put over this gig. . . . Bonito they were not! I had a smash, and the duffer ran off nearly all my line. Thought he'd take it all. But he slowed up, and I began to work. I was a long time getting him up. Too soft for such a big one the first thing. Then I got him up. He was a thumping big yellow-fin, seven feet long and big around. He had long sickle-shaped pectorals. By Jove! he was a dandy. I was congratulating myself and betting I had your three-hundred-and-eighteen-pound record for yellow-fin beaten. He came in on his side. Very beautiful fish, dark blue on the back, silver underneath, with the gold fins. Then the hook straightened out!"

"Well! . . . Oh, say, Cappy, old top, I'm darned sorry you lost him. That would have been starting in great. To have my records beaten doesn't bother me—so long as one of my outfit does it. But, see here, weren't you up to your old trick of handling a fish too rough?"

And that was the start of our 1930 season at Tahiti.

Next morning Cappy took the Guilds out, while I had to wait for my boatmen to go to Papeete to get their passports. They did not return until after one o'clock. Still I thought we would take a run out, just to feel started. It was hot, with what we used to call in baseball days a high sky, and a stiff breeze was blowing outside, kicking up a white sea. That, of course, was to be expected, as we had missed four or five still, dark showery days—the kind that are best for fishing in this latitude. We put out a needlefish bait and a feather gig, and I began this season's siege with old Sol. We ran several miles before we sighted Cappy's boat bobbing up and down. He was running east, against the sea, and we turned likewise.

By and bye we saw a few birds, white terns and noddies, and as they appeared to be hovering over fish we made for them. I stood up, holding my line. Presently I saw a splash, and then a streak on the surface. Though it was fully two hundred feet from the gig, I knew a dolphin had seen it. I let go my line and snatched the gig rod from Peter, who was surely surprised. An instant later there came a quick strong pull, then a smash on the water in the bright sun-track.

Right there we began to make John Loef's life a burden by instructing him how to run the boat—no easy task for Peter and me. However, he did well. The dolphin leaped, presently, out of the glare of sun, and I had a good look at a big broad blue and silver *coryphene*. He leaped four times more, one leap of which I would have given a good deal to photograph. After that he fought hard and came in slowly. When at last he rose to the surface he had turned a deep gold hue, and it was a beautiful sight to see that blaze in the top of the swells. He made awkward dives under the boat, which I frustrated by sticking my rod straight down deep in the water, so to clear the propeller with the line. Eventually we got him in the boat, where, in the absence of any implement to kill him mercifully, he flopped blood and slime all over everybody and everything, until the natives sat down upon him.

Further trolling did not raise a fish, nor bring us again within sight of birds. So we followed Cappy in. He reported a poor day, uncomfortably hot and rolling.

It developed later that he had gotten a bad sunburn. He wore shorts and did not feel any effects of the sun until too late. But he suffered severely during the night and could not go out next morning. Sunburn in this latitude is an insidious, deceiving thing. The sun feels good while it is doing its deadly work. However, I mind it less and think it is easier on anglers here around Tahiti than any other place I know. Cappy was so enthusiastic that he was careless.

The following day was pleasant inside the reef, smooth like a lake, cool and dark, with the magnificent mountains mirrored in the water. Gray misty clouds, with rain, shrouded the jagged peaks and the ragged canyons. We caught a small barracuda and a bonito for bait, and ran out the upper channel into a rough sea.

Coming down with it, the ride was not so bad. Soon we espied birds, and I sighted three sailfish fins and a marlin, riding the swells. Some of them swerved behind us, and one rapped a gig trolled by Carrie-Fin. We hurriedly changed that to a strip bait. Soon afterward we sighted fins again on the surface and I saw one very large sailfish. They did not come at the teasers or our bait, which surprised me, so seldom does a sailfish fail to look at the teasers. Altogether we saw fifteen sailfish without a single strike. After a time we put on the gig again—of course all the time I was trolling a bonito on my big outfit—and seeing some boobies working (circling and swooping above bait), we ran through them, with the result that Carrie-Fin got a smashing strike. I saw this tuna. He flashed gold in the top of a swell. It was fun to see the excitement on board. Ham-Fish went wild; Johnnie Loef stalled the engines; the natives yelled a lot of unintelligible jargon; while Carrie-Fin called for the harness. She was using my rod, and neither it nor the harness fit her. After a very creditable performance on a big fish in a rough sea she turned the rod over to me. I was naturally very nonchalant about it—desiring to show off a little before my guests—but I took fifty-five minutes to pump that plugger up. He was a beautiful fish between 100 and 125 pounds, with very long fins, a striking feature of this species of Tahitian tuna.

We found the school again and hooked Ham-Fish on to another, but it broke the wire leader at the hook. I could not tell how much drag Ham had on, but the rod sagged like a buggy whip when the fish struck.

After that we were charged by a school of dolphin, one of which Ham hooked, only to lose. We came in rather early in the afternoon. I did not want to hook a heavy fish in that sea. It meant hard work for nothing. How many times have we persisted until we got fast to a big tuna or swordfish, which was impossible to pump up! The fish went down deep and the swells lifted the boat, with the result of stripping line off the reel. It would be better never to hook a big one in a rough sea—and that, of course, means not to fish at all. After reading this over a day later, during which the pangs of breaking in again possessed my physical being, it seemed to me to be a wonderful idea. To escape the glare, the motion, and the pain of the sea! That would be easily possible—by staying *off* the sea. Then I remembered having encountered such ideas before, though this one seemed new and novel.

It remained with me until I went down to our primitive pier and sat there watching the many gorgeous little fish and the strange creatures that live in the coral. This many-hued reef, just where it shelves off into deep water, was an indescribable place. It was a scalloped, mushroomed, festooned fringe of coral, one layer over the other, with labyrinthine passages everywhere, caverns and grottos and dens and forests. To gaze at the coral alone was enough to charm any lover of nature. But the fish, the snakes, the octopi, the unseemable things animated by the ceaseless and awful energy of the sea—these were all-possessing to a mind like mine.

I recognized pipe-fish, golden mullet, parrot-fish, various kinds of angel-fish, a *crevalle*, and that about let me out. And there appeared to be a continuous procession of other fish—most of which I had never seen before. There was one very striking little fish, only a few inches long, dark blue in color with a white stripe down its back. He attracted notice among more gaudy fish by reason of his activity. Close observation showed that he bit the other fish. At least I imagined it at first, but I soon decided that, owing to the little fish appearing to like his picks, he was feeding upon parasites which clung to the bodies of his companions. Most of his attacks struck about the gills, though there was really no part of them that was not subject, now and then, to his nibbles. I could explain his energetic habit and the passive reaction of the various species about him in no other way.

There was a lovely angel-fish deeper down, of a kind wholly new to me, and when it swam into my ken, like a fairy from its purple Stygian cavern, my faculties of attention had to do only with beauty. This fish was about the size of an oval plate ten inches long, and it had two broad black bars across its silver sides. The tail was large and deeply forked, and its head narrowed down to a snout, with which it was industriously poking into holes in the coral. The eyes were black and as big as a penny. Last and most remarkable of all, the high dorsal fin had a long silver streamer, fully eighteen inches in length. It floated behind him. Besides the grace and beauty of this streamer there was something that forced itself upon me—of what use was this queer appendage? Most probably it had a relation to the angel-fish such as the exquisite plumage of a bird of paradise has to its mating. Right near the angel-fish I espied an octopus—a small one with tentacles scarcely more than a foot long, but just the same a real specimen of this most inexplicable, most horrible, and marvelous of all known sea creatures. I had watched octopi before and helped catch a few, only one of which was large enough to give me the creeps, but sight of another augmented all the perceptions I had felt before.

This one was brown when I first glimpsed it, but in a moment when it squirmed up on another shelf of coral, which was yellow, it changed like magic to the same hue. The hideousness of the octopus was again presented with exceeding vividness to me, yet it could not be said to lack beauty. Probably a huge octopus would be the most frightful and terrible thing in nature. The gorilla possesses these properties, but in no comparison to that of the octopus. This small one appeared master alike of the action of crawling, holding on, and swimming, which latter movement he performed from one ledge of coral to another. I have tried to describe that action before. It was a propulsion of some kind, getting its momentum from a drawing in of water, somewhat after the manner of certain jellyfish. Finally, when I took a stick and poked at the octopus it shot away like a comet. Indeed, that was the distinct impression I received. Its rapidity of movement seemed incredible. I wondered if that swiftness was used in attack as well as in escape. My curiosity about this marine monster increased in proportion to the dread it inspired.

Another day found Captain Mitchell wholly incapacitated. The sunburn had gone through the epidermis and very likely had raised it from his flesh. He could not walk and his sufferings were acute.

That day I ran forty or fifty miles over a sea of heaving glossy swells, hot as a furnace, the reward of which was sight of one large tuna smashing on the surface, and hours later a flock of boobies circling over a spot where evidently fish had been feeding. A very heavy swell had set in from the south. When we ran in through the channel the fury of sound and movement was stunning. Foam two feet high floated like cakes all over the still water back of the reef. This corner was one that had fascinated us all on former occasions of high tide and storm. But at this moment I was too weary and aching to appreciate it in full. My eyeballs were seared, my neck and cheeks swelled, my forearms red as beets, all in spite of care that I had exercised. Natives and whites alike on Tahiti use cocoanut oil as a panacea for all kind of ills, especially sunburn, but for me it did not work. I had to go back to my old standby, witch-hazel. The night was long and a great deal of it wakeful for me. But it was wonderful to lie awake, to feel the cool breeze, to watch the Southern Cross from my window, to listen to the seething, crashing roar of the sea below on the fringing reef, and the deep booming thunder out on the barrier reef. These were lulling, enchanting sounds.

During these wakeful hours there occurred a former disquieting question, which seemed to have grown more baffling, and it was—how to fish these Tahitian waters? This was my third attempt. And by fishing certain waters I mean locating and catching fish in the most sportsmanlike and utilitarian manner. I was not prepared yet to say that the waters around Tahiti cannot be fished properly; nevertheless I was worried.

The natives are honest, but very little help indeed did they give me. Many of their statements did not pan out for us. Last year we were here from August to December, and still the bait and bonito did not run as we had been led to believe they would. After we left, of course, they came. This December and January the coast up and down Vairao was alive with them, and big fish plentiful. Now they are reported off Papeete, fifty miles away, and evidently working around to the north side of the island.

It was a perplexing problem. To follow the fish was of course any experienced sea-angler's method. But let's see some angler follow them here—and catch up with them! You see a great black flock of swooping, circling, diving boobies. You run the wheels off your boat getting down to that splashing maelstrom, and just as you reach it, slow down and make ready to fish—away they are gone! The bonito or tuna have sounded and struck out for China or the Galapagos. The boobies fly faster than an airplane. In a few minutes they are out of sight. You can go hunt for another flock.

This had not come to us so far on the present season. We had only just begun. But it had been presented to my mind, and it was the most baffling problem I ever struggled with. The incentive, of course, was as great as the difficulty—the driving passion to capture one of these strange new giant species was perhaps, thinking of man as an unconquerable animal, too strong, too relentless ever to be surrendered. It was not so wonderful, beautiful, magnificent a thing as the conquest of Mt. Everest, nor so tremendous and ap-

Wahoo, 62 and 67 Pounds

Zane Grey's Silver Marlin, 618 Pounds. Another New Species

palling a feat as the dash to the poles, but for me it was about as hard and poignant and strangling a job as I wanted to undertake. The tropics is not for the white man; the sun is a devastating element of nature; the sea is aloof, resistless, deceiving in its soft moods, terrible when you learn to understand it.

CHAPTER TWO

I SENT my launch to Papeete for repairs, and motored in next day, and went fishing from there. Peter and John reported very few bonito in the market, but they saw an enormous bonefish about four feet long. We ran toward Point Venus, into rough water, and then down the middle of the channel. Sighted two flocks of boobies. Ran on down into the lee, and about 2.30 went in through the channel to spend the night at Guilds'.

Next morning we were off early toward Moorea. Captain Mitchell had joined us, not really fit to fish, but he could not stay cooped up any longer. Five miles out my natives sighted birds, and we were soon among bonito and tuna. Then I went to trolling. We followed that flock of boobies for miles and hours, during which time I raised four marlin swordfish, the first of which took the left teaser, and then leaped across my line. He came back and I made sure he would take my bait, but he did not.

In the afternoon we ran down toward the other boats and another large flock of circling birds. A heavy swell was running, the boobies were circling, swooping, diving, screeching, tuna were cracking the water, and bonito were boiling it. Cappy was working on a tuna. My natives had out pearl-shell gigs on their long bamboo poles. We could not get a strike. I saw a 200-pound yellow-fin leap high, and when he splashed down there was a crash in the wave, and a large round-nosed shark stuck up his head. The boobies would alight in patches of bait, all with their heads under, feeding on the tiny minnows that the bonito had driven to the surface. Green sharks gleamed under the water; the silver-sided bonito shone in the tops of the swells. It was carnage all around, but we could not share it.

Again we ran across Cappy, this time fast to a shark. He yelled, "Ocean alive with sharks!"

Ham-Fish later corroborated this, having had five sharks take his bonito bait. Also several tuna broke his line in turn.

The scene was wonderful and wild, but not satisfactory from a standpoint of fishing. I followed Ham-Fish in to his pier, while Cappy headed toward Vairao. He made our camp in only a little less time than I in the car, and he reported bonito all the way. Wherefore I was all at sea again. We had decided all the bait, bonito, and birds were around in the channel between Moorea and Tahiti. It seemed quite impossible to tell anything about conditions and fish in these Tahitian waters.

The next day, however, told a good deal. We found flocks of birds and schools of bonito and tuna off Vairao, just as we had found them over near Moorea. These were also accompanied by numerous sharks. Cappy raised one fair-sized marlin, around 300 pounds, that followed him for half a mile, very curious about the teasers and indifferent to a nice fresh bonito. This absolutely explained that the swordfish was not hungry, but only curious. I raised a small one which acted somewhat similarly, though he did not follow us long.

After that we espied a big flock of birds, wheeling and circling to the eastward. It took us an hour running full speed to catch up with them. Some heavy vicious splashes denoted the presence of large tuna. Peter had out a medium-light tackle, and I had a large feather gig on my heavy tackle. We both had a strike at once, and the fun was on. My fish ran two hundred yards or so, after which I pumped him back to within a few hundred feet of the boat, when something took him like a bass takes a grasshopper. Punia yelled *"Mauu!"* which is native for shark, and what I said must go unrecorded. Five hundred yards of line simply melted off my reel. Then he got weary and I halted. It took quite a while to get that line back. When I got most of it I suddenly felt a peculiar slackness, and I reeled madly. But the shark swam up the line and bit it through. There are pretty clever sharks in these Tahitian waters.

Meanwhile Peter had been having a tussle with his tuna. I took the rod and after a while hauled the tuna up. But he was inside a 300-pound shark, as we soon found out. Peter gaffed the shark, which splashed and threshed tremendously, while the natives hacked it to pieces. They found a 60-pound tuna, with the feather gig in its jaw, inside the shark. The hook had not touched the shark at all. He had refused to eject the tuna, and that was all that was holding him. We called it a bad day and quit.

Personally I had found it a most exhausting day. The sea was lumpy and gave the boat a side roll and pitch at once, which made it impossible to sit still or stand up. Then the sun was blistering. Six hours of that without any real action took the sap out of a man. The natives went to sleep, and it was I who sighted the marlin, the flock of boobies, and finally Cappy's boat on the horizon. I was so tired upon landing at the dock that I had the blind staggers.

Our little pier on the west side of the peninsula was in bad shape and needed to be repaired. It developed that the earthquake in New Zealand recently had sent a tidal wave across the intervening sea, to wreck my wooden docks and native huts on our side of Tahiti. I surely would have loved to see that wave come in over the barrier reef. What a grand roar it must have made, when the ordinary high tide sends a thundering boom in on the wind! This is one of the instances that helps to make vivid the moods, the mysteries, the possibilities of the sea.

It was a good thing that I kept my discouragement to myself, and my fears that some condition might prevail which would make fishing almost insupportable. For the next day fulfilled the truth of fishing—it was wonderful, all-satisfying.

There was no heavy sea running, no uncomfortable motion, no glaring sun, no blast of heat down on my head and up on my face. The air was cool. Trade-wind clouds trooped up early in the day to enshroud the great peak of Tahiti, and huge white cumulus clouds lodged against the mountains of the peninsula.

The sea was as blue as indigo. I did not see Cappy until two o'clock, and when we met out there he megaphoned: "Not so bad! Raised five marlin. Had two strikes. All on old bait."

I yelled back, "Thanks, you old life-saver!"

Not long after that Cappy raised another marlin, and while we were circling back to maneuver for position should he hook on, I raised one myself—a swift flashing purple-tailed swordfish that did not tarry long. Then my natives sighted birds. We ran out a couple of miles into the most remarkable mess I ever saw, of its kind—the water churned into a maelstrom with hordes of frantically leaping little bait fish, like sardines, and bonito cleaving the air in beautiful jumps, and huge hog-back tuna literally wallowing in birds, bait, and foam. Not to forget an ugly shark or two!

Straightway my natives began to hook bonito on their shell gigs, and it was up to me to dodge. One of these swinging bonito on the side of the head or in the stomach—as I well remembered—was no fun. Peter got one slam in the side. When the natives get to working among bonito they do not think of the comfort of those on board. Soon the boat appeared to be full of flapping, slippery bonito and blood. Then Jimmy got fast to a good-sized tuna. He could not lift it, nor could the tuna break away. How the line sang in the water! At last Jimmy—who is a powerful fellow—heaved the tuna out, and it came over the side to thump into the boat and make us all jump.

That settled the bait question. We began to troll around among the patches of bait and screeching birds. Some kind of big fish made a tremendous rush at my bait and missed it. Like a lion that failed in his leap, he refused to come again. It was highly exciting to troll here and there, and time flew by. So did both birds and bait. Then we ran in to hunt for Captain Mitchell.

As I half expected, we found him hooked to a swift, hard-leaping swordfish, and we stood by to watch the fight. It was a tough one. The marlin was small but valiant and exceedingly strong and enduring. I thought Cappy would never beat him. The fish ran all over, leaping and threshing, then sounded to stay down a long time. Finally I went on fishing, calling to Cappy that I would come back tomorrow. "He's a sticker!" called back Cappy.

Nothing more happened to me during an hour or so of trolling, and then seeing Cappy's boat on the way in, we followed.

It was sunset and one of those magnificent panoramas for which Tahiti is noted. The broken trade-wind clouds in the west were like a fleet of golden sails; the vast sweep of mountain range was enveloped halfway down in dense cloud, from which long veils of rain hung down, like waving lace; the sea was a shimmering mass of jewel; and the great canyons on the peninsula to my right were full of purple haze, while the points of the headlands sloping down from the summits caught a green-gold vividness from the sinking sun. It seemed too marvelous to be true. But it was true, and one of the rewards for long, toiling, enduring hours. They never fail to come, if we can only go long enough.

Captain Mitchell reported an incident that is another link in the long chain of evidence against the danger in sharks. He hooked and whipped a 400-pound specimen of the common variety here, and while Areireia was cutting it up to get the hook out, Captain Mitchell espied another shark shooting up like a gleam out of the blue depths. He yelled for Areireia to look out. The native jerked his hand and arm up just as the second shark slid his nose over the other and bumped hard into the boat, precisely in the spot where Areireia's hand had been. Captain said the most astonishing thing about the action was its exceeding swiftness. The native, bending over and busy cutting the caught shark, might not have seen the other in time.

It is very easy for fishermen and scientists who scratch around in cold Eastern waters to make the claim that sharks are not dangerous, but they simply do not know what they are talking about.

March 13th was a hot, still, glaring day, with a smooth sea, almost unbearable by two o'clock. About three a little breeze started to ripple the water. Up until then there had been no fish, no birds, no life. Eetuarii sighted a flock of birds way off, and we ran for them. They proved to be a mixed flock of boobies, noddies, terns, spread out over a large area, hunting fish. They were in the main moving to the east, and would slow up and circle at times, giving us a chance to catch up. Finally bonito showed on the surface, to fetch a screaming bunch of boobies and then flash on again. This happened about once every mile. After perhaps a ten-mile chase Cappy gave up or saw a swordfish or something; anyway, we went on, determined to catch some fresh bait.

Soon after that the bonito came up in churning swarms, and the carnage began. The natives jabbered like a lot of monkeys. With feeding birds and bonito all around us, and large fish making pale gleams in the blue, we got among a bunch that were too ravenously hungry to mind us. Then the natives, skittering their pearl-shell gigs over the surface, began to raise and hook bonito. If you watched one of these fascinating bits of pearl shell, fashioned like a tiny canoe, you would see a flash of bronze, a sharp-pointed bonito, then a vicious splash. Seldom did one get his head down after hitting the gig. A heave of the long bamboo fetched him wiggling out, to shoot into the boat, where we had to escape being hit the best way possible. I hid behind anyone when I saw a bonito swinging in, and at that got a smack on the side of the head which nearly knocked me flat. It was when two bonito were being swung in at once.

Soon the boat appeared full of flapping, sliding, bleeding bonito. The floor of the cockpit was, at any rate. This species of ocean mackerel is very delicate. In almost every instance when one struck the floor his gills would burst, and as they are extremely full-blooded the mess in that boat can be imagined. We had made sure to cover the fishing-reels, because blood on a line will very quickly rot it. I was spotted red from head to foot. The excitement of the natives, the sport of it, and especially the great importance of fresh bait, tended to make me yell like the rest of them. When that school of bonito sounded and went on we turned to trolling again. And we had scarcely got under way when we saw a huge splash behind Cappy's boat, and a marlin leap four times to shake the hook.

I had gotten up to grasp my camera, leaving enough drag on my reel to keep the bait from going out. A yell from Peter and the natives made me wheel to see a fine marlin, jaws wide, dorsal up, snatch my bait. But as the line was tight he let go. What a wonder the bonito did not pull off! I rushed back in time for his second charge. It came swiftly, but as he was shy after that first failure he missed the bait. He flashed in again to whack at it, and then left us.

That bad luck, brought about by my eagerness to photograph Cappy and the marlin he had on, filled me with discouragement. The same old thing! The same old rotten balance of luck on the wrong side! I had suffered it for fifteen years.

We trolled on, and somewhere nearer shore we ran under the great bank of clouds overhanging the mountains and reaching out over the sea. Here the light on the water was gray, making it hard to see. Jimmy sat on top and suddenly yelled, *"Beeg feesh!"*

I saw a flash of dim purple. He was far back and not coming, so I let my bait out. Presently a large sharp curved lobe of marlin tail stuck out of a wave, cut the water, and disappeared. He was gone. Jimmy came down and spread wide his long arms. *"Beeg one!"* That information should have pleased me, because it was something to raise one of the larger marlin, to know he was around, but inconsistently I took food out of this for further discouragement. It could not be helped. It made me worse when I looked across to see Cappy had raised another fish. As a matter of fact, I later learned he had raised six marlin that day and had three strike. If I had known that on the moment I might have jumped overboard.

We trolled on, and of course before very long Cappy was fast to a marlin that did not leap and did not get off. I grew tired of waiting for a possible picture, and finally went on.

Peter was dragging a bonito that must have weighed fully twelve pounds, and he was trolling it just inside the left teaser. My bait was an ordinary bonito of about five pounds, and both were fresh. That is the prime requisite at Tahiti, and the most difficult thing to accomplish regularly that I have ever encountered in angling. Fresh bait all the time—which means *when* you need it most—is an impossibility.

We were going along about three miles offshore; and for me, at least, the day seemed about over. Suddenly there was a yellow upheaval under the left teaser, then a flash of silver, a sounding roar of water, and flying spray which went over my bait and clear over the right teaser. The strange thing about this spray was that it appeared red. My stunned brain vaguely realized that this meant a fish of unusual size and action.

"Hell!" bawled Peter, leaping up. "He smashed off my bait!"

I leaped up, too. The fish made a tremendous churning curve that fetched him swift as lightning around to my bait. I saw him gobble it. But instead of sheering away as ninety-nine out of a

MITCHELL'S LONG-FIN TUNA, 128 POUNDS. FIRST TO BE CAUGHT ON ROD.

Nato-fishing

hundred swordfish do, he came on up between the teasers toward the boat.

"He got your bait, too," yelled Peter, wildly, as he dove for the bait tank, and jerking out a bonito he swiftly drew in his line and hooked the bait on.

"Pull in! That codger got your bait. He'll take another. . . . Some fish!"

"Don't drop yours over yet, Peter," I shouted. "He's got my bait all right, and he's coming in for more."

Peter could not believe it, but the amazing fact was plain to me. I could see the brass swivel on my leader, and without any strain on my line it was moving along with us. The swordfish swam pretty deep, and did not look very big. But he was just under the boil of the propellers.

"By Jove! He has got yours. What do you think of that?"

"I think I'd better soak him," I returned, grimly. "Look out, everybody!"

Whereupon I set the drag and struck the fish time and again, six or eight powerful jerks; and after each one I expected him to come up, which at that close proximity would be rather a ticklish situation for us. But he did not come up or change his pace. He did not yet know that there was anything wrong. I jerked and hauled on him again, hoping to make him swim away from the boat. But he stayed with us, and I had to have John speed up a little to draw away from him.

Meanwhile Captain Mitchell had run up, and was waving and yelling, "What you fast to, Doc?"

"Something big and heavy. Keep clear! . . . There, he's coming up," I yelled in reply.

The fish took line, but slowly, and gradually rose, to stick out a short, straight bill and an enormous silver head. The natives burst out into wild acclaim.

"*Beeg feesh!*" Jimmy kept on repeating.

He sounded and sheered away, going faster and faster until finally he had attained the speed of an express train. The line approached the surface.

"Camera, Peter! He's going to jump!"

And when he came out I was petrified. His first was a long, low jump, which revealed his size, his broad silver side, both of which were astounding to me. He struck with a great splash, and then came out again, a high, limber leap, perhaps the most magnificent that any marlin ever performed for me. This time he made a commotion that would have done credit to a fourteen-inch shell from a battleship. Out of the huge upheaval of white he shot again, out and up on his side, to strike like a toboggan and slide for yards before he got under. This last hop fetched the marlin uncomfortably close to Cappy's boat and I waved him back.

Then the swordfish sounded and made the line melt off the reel. At eight or nine hundred feet he stopped and began to plug around down there. This was settling down to steady work and gave me a chance to get my breath.

"Wonderful fish, Mr. Grey!" ejaculated Peter. "Never saw one like him. Looks a little like a black marlin, only he's too bright. . . . That was the grandest strike I ever saw."

I agreed with Peter's observations, but on the moment I did not waste any breath.

"Kind of tough to have your first fish this trip so big," went on Peter. "You'll have some work cut out for you."

So it turned out and time flew by. The swordfish stayed down and made no more flurries. The sea was smooth—a rare and fortunate occurrence—and I was able to work to full advantage. Nevertheless, despite my training on the rowing-machine all winter, in an hour or so I felt the strain, and after that a lessening of the glow of battle and eager hope. I slowed up a little to save myself, pumping and winding steadily, but not so hard.

The sun set in a golden blaze under pearl ships of clouds and the full moon came up in the east. It was very beautiful on the sea at that hour and I should have appreciated it more. Mostly, however, I was concerned with what I felt to be my luck—to hook such a fish before I was in shape to fight him properly.

Somewhere after two hours and a half he sounded again, taking twelve hundred feet of line. He could have taken more, for I certainly could not have stopped him. But he stopped of his own accord, perhaps the tremendous pressure of water at that distance being too much for him. I felt certain it would kill him, and as I did not want him to die at that depth I redoubled my efforts, sparing nothing.

That was a long grueling pull. It required half an hour of increasing toil to heave and wind him up, and when he anchored around a hundred feet or so under me I was out of breath, wet with sweat, hot as fire, and almost beaten.

"If he—sounds again—good night!" I panted. And I rested the rod on the gunwhale, and gripping the bells of the reel, and thumbing the line I essayed to stop that fatal *zee zee zee*. The rod bent almost to the water with every *zee*. But gradually these grew shorter and shorter, and finally ceased.

"You've stopped him," asserted Peter, enthusiastically. "Now get your breath and haul him up. Once more!"

Thus encouraged, I set to work with what reserve strength was left. All I need say is that I hated fishing before I saw the double line. Peter was leaning over the gunwale.

"I see him! I see him! He's on his side! You've got him licked!"

Of course that gave me momentarily the strength of a giant, and soon I had the leader out of water for Peter to reach. The issue then was quickly decided. Peter had a gaff in him and Jimmy had a rope round his tail in a few seconds. He gave a short, furious tussle, and suddenly floated up on his side.

One look proved to me that I had a prize, not only in size, but in species, for he was huge, and entirely new to me. Then I relinquished the rod and bethought myself of dry shirt and coat, while Peter and the natives lashed him fast.

We ran back to camp under a Tahitian full moon, with the grand peaks all silver and the canyons all black. It took two hours to reach the landing. Cappy had stuck it out with me, and was there to offer hearty congratulations.

"He's a buster, old man. I think I photographed a couple of his leaps."

We let well enough do for that day. Next morning I went down to see my fish. Hauled out on the grass, he was an astounding and beautiful spectacle. He was built like a wedge, very heavy at the shoulders and tapering to his tail. We dismissed at once the possibility of his being a black marlin. He was not black at all, but mostly a dazzling ribbed silver, except the curve of his back and his fins, which were violet. The marks that distinguish a black marlin are the black opal color and the hooked lower jaw. This fish had a straight lower jaw. Another mark differing from the black marlin species was a decided hump between the front of his dorsal and the slant of his bill. There was not a stripe on him. The line of demarkation between the dazzling silver and the violet was at least halfway between the median line and the top of his back, all the way down. Hung up where he could be seen and studied to better advantage, he presented a very great contrast to any other marlin I ever saw. Right there I could do no less than give him a name truest to his most striking point—his silver hue. So I called him silver marlin. I did this fully cognizant of the fact that this fish might have been an extreme modification of the striped spearfish species, or a variation of what I have named the black marlin species. But it appeared to be different enough to warrant the distinction. He measured 11 feet 6 inches in length, 5 feet 2 inches in girth, and weighed 618 pounds.

CHAPTER THREE

MY NATIVE boatmen are magnificent chaps, and every day I grow fonder of them. Matured men in years, they are children at heart and as keen about fishing as any boys could be. This is rather an unusual thing in boatmen—an exceedingly pleasant thing. I have had but few white boatmen to stick the game out with the eagerness and enthusiasm with which they began. It is not fun or sport with them, but wages, and in many cases a livelihood. But in the case of these Tahitians they would go just the same for nothing as for the money I pay them.

Punia, or Charley, as we call him, is rather medium-sized for a native, but superbly built. He is half French, very dark skinned, has an ever-ready smile, quick black eyes, and would be handsome if he had not lost some front teeth. He served three years with the French in the war. Upon returning to Tahiti he found that his young wife, whom it is said he dearly loved, had left his home to live with another man, a friend of Charley's.

"All right, old man, it's all right," he is credited as saying. "If she likes you better than she does me, it's all right!" And that is all he ever said.

Eetuarii, or Jimmy, is half English. He is a tall, heavy-shouldered man, rather light of skin, has big eyes more like a white man's than a native's, and a hooked nose. He, too, has lost some front teeth, which does not improve his appearance.

He is said to be the best bonito fisherman on the island, and I can vouch that if there is a better he must be marvelous. His pearl-shell lures are works of art, and the way he skitters and dances them over the surface of the water to raise bonito is assuredly something to see. Then he is so powerful that he can jerk the fish out, in most cases, before it gets its head. However, I have seen him hook a tuna that contested the matter with him for some moments. The stiff bamboo pole is about sixteen feet long, and the line a little shorter. In every case, of course, the bonito or tuna is hooked on the surface; and to lift one out before he gets to fighting is the skill of the game. When I tried it, as I have related before, I was nearly yanked overboard.

Eetuarii is the only man with whom I have ever fished, who could beat me seeing things on the ocean. He can sight a flock of birds that are invisible to me. All these natives are far-sighted, but he appears to be the best. It is a most valuable asset, because we cannot get fresh bait without finding them, and seldom or never do we find them without being guided by birds.

In every phase of fishing these two natives have become invaluable. Likewise Areireia and Peto for Captain Mitchell, and Amaru for my brother R. C. When I take the long-cherished fishing expedition round the world I want these Tahitians with me.

The other day I had a tuna up to the boat, about ready for the gaff, or so I thought, when quick as a flash he darted under the boat and fouled the line on the rudder. Eetuarii dove in like a boobie. I saw his big, brown kicking feet disappear under the boat. Next instant the released tuna went darting away and Eetuarii reappeared. As his head came out he called, *"Fee-nish!"*

They make some mistakes, these natives, naturally, as this rod-and-line fishing for big fish is entirely new to them.

One day I had a large feather gig out on a rod which was tied in the other chair while I trolled with the usual bonito. I thought I might pick up a tuna, as there were some big ones seen with the bonito. After a while there came a whack at that rod and the line went whizzing. Quickly changing over, I found that I had a heavy fish of some kind on the gig. But he did not run off the long length of line characteristic of a tuna.

The sea was calm, glassy, and the sun bright and hot. I hauled away on this fish until I was reduced to perspiration. Finally I drew him up to the surface about a hundred or more feet, where he shone a dull yellow. Punia yelled, *"Mauu!"* which is Tahitian for shark. The third native on board, an older man, agreed with him, and finally Eetuarii grunted, *"Mauu!"*

"Ump-uum!" I retorted. "You're guessing wrong, boys."

I could not see the fish as plainly as they could, for they were standing up on the gunwales, but I based my conviction on the feel of the fish and the action of the rod. An angler after long experience can usually tell what he has on, except in case it is an entirely new and strange fish. The first wahoo I ever hooked had me dumfounded—but that is another story. Anyway, I disagreed with my men about this particular fish. Suddenly he leaped—a glorious shield-like blaze of gold. Dolphin! He slapped back like a broad board. Then he was out again, higher, sidewise to us, and while my crew yelled I was electrified. At last I had connected with one of these big goldfish of the tropics.

That was his best leap, which I certainly would have given much to have photographed. But he tumbled in and out of the water at a great rate, and ended up by sticking his great, strange, blunt head out. After that he made a dogged fight, on tackle too heavy for him—as I had not dared risk hooking a big tuna on light stuff —and was eventually brought alongside.

It is useless to attempt description of a dolphin, or, correctly named, a *coryphene*, while in the water. No words can do justice to the color and beauty. Outside he appeared one long, broad bar of almost solid gold, flecked slightly toward the tail with blue. His head was square and at least a foot high up the front, and his dorsal fin stood up in triangular shape from nose to tail. He was thick, bull-headed, pugnacious-looking. I have never been able to study out why evolution produced this queer-shaped fish. In case of a marlin, or a thresher, or a broadbill, you can understand their particular feature, but the great head of a dolphin is beyond me.

This one weighed 63 pounds, and beat my own world record of 50½ pounds, caught at the Galapagos in 1926, and a later record of 60 pounds. It is needful to state here that such weight dolphin are small compared with the size they attain.

We had a change of weather. Wind shifted a little to S. E. and grew stronger, so that several afternoons we were forced to run in for shelter. Sunday, being a day of rest, did not matter whether it blew or not, but Monday the trade-wind churned the ocean into foam. Aiming to find a lee around the point halfway between Vairao and Papeete, we ran inside the reef for fifteen miles or so and then out the last channel, where the sea was breaking white. I would not want to try that again. Then we scudded before the wind and a following sea. As we got farther along and more out into the open—which was necessary to round the projecting reef, the great white swells lifted our launches and carried them with a roar, so swiftly that at times my hair stood on end. What if a steering-gear broke! This ride was one of those things that just seem to happen. Hopefully we started out, and got in bad before we realized that it was coming. We could not go back. And the following hour was one I shall not forget in a hurry.

At that we rounded the point and reached safety. Still the water was not very good for fishing. Flocks of birds and schools of bait everywhere! The horizon was black with boobies. We caught bonito and went to trolling. We covered the channel to and fro clear to the north end of Moorea and back again—five hours of trolling with fresh bait and never a sign of a swordfish.

It was sunset when we reached the pass opposite Guild's pier, and we were more than glad to run into calm water and call it a hell of a day.

We left our boats there and motored back to Vairao through a deluge of rain. It rained all night, and the morning broke, lowering of sky, black out at sea, and shrouds of gray over the mountains. All the same we went back to the boats to find conditions off toward Moorea worth chancing, at any rate.

Outside, we found the sea had gone down, and up in the lee fishing was not only possible, but promising. We soon ran into birds and bait, and for the remainder of the day never lost them, nor the squalls of rain, either. But nevertheless it was fascinating fishing, and surely different from any other kind. On all sides bonito were smashing the water white and birds were hovering, swooping, darting for their share of the carnage. A path of silver-yellow bait would show up, and then would follow a perfect mêlée of birds, bonito, and bait all mixed in a white lather of water. Here and there a big tuna would crack on the surface, sending up a great splash, and the dim moving green shapes of sharks were always present with a school of bonito.

We had nine sharks after our baits at one time, and had to haul in and put on speed to elude them. Finally we connected with one on a feather gig, which we trolled out far back of our baits, and then we had to halt, drag everything in while I pumped the ugly brute up to be dismembered. We made short work of sharks. These are the tackle-destroyers, and always dangerous around the boat on our swordfish leaders.

It tickled me to see Cappy in the same trouble. We trolled among the schools of bonito, hoping to raise a swordfish. One of the natives, the day before, while fishing from his canoe, had a swordfish rush him and steal the bonito he was hauling in. Probably the swordfish was as large as the canoe. These Tahitians are real fishermen. We watched them catching the bonito from their canoes, and it was a dexterous, strenuous business. The canoes are hardly more than a foot wide, and to jerk a wiggling bonito out of the water and into the canoe must take a nice sense of direction as well as strong arms.

The area covered by the flocks of birds and schools of bonito was fully ten miles square, in the middle of the channel. The birds were sometimes like a hive of swarming bees, and then again they would be sailing all over the ocean. When the bonito drove the bait to the surface, then the carnage began. Seldom did it last longer than a few minutes, and many times we arrived just as it was over, and birds and bonito away again.

Moorea was half hidden in clouds and Tahiti was almost wholly hidden, except the long slopes at the extreme ends of that west side of the island. Squall after squall gloomed over the sea; the sun shone at intervals, shining silver through the clouds, and the sea was either gray, or blue and white. All the while our natives had their pearl gigs overboard, and every little while they would hit into a school of bonito, or small tuna, and that was when Peter and I had to dodge. It is no fun to be hit by a ten-pound bonito, swung aboard by one of these excited, yelling Tahitians. I dodged one and then got the next square in the stomach. About my feet, flapping, sliding bonito covered the floor of the cockpit. And the rain came in mists and sheets. All about us was intense elemental life.

It was a most wonderful day on the sea, but we did not raise a single swordfish.

Such days passed until we counted eight of those trade-wind

white seas; and we were—well, disconsolate and impatient. We had not gotten down to essentials. Three weeks is not enough to break in. This was just a foretaste of the endurance necessary.

Then, out of exasperation and bull-headedness we stayed ashore the ninth day. Lo and behold! It was a perfect day. That illustrates the nature of this freakish Tahitian weather. None of the prognostications I ever heard were justified. No two opinions on weather, rainy season, summer, trade-winds, or anything in Tahiti are ever alike. I have never yet found what the rainy season is, unless it is every day.

The little brook that babbled through our camp, to our delight and convenience, went dry, to the mystification of Captain Mitchell and Mauu. They claimed it was the dry season, and we had many and diversified arguments about it. But the real reason, which I discovered myself, was that the east and south hills had been burned over, leaving no vegetation to hold the rain after it fell. I was sure the brook would come back.

Weather and climate are perfect, according to the white men who live on Tahiti, and the tourists who make a visit between ships. And I am bound to admit that for the person who does not exert himself mentally or physically the climate of Tahiti is about as near Paradise as humans ever find on earth. But it is too hot and too moist during the day for prolonged writing, and at night, though it is delightfully cool, the light draws so many insects which can come right through the screens, that it is almost as uncomfortable as the daytime.

Physical exertion is enormously more difficult to achieve than in temperate zones. Away from Papeete the natives wear only the *pareu*, which amounts to no clothes at all, so sweat does not bother them. At that, I never saw a native sweat. But a white man is bathed in a liquid fire that exudes from his pores. The strain of a three-hour battle with a big fish is felt more severely here.

The worst I can say about the climate of Tahiti is its tendency to cause extreme depression of spirit. Without any reason at all, I find myself going clear down to China. At night I will go to bed in fine mood, and have the most horrible dreams, or wake up with a leaden weight upon my chest, and an exceedingly dejected, hopeless mood. This must be continually fought, and during the night hours, for me at least, it is almost impossible to overcome. Daylight and sunrise, however, quickly dispel it, and I wonder that I could have had such thoughts. There is a strong tendency to inferiority complexes in all their mysterious phases.

I can understand now why the great majority of white men who live here for a time drink the French wines and liquors. Probably there are many who drink solely as a means of self-preservation, so to speak. These escape, in the main, such depression as I have intimated. But that way is closed to me and my party; and even if we were to pay Tahiti an extended visit, I am sure it would remain closed. The evil of drink is far graver than any good that may, even under peculiar conditions, accrue from it.

Accidents on fishing trips such as this are so numerous that only important or amusing ones can be recorded.

One beautiful day we spent nine hours running to and fro between Moorea and Tahiti, doing close to a hundred miles of trolling, all the time among screaming flocks of sea fowl and smashing schools of bonito, without raising a swordfish. These were still offshore or down deep, in my opinion. Still the day went fleeting away, enjoyable in every moment. The dark-blue heaving ocean, the magnificent cloud-wrapped islands, the manifestation of fierce marine life and struggle ever around us in its varying aspects, the excitement of our native fishermen, the fun of having a try for the bonito with the shell gigs, the fascination of endless opportunities for unusual pictures, and lastly, of course, always the chance of raising one of those striped tigers of the deep—these were all-sufficient.

It was sunset when I ran into Guild's dock, intending to ride back to camp in the car. Captain Mitchell had sent his boat ahead inside the reef. His natives had caught sixty-three bonito and tuna, which they were keen to take home. My natives, Eetuarii (Jimmy) and Punia (Charley) were not familiar with the intricate inside passages, which fact occasioned me concern. But as a matter of fact, I did not think seriously enough about it, though I said that Captain's boatmen should have waited for mine, and let them go.

Darkness had settled down over Vairao before we reached camp. The heavy clouds hung low over the mountains. More than once I thought anxiously about Peter and John and how they were faring.

After supper I went to bed early, tired out, and I was awakened about eleven by Peter, who said bluntly that my boat was on the reef.

Not until next day did I learn all the details. Charley was at the wheel and John had the engines hitting a good ten-knot clip. They had gotten about five miles east of Guild's. Jimmy was on top, trying to see Cappy's boat; Charley was standing with one foot on the rail and the other on the wheel, looking out ahead; Peter was cleaning a tuna at the back of the cockpit, and John was winding a line off one of my reels, when they struck.

It was still broad daylight. Charley went overboard as if propelled from a catapult, Jimmy was thrown out of the chair on top, Peter went banging clear down into the cabin, while John went crash against the forward house.

Charley swam ashore as if the very devils were after him, and he disappeared. When the remaining three collected in the cockpit blood and bruises were in evidence.

The launch was stuck fast on a coral head, cantled over somewhat, and she was leaking. Peter got in a native canoe that happened along, and going ashore walked five miles back to Guild's, where a wrecking crew was telephoned for. Then Peter, with Mr. Guild (or Ham-Fish, as I call him) motored back to where the launch was, and took off all my tackle. John and Jimmy stayed with the ship, but poor Charley never showed up all night.

Next morning the crew got her off and patched up the holes so that she could be taken to Papeete for repairs. The incident caused vast excitement among the natives. The old fellow, Matatuapo, whom I had hired for a month and then let go, vociferated that the accident would not have happened if he had been kept aboard. I have an idea he was correct about that.

Other natives claimed the disaster was owing to the fact that I fished on Sunday, and that God had seen fit to wreck my launch as a punishment. I didn't know whether they were right or wrong. The fact was that I did fish occasionally on Sundays.

During the process of working the *Tahiti* off the reef Charley reappeared, looking as if he had spent a miserable night. His great concern, after ascertaining that the boat had not been wrecked, was in regard to my attitude. "What boss say?"

The boys had considerable fun at poor Charley's expense, assuring him that I would do little less than kill him. Nevertheless, in due time Charley presented himself before me like a man for expected sentence. He was white of face—and for one of these natives to look white is remarkable—he was sweating, and most grievously affected. On the moment I happened to remember some of the high-salaried, commission-grafting, conceited boatmen that I had been compelled to engage in my fishing experience. My reaction in any event would have been kindly toward Charley, but under the influence of this recollection it was something that made the sincere honest fellow gasp with relief and joy.

Every day I liked these Tahitians more and more. They were simple, elemental men. They loved fish and loved to fish, which things surely bound them to me with brotherly ties.

One of the most fascinating places around our camp, Flower Point, is the dock that projects from the south side of the peninsula a hundred yards or so out over the shallow fringing-reef to the deep water, where we moored the launches.

This dock or pier is not much in itself, being merely a narrow bridge built by natives out of wood from the hills. It is rickety at certain points and shakes when you walk over the poles laid endwise. Posts have been driven down into the coral, and in many cases the worms that infest all tropical waters have eaten them partly through, and we need often to put in a new one. I could almost call this pier an eighth wonder of the world.

This is because it runs across the coral, giving opportunity to see that most amazing and mysterious of all growths, with its exceedingly marvelous life and beauty.

At low tide the coral bed is covered by less than a foot of water, which is, considering the exquisite transparency of this Tahitian water, almost the same as exposed to the open air. Only the ruffle caused by a breeze or a swirl made by a little fish, proves that there is any water there at all. I spend many idle hours walking and sitting upon that pier, lost in contemplation of its ever-varying changes.

There is never an occasion when I do not see fish or marine creatures of some kind that I have not seen before. And always the same beautiful specimens of angel-fish and other colorful fish that I have come to know. Gradually I have lost my boyish instinct to capture, first because it proved next to impossible to catch any of them, and secondly because I learned to view the reef as a natural aquarium of my own. At the end of the pier, where the bank of coral steps down in plumed and diademed benches, many species of larger size were always visible, while back on the shallow reef only small fish disported. And these ranged from the size of your hand to tiny fish hard to see at all. This morning, in particular, there were many varieties of angel-fish out.

To give an adequate idea of this aquarium is as difficult as an attempt to describe the Grand Canyon or Death Valley. Coral growths are as infinitely various as the most exacting artist could desire. They take on some semblance to ferns, moss, leaves, vines, plants, and forest jungles. The color is like that of a New York woodland of maple, chestnut (alas! the noble chestnut trees are almost gone, victims to the Japanese buffalo-beetle) hickory, oak, pine, hemlock, spruce, birch, in mid-October, when frost has worked its magic painting.

In the shallow water the formation holds to that of deeper water, except on an extremely small scale. There were areas where the coral stood up like pine cones on end, where toadstools of gold and green stood guard at dark little apertures, where miniature groves of slender points resembling aspens merged on flat plots of gray and yellow, where a meadow of clover made a pasture for heaps of sea animals like chestnut burrs, where rose-like coral heads, of different hues, stretched away farther than I could see. But to appreciate best the marvel of coral it was necessary to approach the edge of the reef where it sloped off into deep water. Here were the jeweled mansions of the gorgeous fairy-like little fish, the rows of scalloped shelves, the mushrooming flowers of purple and violet coral, studded with precious stones, the mosaic of floors, beds, nooks, nests, from which everywhere led lanes and subterranean passages, black holes and blank spaces, down into the labyrinthine maze of the interior.

Presently I was halted by sight of a small angel-fish, one of the species with the silver sides and black bars, and the short streamer from the dorsal fin. It wavered close to the bottom in a little open space surrounded by tiny copses of bronze coral, and it appeared to be ill or very sleepy. I had to look closely to make sure that it was alive. That it happened to be comparatively alone was surprising.

Then I was startled to see that it was indeed not alone, that the menace of the sea was here terribly present. Out of the ragged leaf-like edge of coral protruded the sharp gray head of eel or snake, directly behind the angel-fish. It advanced stealthily, this gray shape, and soon showed half the length of a serpent-like creature, silver gray in hue, circled with black rings, and as beautiful as it was horrible to gaze upon. All the instinct and cruelty of the sea seemed to be manifest in its action. It was a snake in the grass, an anaconda hidden in the rushes. It kept close under the edge of coral until suddenly with the strike of a cobra it darted to snatch the angel-fish in pointed jaws. Then indeed I saw that the little fish had been sleeping or dreaming, like so many humans, its precious life away. How violent and ferocious the action of the snake creature when it had its prey! Retreating into its hole, it dragged the wiggling fish in. I caught the last gleam of silver and then the hole in the coral was vacant and blue.

Soon after that I espied an octopus. The thrill I sustained was appreciably stronger than that occasioned by the one before. For no apparent reason, unless to watch the little electric-blue, black-lined fish that so kindly removes parasitical things from his associates of all species, I kept looking at one spot, until all at once I made out the octopus, half under the coral. He was in the act of changing color to match the bronze and violet of his background, and in a few more seconds he had accomplished the change perfectly. Then if I had not known he was there I would have passed him by, even with close observation.

This rooted me to the spot and offered unparalleled opportunity. He was scarcely seven feet distant and in water so shallow that there did not appear to be any. At first I imagined the creature had seen me and had resorted to his chameleon power of changing coats, but presently I began to think this a hasty observation and resolved to stand still as possible. It might result in one of those rare and never repeated phenomena of nature, only too few of which I had seen.

The body of the octopus, that half exposed, resembled a delicate transparent sack of some exquisite bronze and purple mottled silk, through which I saw the palpitation of lungs or heart. This was a quick, regular breathing of some kind. The queer eyes stood up or out, far apart, like the eyes of a ghost-crab, on protruding appendages, and they were somehow hideous and fascinating. What would the plate-size eyes of a full-grown octopus reveal in hypnotic and devastating power? I shuddered to imagine. But how surely was the fact forced home to me—of the extraordinarily strange nature of this most ruthless and horrible of all the creatures of the seas! Even the sperm whale, the fast disappearing cachalot, that preys upon the octopi in the abysmal deeps, seems tame in comparison. The mind conceives much of its distress and pain from the hatefulness, the ugliness of a beast. A lion or a rhinoceros can kill a man much more quickly than an octopus, yet inspires nothing of the terror.

Little fish came closer to this octopus I was watching, and when one of them, a slender, yellow, pugnacious fish, swam within a foot of it a lightning-swift and astounding thing occurred. Simultaneously with the darting out of one of its feelers there passed a marvelous flashing change over the octopus. From bronze it flashed to a pale opalescent hue, like nothing so much as a blush. This lasted only a second, so fleetingly that I doubted my sight. I had never read of this phenomenon. Again the octopus resumed its verisimilitude to the coral, and again the little fish ventured closer. I watched breathlessly, absolutely certain that this was one of the most fortunate and wonderful moments of all my nature-loving, the reward of watching and patience.

Out shot the curling feeler and with that action blazed the magic blush. Like a breath it faded. I was mystified, inexpressibly fascinated. That marvelous change of hue could not have been defensive instinct. It brought the octopus into strong relief against the bronze coral.

In the succeeding moments I watched this singular action and change no less than half a dozen times, the last of which appeared to be the most dramatic. He got hold of the pugnacious little fish, or at least struck it, and sent it scurrying away out of danger. Eight times had I watched this turning from dark bronze and purple, the shade of the surrounding coral, to a mottled, bluish pale gray, a ghastly, deathly hue that had no similarity in any background of coral near. It struck me that that metamorphosis was one of anger. It might have been hunger, too. I saw it and regarded it as an epochal incident in my study of the sea creatures.

Then it sank down to assume its former color and resemblance to its bed. I watched for long. Then when I moved the octopus squirmed down deeper. Picking up a long stick that happened to be handy, I poked the octopus. It tore loose from the stick and apparently turning inside out, to assume the shape of a comet, it sped away with incredible speed to hide in a recess out of my reach. Only then did I become aware of a thick spreading cloud of bronze ink in the water. It was the ink this creature secretes and can exude at will. But I always read that this ink was black. Here it was bronze, or a pure cinnamon, and as I touched it with the stick it disintegrated, spread in stringy patches, and gradually thinned out, finally to disappear before my very eyes.

The octopus will bear all the observation a naturalist-angler can devote to it. I have no particular yearning to hook one with forty-eight-foot tentacles, such as was washed up on the shore at Cape Breton, nevertheless, I would like to see a big one, and to engage in combat with one of reasonable size.

CHAPTER FOUR

CAPPY went out alone the following day, while I waited for the *Tahiti* to be repaired. I was hopeful for him, a change of luck and conditions, and somewhat rueful because I had to stay in. Not that the time lagged! If I could not write or leave the cottage, still there would be ample to keep me satisfied. It was a wonderful day. The wind came from the north, a very unusual quarter, and it blew briskly and lulled by turns. The sun shone brilliantly and hot or was hidden under huge rain-clouds, from which thunder rumbled. When it was not raining the sunshine was glorious, and the lagoon a rarely dazzling mosaic of sky-blue and purple, white and gold. I could not keep off the porch.

At 5.30 I espied Cappy's launch with flag flying. I let out a whoop. The Old Sticker had found them again. I made a run for the pier. Cappy had a marlin that weighed 172 pounds, and he had hooked and lost another around 400 pounds, and he had raised a third of still larger dimensions. All in three-quarters of an hour's trolling! He did not have any bait until late.

But all day he was among tuna, and caught nine, the largest of which belonged to what I call the long-fin tuna, in a way resembling the Allison tuna and perhaps a variation of that species. It was a splendid specimen, 128 pounds in weight, and the extremely long, thin, sickle-like dorsal and anal fins were remarkable to see. I had seen two photographs of this species, taken by schooners, one near the Figis, and the other in the eastern Pacific. It must be rather generally distributed, and probably rare because hard to catch.

"By Jove!" ejaculated Mitchell. "I had a fight with that tuna.

And all the time there were some old soakers breaking water around the boat, some of them much larger than this one. Big as hogs!"

The natives had been right about the new moon bringing in the fish. At least their return was coincident with the change of moon. This is an interesting development to watch and verify.

The day after the equinoctial period was dark, still, cool, with a heaving, glooming sea, and rain-veils dropping all around. Yet strange to note, the mountains stood up black, sharp, in clear relief.

We ran far east, and sighted birds six miles off the east end. They proved to consist of two flocks, boobies and noddies in great abundance, spread all over the ocean. Bonito and tuna were in evidence, though not in proportion to the birds. The natives soon caught a dozen rather large-sized bonito and some small tuna. Amuru hooked a larger tuna that resisted his strenuous efforts to lift it, and not until the boat halted could he do so.

There were many logs and branches of trees, débris of all kinds—an unusual circumstance; and around one big piece of driftwood a school of bait had collected for protection from the sharks that hemmed them in. I counted ten sharks, some of them two fathoms long, and one of them was black. They were milling round that driftwood, jaws agape, gulping the paralyzed little fish.

We ran away from that locality, and several miles inshore, as I watched my bonito, I saw the color of a swordfish loom back of it, and I yelled the old battle cry, *"There he is!"*

It required some skill to make that bird take my bait. When he did and sounded, I struck him, and then there were some pyrotechnics. He did not leap at once, but he skittered all over the ocean on his tail, once cutting almost a complete circle. Then he sounded, going deeper and deeper, until he was twelve hundred feet down. It took me an hour to pump him up. We were surprised to find that a husky shark had bitten at least fifty pounds out of him. At camp he weighed in at 217, so we were sure he would have gone 267 in a normal condition.

Cappy had a blank day. This day was the first in my three trips to Tahiti that the sun did not shine at some time.

The next day was the most perfect so far this trip. The clouds were high and not thick, though they obscured the sun. The same magnificent southwest swell was running, only like dimpled glass. We found birds and had to chase them full speed for miles at a dash in order to catch up when they were feeding. Bonito scarce, big tuna plentiful. They were leaping in bunches, out of frothy water, where the bait was boiling. Peter hooked one of these tuna, a husky fish between 60 and 70 pounds. After it struck it sheered to the surface in a wide curve. Then we saw a crease on the water, going at lightning speed, showing that a great fish of some kind was after the tuna. Suddenly Peter's rod jerked violently, and the line slacked.

"He knocked my bait off!" yelled Peter, excitedly. "I felt him whack it."

"That was a swordfish," I replied. "The wake was not like one a shark makes, and the speed was too terrific. If it had been a shark there would have been a crash at the instant of contact, and either a juggling or a hard pull. . . . I'll bet that was a giant marlin!"

We made haste to put on a smaller tuna, and began to troll all over the place, following the birds. But all to no avail. We raised another marlin that soon faded away in the blue. Cappy raised and hooked one of about 250 pounds, which threw the hook. We trolled in toward the reef and camp, arriving at the pier after dark.

In the morning I was awakened by the roar of rain on the roof of my cottage. It had a thrilling sound. I love the rainfall in Tahiti. A gray light shone in my window, and when I looked out I could see the pale reef below, crawling in with its melancholy dirge. Dawn had come. I got up and went out on the porch. All appeared lost in obscurity, and from out the gray pall broke the sound of surf and above that the boom of the outer reef.

The rain stopped by seven o'clock, and soon the sun came out brilliant and hot. Flowers and foliage glistened as if hung with diamonds. The flaming red blossoms stood out startlingly from the green, and all the other flowers, particularly the frangipani, shone with sweet and dewy beauty. The fragrance was seductive. Soon the garden reeked with it, and a hot steam appeared to be rising.

White Wild Horses of the Sea

This is the name I have given to the breakers at the west end of the Pass. Out of a dark-blue level sea would rise a long, slow, uneven line of water, a growing swell, that moved inward and climbed at the same time, and mounted to a green wall with a shining ripple on top and a green cave underneath. How majestic and beautiful! The motion was so gradual, so processional and stately, so expressive of the eight thousand miles of Pacific behind it. The grand swell heaved all along its length and the center mounted to a white crest of spray. It held that position for a marvelous forward-coming moment, a curved emerald cliff forty feet high. Then the crest curled and instantly, as if by magic, pearly waterfalls streamed down the face of this marching wave. Its bulk lifted higher until it loomed colossal, and then the whole curling tip fell forward in a rolling, thunderous crash, from which mighty chaos the glorious white horses leaped to plunge and boom upon the reef.

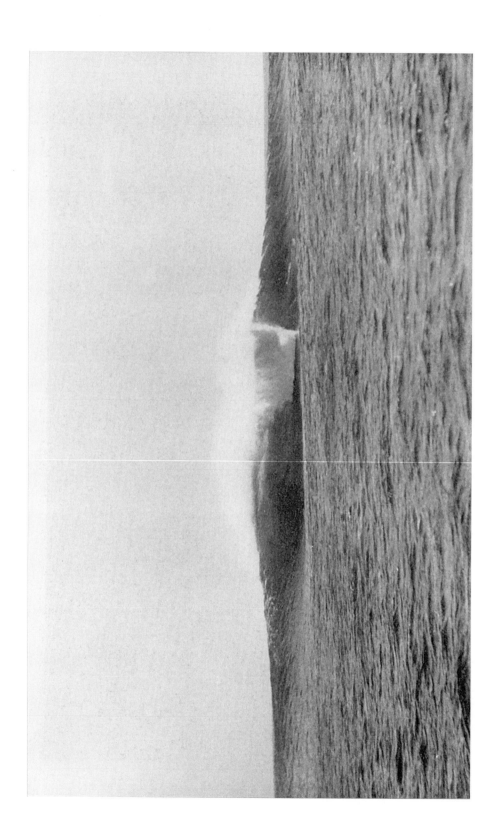

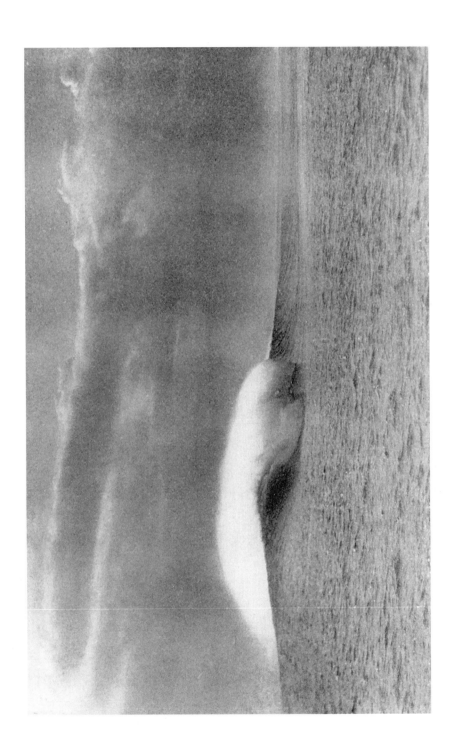

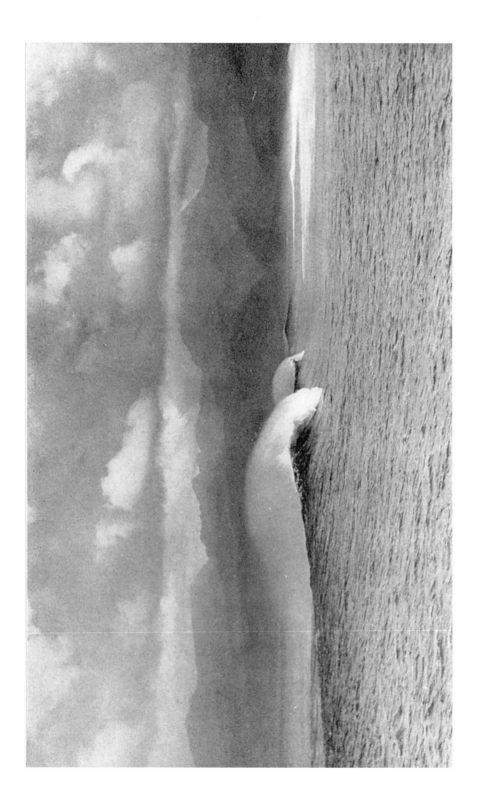

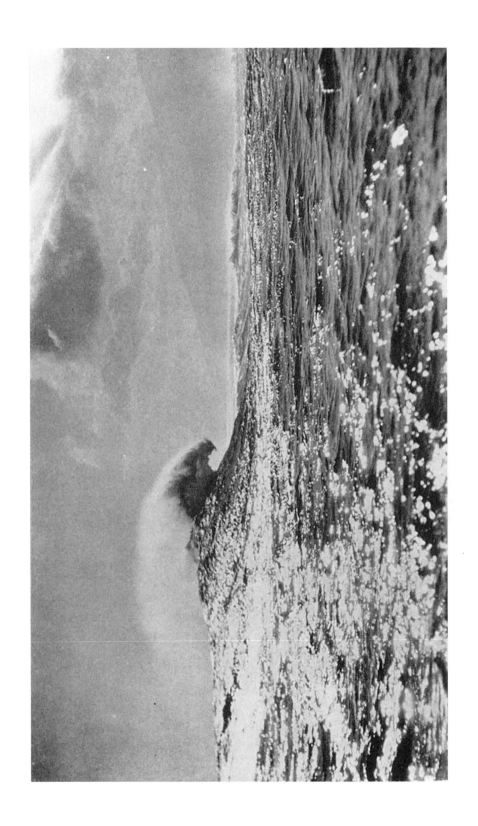

A cloud bank hid the sky except in the east, from which clear rent the sun blazed. This curtain lent a strange and glorious effect upon the sea. It was the deepest, most vivid blue and the reef shone dazzlingly white, and in between, the other hues were emphasized accordingly. Through the tops of the palms and the breadfruit trees this glorious color shone so miraculously as to seem unreal. All the way down to the pier, I felt in a sort of trance, realizing, yet somehow imagining, that I was not appreciating this magic isle to the full. But there did not seem to be a single hour when some time or other its glory was not omnipresent.

My white horses were running and charging wild this morning. This is the name I have for the breakers on the west end of the pass. Out of a dark-blue level sea would rise a slow, long, uneven line of water, a growing swell, that moved inward and climbed at the same time, and mounted to a green wall with a ripple on the edge and a green cave underneath. How majestic it was! The motion was so slow, so processional, so stately, so expressive of the eight thousand miles of Pacific behind it. The grand swell heaved along all its length, and the center mounted a white crest of spray. It held that position for a marvelous forward-coming moment, a curved, green wall forty feet high, shining emerald. Then the crest curled, and instantly pearly waterfalls streamed down the face of the marching wave. Its bulk mounted higher, until it loomed colossal, and then the whole curling tip fell forward in thundering, rolling crash, from which ruin the great white horses leaped to plunge and boom on the reef.

I trolled up the outside of the reef, about two hundred feet out. We had not tried this for days, owing to a scarcity of fish. Upon the two former occasions here at Vairao, we had good sport with wahoo, *crevalle*, bonito, dog-tooth tuna, and other fish; but this time we had failed to raise any kind of fish.

This morning, however, I soon struck something heavy and fast. The smashing strike was somehow familiar, still I did not recognize it as that of a wahoo until the bewildering runs so characteristic of this game fish and so productive of slack line forced me to remember. Then indeed I settled down to careful, hard work. As luck would have it, I landed the finest wahoo I had ever caught. At Long Key, Florida, in 1912, I caught the first of this strange species, 38 pounds, and never forgot the experience.

In very short order I was fast to another and a larger one, which eventually came the way of the first. What a pair of fish! Wahoo appear to incorporate all the greens, blues, silvers, and mother-of-pearls that belong to the coral reefs. Yet this fish is as cruel-looking as a barracuda. *Paire*, Eetuarii called it.

Captain Mitchell came along to photograph it in action, and he called: "Bully! I see the wahoo are back. That's a big one!"

Soon afterward I had a cracking smash from a third wahoo, but he missed the hook. This was unexpected and exciting. I trolled on up the reef on edge. And sure enough a fourth and heaviest strike nearly jerked my rod out of my hands. This fellow made a run of two hundred yards in what seemed two seconds of time. We chased him. He broke water here, there, everywhere, at least a dozen times, but did not show above the surface. I could not keep a tight line on this wahoo, and soon lost him. It was hard not to be disappointed, but this fellow would surely have weighed over 80 pounds, possibly 90. Then Eetuarii took the wind out of my sails by saying: "Small! Small! Beeg one like this!" And he stretched his long arms wide, then made a circle of them as large as a telegraph pole. Later we found out that one-hundred-kilo (two hundred pounds) wahoo were common in Tahitian waters, and very large ones not rare. All I could do was to groan and beg the fish gods to lead me to a wahoo of such incredible proportions. So that I could confound my Long Key angling friends! My two wahoo this day weighed 62 and 67 pounds.

We ran out to sea, where we put in a long, wonderful, fruitless day trolling fresh bonito and tuna for miles and miles, to and fro with the immense flocks of birds.

On April 3, which was a fine day, I noted shearwater ducks, both the sooty shearwater and the silver-breasted shearwater, flying along in considerable numbers from the east end of the island. This struck me as unusual, because I had seen only an isolated shearwater here and there during March, and I kept watching. All morning they continued to come, twos and threes and flocks, flying with their swift erratic flight toward the west. Altogether, I must have sighted hundreds, yet none of these sea fowl lingered with the flocks of boobies and noddies that hovered over the schools of bonito.

Another day, when it was clear and hot, with an azure-blue sea, I saw some large fish breaking water far away. We ran over to sight several long, whitish-yellow, mottled animals, fifteen to twenty feet in length, rolling and puffing among the bait. They sounded before we could get close. I had never seen any sea beasts like them. They had the shape and action of blackfish or grampus, but a very low dorsal fin. They must go nameless. In unknown waters, one of the great fascinations, if not the greatest, is always the prospect of seeing strange new creatures.

The flocks of boobies and noddies have thinned out, and those that remain swoop over the ocean so swiftly we cannot keep up with them. Bonito are on the run. They are finding bait scarce, and run farther and faster than at any other time this visit. Conditions have altered markedly. For days the wind, when it blows at all, has been north, northwest, west and southwest, which is new for us, and very favorable, as it makes a lee off the east end, our favorite fishing-grounds.

On April 7, a clear, hot morning, we had a job catching a few bonito. We chased birds for hours. At last we caught four, and then turned to run east. At noon the sea was blue, with a brilliant ripple, perceptibly increasing. It was the kind of water I liked, for I could see a fish quite far, and pretty deep. The boys were at lunch when I yelled, *"There he is!"* And there was a scramble.

It turned out that we had raised two marlin, one approaching 400 pounds easily. His small companion vanished, but he made a rush at my bait, and going under it, like a surly lion, he would not return.

About the same time Captain Mitchell raised a marlin. We could observe him trying to coax it to bit. The fish must have followed him quite a distance.

I expected we would soon raise another. We did, but it was a big yellow shark. I had to wind fast to save my bait. Then he followed us. We hooked up and ran away fast. All the same, this hound trailed us. I could sight him plainly fully two hundred yards back. We would lose him, only to find him again, or maybe it was the other way around. Then I caught his yellow-green color farther back.

Just then a darker shape loomed up out of the depths to my right. I had only to see that shade of purple when I called out the familiar slogan. He came forward, steady and straight, all his fins closed in. I caught the lilac gleam of a high tail. He was big. And he was wary. He hung back. All at once I remembered the shark. "Gosh! Pete, that shark will about rob us of this strike!"

I let my bait out a little, and instructed Peter to do likewise. Johnny had thrown out the clutches. And then when all was favorable the marlin charged my bait. He came like a bull, not so swiftly, but ponderously, and he broke water as he surged for my bait. He struck at it, and I let my line go. As he swept on with the impetus of his drive, I caught a fine glimpse of him—easily twelve feet in length and 500 pounds in weight—a splendid striped marlin of the ordinary species. He wheeled for my bait, which was sinking, as was Peter's. Out of sight he dove. I felt a touch on my line. But it was not what I wanted. Just then Peter began hauling his bait in for dear life. "Shark! That pesky shark! . . . He's got it! . . . He's got yours, too!"

So it proved. The ugly brute swam leisurely up to the boat with both leaders projecting from his mouth. He wanted more. Peter grasped his leader in his gloved hands, held on desperately, and yelled to the natives. They made mince meat of that shark in just three minutes. Sharks used to play the very devil with us, ruining tackle and endangering hands, and even more, but now only a very big one can give us any trouble. We know how to treat them. Peter is a whaler, and my natives natural-born fishermen. When a shark follows us it is just too bad for him.

But there was a sure strike lost, and from a magnificent fish. These opportunities are rare. It hurts when we miss one in that manner. I got a little satisfaction out of the bloody water and the sinking shark. An angler for big game in the open seas after some years learns to know and fear and hate sharks.

The Great Tahitian Marlin Hooked at Last

HIS PLUNGE AFTER BEING GAFFED

I swallowed my disappointment and cheered the outfit back to patient continuance. No other way! It must be done.

We had just raised our hopes again when the breeze freshened, the sea rose to white-crested swells, and we had to run for a pass in the reef.

CHAPTER FIVE

THE weather continued ideal, and consistent with this was the scattering of flocks of birds and bonito. Every day for ten days I made note of the diminishing supplies of anchovies, or small fry that bonito and birds live on. Still we continued to raise a marlin here and there, without getting a strike.

April 9 was the best of fishing days. We started out in sunshine, caught bonito inside the reef, ran out into misty rain, and on up to the east end, where the sea was gleaming dark blue, and fine to troll. I could have seen any color back of the teasers. But there was none. We ran sixty or seventy miles—all in vain. Towards sunset we ran into a school of bonito, breaking at far distances, and we saw two flocks of birds, one to the south, the other to the north.

The moon at this date was a little more than half full. All conditions perfect. Yet the fish are gone, or deep down, or far out.

When we arrived at camp our good Tahitian friend, Mauu, was at hand to meet us with good news. The chief of the district of Tautira came over to inform him, for our benefit, that a twenty-five-foot swordfish had been feeding among the bonito schools for several days off Tautira, and had been seen by numerous native fishermen. All verified his length and size. They were afraid of him—not he of them. Several natives saw him lunge high out of the water with a bonito wiggling on his spear. What a picture that would have made! If I could only have been there! Never the angler and the fish at the same place and time together!

We are going to run around the east end to Tautira, and try to find this twenty-five-footer. If he was that long he would be, at

the very least, eight feet deep and five feet thick. He would——
But I have tortured myself enough.

As luck would have it—my luck—the next day broke dark, windy, rainy, with a stiff swell from southeast. We ran out and up the reef, hoping against hope. Halfway to the east end I had a smashing strike from a wahoo. He missed the hook.

It began to rain fairly hard and blew harder, so we gave up and ran back, and got to chasing birds and bonito. At the end of that chase the squall had passed and the east had lightened. We turned and went on.

Southeast of the island point there is a gap in the reef several miles long, and this place is shallow. The blue, purple, lilac colors of coral showed clearly, and also pale green. High swells rode in, and heaved aloft but did not break.

We trolled along the outer edge of this long shallow, and soon were in trouble. We hooked three heavy fish simultaneously on both boats. As we were trolling for bait we had out three lines. My fish was a soaker and broke my light rig in short order. Peter got his in—a dog-tooth tuna of about 50 pounds, and then I took the other rod from Jimmy and landed a smaller one. We saw that Cappy and crew had hooked into the same species. They were fighters. I saw a line break on their boat. These were the first of this variety of tuna (which I called dog-tooth, because of their big, white, vicious teeth) seen this trip, 1930. They are a game variety of tuna and deserve the name.

When we rounded the east end, and got abreast of the little island that stood out between the reefs and the headlands, we found a calm sea, without even a swell. And I was not long in appreciating the fact that this end of Tahiti was magnificent in the extreme. It was very wild, verdant, and the great canyon slopes sheered up several thousand feet. The peaks standing up in the notches of the canyons loomed twice that high. Waterfalls poured off the velvet-green cliffs, and the patches of dark green and dark gold were exceedingly beautiful. The island was a gem. The moment I realized its isolation, its beauty, and wildness, I had an overwhelming desire to own it. It had a horseshoe-shaped reef between it and the outer reef, in fact it was almost surrounded by reef, and had its own lagoon, blue as the sky. Only no blue sky shone at the moment. All was dark, glooming purple on the sea, and shoreward the mountains climbed aloft to hide their green heads in the clouds. The many waterfalls enchanted my eyes. Low down a strip beach and cocoanut palms fringed the shore, except in places where the precipitous bluff fell sheer into the sea.

As we ran along inside the reef, presently we began to note palm and bamboo huts of natives. But there were at least ten miles of that round east end as wild almost as the peaks. We saw the exquisite beach and grove where the nature men lived. I saw this secluded paradise once before, at quite a distance outside the reef. This time I had a strange thought—what did these nature men know that was beyond my ken? I began to fear they had something. Terribly fascinating was the idea of living there, where no human being intruded, where cocoanuts, bananas, breadfruit, pawpaw, were to be had with ease, where the reef boomed in front of the curved beach and creamy spray, and behind from a purple cleft dropped a lacy waterfall, like downward smoke.

I resolved to go there, scrape acquaintance with these white men who go naked and do nothing.

We ran off Tautira, and trolled out to sea. There was only a slight ripple on the surface, and only a perceptible swell. From six miles out the view inshore was simple stunning. One vast V-shaped canyon opened in the lofty range. The sun came out and made the scene unforgettable. Tahiti may well be called queen of the Pacific. It is marvelously lovely.

We ran out to about eight miles, and found no birds, no bait, nothing but a gentle, empty sea. Trolling back about four miles out, I had a vicious strike. The fish took my bait and shot off swiftly. But he doubled back and came up to break on the surface. I could not get up the slack, and when he leaped he threw the big hook fully thirty feet in the air. We anathematized our luck.

But it turned out that all was well. We had two baits out, one large and fresh, the other small and stale. Suddenly I saw a tremendous boil behind the larger bait. Jimmy saw it, too, and yelled, *"Beeg feesh!"* I leaped to let the line run free, while calling to Johnny to throw out the clutches. The large bait drifted back and the boat slowed. Then a gigantic purple shape flashed up, broadside, just back of the stale bait, struck at it, and sheered away. I heard the natives yelling. Peter happened to be down in the cabin, so did not see. I expected the monster to take one of the baits, as he had gone down. I waited in a state of perfect trepidation, rapture, and suspense. But nothing happened. I became aware of my wobbling legs—the old thrill not experienced for years! My heart up in my throat. Then a bursting gush of blood flashed over me, and the supreme sensation—whatever it was—ended in anguish.

I had raised one of the giant curved-bill marlin. If I had not slacked back that first bait I surely would have gotten a strike out of him. But how was I to know he had swirled at the bait on a forward charge, which carried him up to the teasers. Still, he was not very hungry. If he had been, nothing could have stopped his getting those baits.

He was twenty feet long, without his spear, which I did not see, as he never broke the surface. He was a wide, deep, heavy fish, and to imagine his weight was to approach madness.

After I had recovered somewhat from the shock, I realized that this incident had not been unfortunate, but the very best of luck. I had seen one of these Pacific wonders, so rare and marvelous. To be sure, I had seen one or perhaps two of the same species before, but not close up like that, not within an ace of taking my bait. I shivered at the thought and there was a sinking sensation in the pit of my stomach. All the same, I had tackle for just such a fish, and it trolled the bait he had struck at. A narrow shave! That was getting close to a majestic, royal fish which millions of anglers would not believe existed.

We left the launches at Tautira and motored back to camp. Returned bright and early next morning, with all the exuberant hope of a fisherman.

Peter and John, with our natives, had acquired a lot of information. For a week past bonito had been coming in close to the reef at dawn, and the swordfish showed with them. The largest of these monsters was a good arm's length longer than the chief's canoe, which we measured to get it correct—twenty-four feet!

So after all the great marlin I raised the day before was not really the big one! That knowledge gave me the queerest sensation of relief. For what if I had hooked the real giant!

There seemed to be no valid reason for us to doubt the natives. We have had experience enough now to know they are truthful. It was a simple thing to them. Such swordfish had come in at Tautira every year as long as they could remember. The very largest, however, are far from plentiful. It scarcely need be stated that a twenty-six or twenty-eight or thirty-foot spearfish will be a wonder to the angling world—when he is caught!

The natives said they were afraid of the large ones. This monster had a habit of sidling up alongside a canoe, out of which a native was fishing. He often charged them when in the act of jerking in a bonito. This rather makes it evident that so huge a fish requires a good many bonito for his dinner, and finds it hard to get them. Bonito falling overboard, as many do from these narrow canoes, or coming unhooked while being swung in, are invariably gobbled by one of these giant marlin. How absurdly easy to get a bait to one and hook him, in this case! It may well be that a launch with propellers will put such fish down. The one that I raised on our first day at Tautira acted as if he were scared.

We did not have any fresh bait this second day and could not procure any. No birds, no bonito, no fish! And the day was simply perfect. We trolled rotten bait until they wore off our hooks, one after the other.

Nine hours of riding, watching, hanging on to a line, to and fro over the ocean, now close to the reef, again miles out, with never the sign of a fish! It was a hot day, bright a good part of the time. My face and arms and eyes were burned black. And when I quit that afternoon I had the blind staggers.

Nevertheless, next morning early, we were on our way to Taravao, where the boatmen had run from Tautira to spend the night. We found them in a protected cove, with a wide-eyed audience of natives lined up on the beach. Areireia was amusing them, wading about, catching octopi.

The morning did not promise well. There was a quickening breeze out of the northeast. But as the boats had to be brought back to Vairao, we set out, passing a beautiful little white coral isle with a few lovely palms, on the way to the reef. It was a ten-mile run to Tautira. We trolled outside the reef, catching a bonito, a small dog-tooth tuna, and I had a splashing strike from a wahoo.

At Tautira, we ran out to sea, headed for the east end, trolling our fresh baits. Soon we went out on the big long swells, much more fearsome to behold than actually to ride. It was a comfortable sea, and a beautiful dark blue, without any white.

By noon we were abreast of the island I had determined to explore some day, and it was seemingly another place, a sandy strip and a jungle of green begirt by a blue lagoon, and cut off by thundering surge. A strong rip-tide was setting in. We had all we wanted to churn out of the maelstrom. On the south side we ran into a heavy sea, white-crested, but still easy to fish, and a multitude of birds, working over scattered tuna and bait. They moved too fast for us, so all that we had of them was sight of leaping fish and high spouting splashes.

After holding my rod for seven and a half hours straight, I needed a rest. I never eat any lunch, and usually fish through that period, when the boatmen are busy. Still, I held on until 3 P.M., when we were halfway down the south side of the peninsula and opposite the sharp peaks. Here I let Johnny have my chair, cautioning him to be sure to "let go" if he had a touch. Nevertheless, I stood up back, and holding to the straps I kept my eyes on the baits. There were birds all around us. Jimmy was skittering a pearl gig all over the water. Peter was out on the bow, taking a smoke —which is the only place on a gasoline launch that it is half safe to smoke—and Charley was holding the second rod.

The baits made considerable splash. It was rough and we were skipping along at a good fast clip. Nobody but I saw a marlin slip up behind my bait, his jaws wide open, his tail wiggling. I yelled and leaped at Johnny. He was so startled that he clung to my line, which I had to jerk out of his hand, just as the marlin seized the bait. Johnny fell out of the chair, while I straddled the rod. He never saw the swordfish at all. It was a fine strike and clear run. When I came up hard on the fish, and jerked, I thought I surely had him hooked. He ran toward the boat and came out in a beautiful leap—a greenish-silver striped marlin of about 200 pounds—and then shot toward us with that wagging motion so marvelous to see. I reeled madly, but never got the line tight again. And at the end of that dance he flung the hook out over the waves.

Cappy ran alongside after a while and called that he had raised a fine marlin, which refused the only bait he had—an octopus.

"Don't blame him!" I shouted back, and called it a day.

Despite the extreme difficulty and strain of this Tahitian fishing, it grew more fascinating as I learned more and more about it. We had Alistair Macdonald, the English artist, visiting us at camp, and he went out with us occasionally. Once he complained to Captain Mitchell in this wise: "My God! man, if you don't stop eternally watching that bait, I'll go mad."

That is a clever way to illustrate one of the features of this class of fishing. Not one man in a million would want to do it, and less than that could stand it. Yet it is really nothing for Cappy, or R. C. or me to watch a trolled bait for hours at a stretch. I have a peculiar habit of watching my bait, then shutting my eyes for a second, and so on, over and over again, endlessly.

It would take more than one volume to make clear and attractive what there is in this great game of sea fishing in unknown waters. Ours are the only launches that *ever* ploughed the swells off the east end of Tahiti; or, for that matter, all sides but the Papeete side. This in itself is something wonderful to know and feel. Then again there is always the possibility of a terrific strike from a monster that has to be fast and ferocious to get his meat in the amazingly clear water. There is so much, too, besides the mere fishing, great game as it is.

As I write here at night the sea crashes on the cliffs below, and above that sound comes the boom and thunder of the outer reef. Huge moths as large as bats fly against my screens, attracted by the lights, and slim, croaking lizards dart around over the wire to try to catch them. A strange bird called a puffin, a night feeder, flies over the cottage, emitting a wild, doleful cry, like nothing I had ever heard before. There come moments of absolute silence, then a slow swish below, the crawl of surf up on the coral, a subsidence of splash, and then a mounting crash against the rocks. Out on the front line the cannonading runs all along for miles, yet

Showing the Sharp, Almost Flattened, Small Head, Something New in Spearfish

Weighing the Monster. This Picture Shows Where the Sharks Tore Off Flesh

a moment here and there is quiet, only to break to hollow thunder. The fragrance of frangipani—than which there is no sweeter on earth—floats through doors and windows. And when I step out on the porch to gaze down upon the lagoon under a full moon, and out to the broken silver line of surf, and across the bay to the grand, black range, crowned by white clouds, I am not sure that it is real, that I am not in some enchanted land of dreams. The red cocoanut-hull fires burn along the curved shore line, and the smell of smoke rivals the perfume of flowers, at least in memory-probing power, and the lights of the canoe fishermen flicker in the pale obscurity. Natives pass along the shore trail, thrumming a guitar, and chanting a melancholy refrain. The whole effect rouses a stinging sadness.

CHAPTER SIX

JUST what effect the moon has upon fish I have never learned, though I have kept careful data. But if the moon affects tides it certainly affects the fish. In the Gulf Stream the very best time for sailfish is just before and after the full moon. I have seen thousands at that time, one school after another.

Full moon here at Tahiti appears to be opposite, according to my notes. The day of the full moon, April 13, and the following day, were perfect fishing days. But we saw nothing except a few tuna chasing flying-fish, and had not one strike along ten miles of reef fishing. I have noted that trolling never is good when the sun is bright and hot.

On this second day, however, I saw a remarkable spectacle, as new to me as it was striking—no less than boobies feeding on flying-fish on the wing.

We ran across a bunch of scattered tuna, chasing flying-fish over a wide area of glassy sea. Some of the tuna were hundred pounders, and to see one of these leap with his wonderful driving power, and the quiver of his fins, is something for an angler to remember. These larger tuna knock flying-fish out of the water, crippling or dazing them, and smashing them when they fall back. After a long fly and a long run a flying-fish appears to be spent, and flops out with amazing clumsiness, considering his usual speed and grace, to be gobbled by the pursuing tuna. This could be seen in all directions and applied to good-sized flying-fish.

The boobies were sweeping and swooping over the tuna, and not, as usual, diving like a plummet. And I soon saw what they were up to. Out would dart a bevy of little flying-fish, to scatter and sail every way. The boobies were swifter and even if far behind often gained on the frantic little bird-fish, to catch them on the fly. It was a graceful, dexterous, tragic action. Between the tigers of the sea beneath and the falcons of the sky above, what chance did these helpless flying-fish have for their lives? Nature is merciless, and in every instance it is the survival of the fittest. I should say luckiest, too. The wonder is that any of these flying-fish survive at all. Sailfish, dolphin, and that lantern-jawed wahoo all feed on flying-fish.

The boobies reminded me of the great gulls of New Zealand, that catch the little Mother Carey's chickens and swallow them alive. Many a squirming little flying-fish, plucked up by a voracious bill just as he was about to alight, went wiggling to the craw of these hawks.

That day I came in early, about one o'clock, tired of looking for bait and riding the sea without fishing. During the afternoon the wind fell and the sea smoothed out. I went to engage natives to seine bait. When I returned at sunset, Cappy was still out. No sign of him with my glass! Supper passed. At seven o'clock I picked up a light flashing, and I answered. We have a set of signals. Cappy was O.K. He was quite far out, and it took half an hour for him to get in. Here is the story he told:

"After you turned in, we went on till we came to white caps, and then worked back. About two o'clock the sea grew calm, and it was really beautiful out there. I had trolled a bait until it was so rotten the eyes dropped out.

"All of a sudden Areireia yelled so loud I nearly lost my hat. There was a gigantic marlin back of the teasers. He hove up like a barge, and scorned the rotten bait. Then he sailed from one side to the other of the teasers, and finally swam alongside so that I could see him fairly well. By Jove! he was a buster! Eighteen or twenty feet long and as big through as an ox! He swam around the boat, dropped back, followed us, and repeated the circle of the boat. He was hungry. I nearly leaped overboard in my despair. He went round us a third time, and then dropped astern to follow us still. The natives saw birds. We ran for them full speed, hoping to catch a fresh bait and come back to hand it to that impudent swordfish on a platter. But we could not quite come up with the birds, and at last gave in.

"We were eight or ten miles offshore, and I still trolled the rotten bait. Would you believe it—I raised two more swordfish, the larger of which was a wonderful fish fully twelve feet long? The smaller would have weighed all of 400 pounds. These marlin were hungry. They came in close. The big one took my bait and spat it out! The other did the same. My disgust was supreme. Then to cap an awful climax, the twelve-footer came back, snapped my bait again, mouthed it as if to make sure he had not been mistaken before—then ejected it. They left us. And I reeled in that rotten bait, threw it off, and waved for the boys to beat it back to camp."

Cappy's report thrilled me exceedingly, and renewed flagging hopes. Anything could happen in this Tahitian sea. We had to run the wheels off the boats.

Engine repairs kept Mitchell in next day, which was a continuation of fine weather. I went alone, and caught some fresh bonito on the way out. We ran southeast until the two little islands off the east end stood out from the mainland. Captain raised the giant marlin in this vicinity. The sea was blue, with a big ripple—ideal for marlin fishing. Birds and tuna, and some bonito, appeared to be scattered all over the ocean.

I trolled across this area, to and fro, up and down, around, weaved over it, and in short, watched my bait for nine solid hours. Late in the afternoon I raised two marlin together. When they come in braces like that or more, you are pretty certain of a strike. But these birds had fed. They were curious, not hungry. The larger, about 400, soon sheered off, while the smaller, about 300, followed us several hundred yards. Then he flashed purple in a swell and vanished. We headed campward, and the run took three hours, getting us there long after dark.

Cappy and everybody were at the dock to meet me, having seen our lights out at sea. They imagined and hoped I might have been tied up with the monster Cappy had raised. "Nothing doing," I said, wearily. "Tomorrow—maybe!"

And tomorrow the full-moon blow came on, which lasted three days.

In town we met Captain Rassmussen, a trader in the islands, and he told us a fishing incident. He always trolls with a hand line out. Somewhere over in the Cook group he hooked a gigantic sailfish which leaped close to the schooner, almost coming aboard, until it broke free. Positively and without hesitation Rassmussen declared that sailfish to be twenty-three feet long, not including the spear. He was slender, thin, and had a sail like a blanket.

We met another seafaring man who had lately come from New Caledonia, an island northwest of New Zealand, and one I had had my eye on for some years, having heard vague untraceable rumours about the fish life there. New Caledonia is remote from any place, a French penal island, and rarely visited. Not until I met this captain did I ever get authentic data. Swordfish, sailfish, great tuna—all kinds of fish abundant from June to November. No one ever fished those waters, and what *might* inhabit them could only be conjectured.

It is such incident as Rassmussen's and such information as we got from the other trader that drive me nearly crazy. How on earth—I mean how in the sea (or hell) are we *ever* going to fish all these fascinating places?

The full-moon blow, as we called it, passed in three days, and we had fine weather again. It left a southeast swell that was magnificent in the extreme, some of the slopes being fully a mile down or up, and to ride aloft to the summit of one of these lifting mountains was to be exhilarated to the point of yelling for sheer joy. The assault on the corner of reef of these great Pacific swells shall be left till a later chapter. I could not do them justice without time for my impression and sensation to subside.

Here at Tahiti fishing conditions change all the time, some imperceptibly, others overnight. For weeks we have not seen a sailfish or dolphin. These were abundant in early March. Where have they gone? I have recorded on former trips how we sighted them in June, July, August.

Wahoo and dog-tooth tuna have arrived, and a few *crevalle*, but none of the little pearl-white tuna with the big black eyes. Yellow-fin tuna have been sighted almost daily, but they are fast thinning out. Bonito in mid-April come through in scattered schools, going like the wind. Formerly they schooled around bunches of bait and threshed the water white. There is also an appreciable (and much appreciated) diminution in the number of sharks.

This heavy southeast swell terminated in an onslaught upon the reefs that beggared description. It was not a storm, though I imagine there had been a blow far out at sea. But at night the continuous roaring seemed equivalent to the most violent of wind storms. It drowned the lesser contention on the fringing reef beneath the promontory on which my cottage stood precariously. Almost, my bed appeared to hang over the sea. And in the dark, starless night this roar was productive of many thoughts and emotions. I cannot confess to fearing the sea when I am safely on land, but the thought of being out there, at night, in all that tumult was certainly terrifying. There was no remembered sound to which I could compare this unearthly, solid, thumping thunder of waters thrown with all the majesty and might of the Pacific upon the coral reefs.

It was different because it swept in out of a bottomless sea, to encounter suddenly an insurmountable obstacle. The pound of the Atlantic main along New Jersey's shore in a nor'easter is no light thing. It engenders respect and fear. But this thing was the voice of Jove in wrath of heaven against the earth. It was titanic, insupportable.

Then to think that with all its appalling power and weight the ocean not only could not destroy the coral reef, but actually furthered its growth—this seemed to stagger one with its incredible truth.

By day the reef was terrific to behold and hear. My white horses had augmented to an army of cream-white leaping steeds of gigantic proportions and superlative strides. This day they mastered the blue waves and over-rode the reef in array so formidable that they never smoothed out until far across the coral into the lagoon. All day long this din, this action, persisted. Ceaseless ebb and flow of the sea! Yet how immeasurably more than that. It swung to the attraction of the moon and answered the call of the wind. It permitted the stately steamer to go on and foundered the white-sailed bark, or it was just as likely to reverse that order.

Where were the birds, the fish this day? Assuredly these never came ashore, as humans do, to escape the conflicting tides. No doubt the birds float like thistle down over the waves and the fish seek the abysmal deep.

Mountain seas ran for eight days, beginning the third day after full moon. Sometimes the sky was clear, with a hot sun shining, and other times it was overcast with lowering storm clouds. Rain? No Californian or Ohioan ever saw it rain! You must come to Tahiti to see a glorious downpour—to see a hundred waterfalls sliding off the great steep slopes at once—to see the brooks come roaring down out of the canyons, to see the dark swamps, with their huge gnarled and serrated-trunked *mape* trees, and the tree-ferns and the clinging vines, dripping a flood down upon the elephant ears, the broad lily pads, the moss.

We went nato fishing a number of times, and I declared that as soon as I could catch some of these beautiful, delicate cute, little silver-and-black fish I would write my impressions of them. So far as I am concerned they have trout tied to the mast for cleverness and wariness. Cappy can grow in one spot until he resembles a tree with a swinging branch, and after a while catch a nato. But I have to cast and cast, then wade on. There is always a hope that I may raise a deluded nato.

Then the weather cleared so wondrously that we forgot about the bad, and reveled in white sunshine, azure sea, sweet-scented zephyrs, and the blaze of flowers, and gold-green tropical luxuriance.

We ran down the reef twenty-odd miles, and across the wide channel to Moorea, as far famed as Tahiti. Captain rounded the north end of Moorea and I the south. The whole trip of about seventy miles took me until sunset, and I never knew where the time went. I had fresh bait and trolled the whole distance without raising a fish. We passed through three flocks of feeding birds—a most welcome sight again—and along the fifteen-mile, irregular south shore of Moorea. The island with its long slopes, its green hills, its spires and monuments, bare and gray, its winding beaches of gold and crawling reefs of white, had an intimacy not possible to feel regarding Tahiti. And it was therefore possible to grasp and possess its rare and exotic beauty.

We stayed all night in the deep bay on the west side, and learned from the natives that two big "feesh" had been seen lately—one a swordfish of seven meters (twenty-one feet), that had been seen with the bonito every day, while they were running a few weeks back, and another kind of fish which appeared to be all head, larger than the canoes and so very ferocious that the native fishermen gave it a wide berth. "Too late again!" groaned Cappy. I felt that some day I would meet one of these monsters on my lawn at Altadena—in one of my dreams.

So we went bonefishing. This has happened before, though very little of our luck and trouble has crept into this notebook. Always waiting for the day when we land one!

There is a lake on Moorea, fed by the ocean, and it is full of two kinds of bonefish, one the common species, such as are caught in Florida, and another species that I am sure remains unclassified. The first named has the name of being one of the gamest fish that swim, and perhaps the hardest to catch. In another book I have related what befell R. C. and me when we started after bonefish at Long Key. For years I held the record, 10 pounds 2 ounces, which at last was beaten by that wonderful, good, and lovable old fisherman, Gus Meisselbach, lately gone on to a better and happier fishing-ground. His fish weighed 10 pounds 7 ounces; and this record was then beaten by some one at Bimini, with a weight of 13 pounds 4 ounces. This fish is a record, but I never heard that it was qualified by any club rules.

These are the three largest taken in recent years—not so very recent, either—and it will interest my readers and probably paralyze the dyed-in-the-wool bonefishermen to learn that bonefish here run to 40 pounds, and the other species, that of the forked tail, go as high as 60 pounds. Shades of Fisher, Thompson, Bohmfalk, and others of the noble bonefish brigade! Wait till I can show a picture of one of these giant bonefish. Then notice the exodus Tahiti-ward. It is sad to relate that these mild-eyed, leisurely, soft-voiced gentlemen anglers would never, never believe me unless I furnished a photograph. And when I do Thompson will knit his brows and say: "By thunder! that's the very bonefish I hooked near the viaduct three years ago! He sure swam a long way—clear to Tahiti." And Fisher will correct him.

On the way campward from Moorea we fell in with bonito again. It was like getting home after a long absence. The birds flew leisurely over a scattered school of fish. No sharks, wonderful to relate. And our native boys got busy with their long bamboos and skittering pearl shell. After so long a rest it was fun to dodge bonito; and soon we could not move around the cockpit without falling over a mess of bonito.

I raised a good-sized sailfish, the first we had seen for six weeks. He hung so close to my bait that I was sure he would take it, but he did not. And that was all for that pleasant day.

Toward the approach of a new moon we inclined to the natives' conviction—that it would bring good weather and fish. There was one fine day just before the onset of this new moon—a sunny, hot day with a fine sea to troll in the lee of the mountains. Outside, either to east or west, there was a heavy chop and uncomfortable roll. So we hung to the lee.

In the afternoon I grew tired of everlastingly watching my bait and hanging on to my line, so I put Jimmy on the job and went up on deck to bask in the sun. Soon I espied a long, black, sickle fin sticking up out of a swell. I was so surprised that I yelled, "swordfish!" when it really belonged to a sailfish.

We maneuvered to get the boat in front of him, and either failed or he missed us, so I had Johnny turn to go back. We ran several hundred yards and turned again. Presently I saw a long, dark, slim shape shooting up back of us, and I shouted to the boys below. At that the sailfish was up between the two baits, undecided which to charge. Calling Peter to haul in the large bonito. I sat down and took the line out of Jimmy's hands. He had it over the handle of the reel and if the fish had charged the bait then—good night.

I had some difficulty in coaxing that sailfish to take the bait, which was a little large for him. But at last he struck and snatched it, and was off. Whoopee! A strike again! The reel was not the only thing singing. He went off fine, slowed down, and presently started again fast. Then I hooked him. He felt heavier than he had looked, but you can never tell the size of a fish under water.

He ran a hundred yards before coming up. When he got clear out, standing on his tail and flapping his blanket sail, he presented a superb picture. Not only that, he showed his size, and he certainly was a sailfish most desirable to capture. He was over twelve feet long and fairly deep. The huge sailfish are humpbacked. This fellow was not so big as that, but he would have tipped the scales at 125 pounds. Down he plunged, to sound deep, and to my surprise and chagrin, pulled free of the hook.

A swordfish tackle is too heavy for sailfish, and very probably I had gotten only a light hold on him. It was all in a day's work.

"Reckon the sailfish have come back," was Peter's comment.

"Yes, I reckon they have," I replied, dryly. "But where have the swordfish gone?"

"Beats me, sir. Hard place to fish—this Tahiti."

In these waters wahoo and barracuda grow to enormous size— exceeding 100 kilos, which is 200 pounds. Three-hundred-pound barracuda have been caught by natives fishing deep for tuna with hand lines. Jimmy told me he once saw a wahoo—*ono*, he called it —that was four meters long. Naturally, as in case of the giant marlin, we were keen to capture one of these prizes, and seldom failed to try where opportunity afforded. That is why continued and persistent fishing in these waters is at all endurable.

Both fish haunt the deep water close to the coral reef, or what the natives call the "tuna holes." This day I hooked one on the lightest tackle we dared use—an eight-ounce tip and twelve-thread line, with the Templar reel—which I like exceedingly for this kind of work.

You can always tell a wahoo strike. It is thrilling in the extreme. You can see a vicious swirl, then a circular splash, and feel a solid snatch at your tackle. This one took three hundred yards of line so swiftly that I yelled good-by. But I stopped him short of the end of the line, and had him at that distance for some anxious moments. He felt like a ton of bricks. I had caught enough wahoo, altogether, to be on to their tricks, and to despair of always keeping the line tight. You simply cannot do it. They dart here, there, everywhere, as quick as lightning, and if it happens to be toward the boat they get slack line, which is bad. It is then you lose as many wahoo as you catch, even after you become expert.

Eventually I exhausted this one and led him to the boat, where we all looked down at him. Probably no other fish can excel a wahoo in color and beauty, seen thus in the clear water. He is iridescent, green, purple, silver, with vivid stripes, all of which fade almost at once, when he is pulled out. Then he has a strangeness not striking in any other fish I know, and all of the savage wolfish look of the barracuda.

This one weighed 40 pounds, a small wahoo for Tahitian waters, but quite large for any other place I have fished. He made me speculate upon the unwisdom of risking a large one on light tackle. There should be used a fairly stiff rod, and five hundred yards of twenty-four-thread line. With that you might see one of the monsters.

CHAPTER SEVEN

THE day of the next new moon dawned auspiciously—calm, warm, sunny, and a smooth sea. Cappy went to Papeete to meet the mail ships, so I had to go fishing alone. I spent an hour photographing my white horses of the sea, always different, and this morning on a wild rampage.

To catch bait was the next thing. In ten miles up the reef, I hooked and lost three wahoo, one of which was the largest I ever had on. He ran nearly all the line off and we had to chase him. After we caught up with him he made short queer runs and eventually liberated himself from the hook.

Our next bad luck was to get among small tuna, three of which we had on, only to lose. We ran out to another flock of birds. A hand line Jimmy had out trolling for bait was snapped like cotton thread by a big tuna. We lost three gigs to sharks, each of which appropriated the bonito we had hooked. The last shark of the bunch fastened to my line and I determined to make it his last greedy action. He turned out to be slow and heavy, hard to work up on a medium-light rod and line. I was an hour pumping the leader to Peter's gloved hands. Meanwhile he and Jimmy had been amusing themselves by counting the sharks around the one I had hooked. At length I saw five of the green-yellow devils. My quarry proved to be one of the black species, a short, thick, fat shark, upward of 450 pounds.

After the boys had massacred him I told Peter to cut him open to see if the bonito he had swallowed would still do for a bait. Peter found only the head. But he found also seven baby sharks, about two feet long, all save one of which we caught in a dip-net.

Small sharks make good bait. I once caught—or at least hooked—a marlin on a small shark.

So that was how I came to troll a shark for bait this provoking day. Not to catch a single bait before one o'clock was very bad luck.

The wind had been coming from all directions, bearing huge black rain clouds, moving slowly. All the mountains were lost. Dense gray veils of rain were falling in at least three points of the compass. From the southwest a storm kept thickening and coming our way, and at last we saw we could not escape, so we put down the curtains and headed toward it. A level dark cloud bank hung over the whole southern and western horizon, here and there letting down curtains of rain against the background of strange luminous yellow. After a while all appeared swallowed up in a pall of gray rain. It roared down upon the boat, so that the cockpit was inches deep in water; it roared all around us, instantly flattening the sea. Without exception, this was the heaviest fall of rain I had ever experienced. In a few minutes it filled a bucket sitting out in the open. We were lost in the silken pattering roar and steely gray.

And in the thick of it something hit the feather gig on the light rod, making the reel screech. I had to sit out in the deluge and fight a fish of some kind until he escaped.

Then like all these wonderful storms this one moved away across the sea and mountains, letting the sun shine once more. Such emerald green as blazed on the slopes would have to be seen to be thought possible. Rainbows everywhere, and waterfalls pouring down the canyon notches. Cold and uncomfortable in my wet shorts, I was glad to sit in the sun a while.

About four o'clock, Jimmy let out a great Tahitian yell. He pointed to the west, where the sky was clear again. Once—twice more, he yelled, and finished in English, *"Swordfeesh!"*

Suddenly I got the direction and saw a high, white, sheet-like splash go up, such as is made by a sixteen-inch shell when it hits water. I knew swordfish splashes when I saw them. But I was not in time to get a glimpse of the swordfish. Jimmy was excited, an unusual circumstance for him. He raved in Polynesian, French, and finally English: *"Beeg.* Most *beeg swordfeesh.* Seven meters!" And he spread wide his long arms.

I groaned. Seven meters made over twenty-one feet! We ran that two intervening miles in fast time, then slowed down to troll all over and around the place where we had seen the tremendous splashes. All to no avail!

The next fish to engage our attentions showed several days afterward, at the end of Captain Mitchell's line, when he was fishing for bonito with a feather gig. And it was a sailfish! To hook one of these hard-jawed small-mouthed fish on an artificial bait is about as likely to happen as thunder out of a clear sky. Still, in fishing, anything can happen. That accounts for the amazing, incredible feats of novices, or what seems to be deliberate suicide of a superb fish.

This sailfish of Cappy's was a long, limber cuss, and like all this species, a surface-fighting fish and a jumper from way back. He had a wonderful sail which he waved in the air like a flag as if to summon aid from his piscatorial comrades. Naturally we waited to see him dislodge the hook. But it stayed fast, and astonishing to see, Cappy landed that sailfish. The hook had caught in the small soft notch in the middle of the upper bill, just the one spot where a hook might hold. The sailfish was a perfect specimen, 107 pounds in weight, and dull bronze in color, with a very dark sail and no dots or stripes.

By way of diversion from rough empty seas, we tried nato fishing again. Tautara and Hitiaa rivers yielded their usual few nato, and small ones at that. But merely to wade Hitiaa and cast under the magic of its dreaming cliffs and murmuring waterfalls, or to wander along the rocky shore of Tautara watching the nato shine like gold as they turned their sides, or the yellow blossoms go floating down the stream, and listening to the thunder of the surf just over the palm-fringed bar—these were enough not only to satisfy my cravings but to remain with me for days.

Ten miles east of Flower Point, far beyond the road and trail and accessible only to canoes, two rivers came down out of huge canyons to empty into the lagoon. They are out of the way. But while Cappy and I had fished miles offshore, we had seen the numerous waterfalls which fed these rivers and the magnificent slopes of verdure, and we wanted to have a go at these wild rivers.

We did. It was an experience of a lifetime of fishing. I could not attempt a detailed description or narrative of it, for fear of being credited with hyperbole.

We towed a skiff and found our way in and out of the numerous and dangerous passes through the reef until we reached the extreme southward-facing side of the island. The mountains stood up like green clouds over our heads. Around the point from this place lay the inaccessible beach where the nature men live. We meant to pay them a visit some day.

The mouths of these two rivers were perhaps a mile apart, with a precipitous mountain sheering up between. Both rivers had built up deltas of sand and gravel that had projected into capes out into the lagoon, and had grown a mass of tropic verdure, the front of which was a fringe of cocoanut palms. Our native guide told us that an American and an Englishman lived on these points, at the mouths of the rivers. The wild, primitive isolated surroundings would have appealed to any man. Bamboo and thatched palm cottages nestled under the rustling trees; the bright red of native *pareus* shone against the green and gold; ducks and geese dotted the tranquil mouths of the rivers; and native women and children stared at us as we rowed ashore.

I saw a white man, rather young, and undoubtedly an American, watching us from amid his native flock. We rather expected to be hailed. It was a lonely place, and white visitors should have been welcome. This man watched till we landed—his pale face contrasting markedly with the dark ones around him—and then he went within the cottage. We landed on the side of the river opposite and thought best not to go farther in that direction. I saw a pretty young native girl carrying a white baby in her arms. Herein lies the delusion and lure of Tahiti for so many men. Gone native! I wondered what was in this man's mind as he saw and heard his countrymen approaching, gay and noisy, eager and enthusiastic, as befits fishermen who are boys bent on another adventure.

I love the wild as well as any man. I know its power, its worth, its danger. But after a sojourn under its influence I want to go back to civilization and put my shoulder again to the wheel of work, of progress, of hope.

The first pool I came upon in this river quite enchanted me, if it did not drive me quite mad. A rushing stream poured out of the green wall of jungle to make a curve in the open, shaded by one magnificent *mape* tree. That tree alone was enough to make even a fisherman stop and gaze. It had a fluted trunk, between each outstanding rib of which grew moss and ferns and flowers. Its foliage was heavy, bright-leafed, and spreading. The water was so crystal clear that it did not appear water at all. Behind opened the cocoanut grove, sunny and shady in spots; and above the jungle banked the grand green cleft from which this river flowed. Between the thundering booms of the reef outside I could hear a distant thunder of another kind—that of a waterfall. Bob, running around with his cameras, raved like a lunatic. Cappy, true to his instinct, began to cast below me where the stream ran fast, and suddenly was fast to a lively and strong nato. Jimmy grew as excited as any of us, and pointed into the transparent pool under the tree. "*Nato! Beeg nato!*" were his thrilling words.

I slipped around behind the *mape* to peep out. And for a minute I was petrified. It was full of nato. Like the Fairy Pool at Rotorua, in New Zealand, a famed spot where everyone goes to see the trout, this magic well not only contained hundreds of nato, but larger ones than I had ever seen. One was a foot long, all spotted black and silver. I actually trembled when I cast. And when he opened a wide mouth and took my tiny fly, wop! right there the past between then and my boyhood was bridged and I was so paralyzed with rapture I could not jerk. I stood there and watched the great nato eject the fly.

I caught thirty-eight nato that day and lost as many, some too large to land on the delicate two-ounce rod and flimsy tackle. Cappy caught nearly fifty, two of which weighed close to a pound. I saw him raise and hook one of these, and not only his skill was needed to land it, but all of Areireia's fish-like proclivities and dexterity in the water.

Mosquitoes as thick and savage as black flies in Newfoundland could not dampen our ardor, nor could the deluge of rain and the dripping foliage. We penetrated the jungle up these rivers and it was as if we had entered a different and unknown world. When the sun shone above, a few shafts of gold penetrated the thick canopy overhead, and a diffused amber gloom pervaded the jungle. Once I heard a shrill, strange bird note, but that was the only sign of life, except the nato, I came upon in that excursion into the tangled web of trees, ferns, plants, vines, and moss. More than once I went up to my neck in a mat-like grass which for the most part sustained my weight. When the sun went under a cloud, then it seemed night had fallen. What a dark, weird green-and-black tent! We went through a swamp of *mapes* that dwarfed those made famous in the motion picture, "White Shadows." We threaded almost impenetrable thickets; we waded over a long waving white moss that grew underwater. While a rain storm passed I stood a moment under a leaf of the elephant-ear plant, five feet long and very wide, and it beat any umbrella I ever owned. There were long, pale saplings, so high I could not see their tops. Nearer and nearer the waterfall sounded until the boom of the reef was lost. Great *mape* trees lay across the stream, to surmount which was no easy task. A sweet, sense-deadening perfume pervaded the dark jungle. There was nothing dry—not even on me. But the feel was not that cold, uncomfortable wetness a trout angler experiences in America. I did not mind being wet. I was obsessed with the enchantment of the place. And my eagerness to catch nato quite inhibited my faculty to observe and remember. Still I saw wonderful broad-leafed vines strangling trees, even while I fished; I saw beautiful, lacy ferns higher than my head, and parasitical moss and lichen that completely hid the trunks of trees, and the gold of wild oranges hanging high, and wonderful red bulbs that resembled pineapples, and strange exotic wild flowers, and purple fringe on the under side of branches. From the cliffs above and the dripping foliage and over the mossy ground rushed water.

The second river was different. It was broad and deep at and near the mouth, running under a tunnel of flowery foliage. But up a little way it opened into the clear, where a long succession of runs and ripples, pools and falls, all bordered by the luxuriant sunlit verdure, furnished the finest nato-fishing we had ever found. We could wade and cast far and see the nato rise like a flash of gold, or make a circle on the surface and come again with a little splash. Nato were coming up from the sea. They were feeding on tiny black gnats, and when we simulated them with our flies we raised them everywhere. It was too good to be true. Captain Mitchell said nato-fishing reminded him of trout-fishing in the chalk streams of England, only, if anything, it was superior. That admission from an Englishman meant much. The trout-fishing in the high Sierras and the grayling-fishing in Colorado came nearer to this nato game than any I had known. But nato-fishing surpassed them. The nato had the advantage and influence of being from the sea; he was as cunning and wary, as beautiful and strong, as delicate a biter as either of the two mentioned; and lastly he lived in rivers bewildering for the beauty and glory of their environment.

For me it was unforgettable to cast over floating blossoms, mostly pale-yellow lily-like flowers, though now and then came a large blossom with silver thread filaments, and a center of purple, and rarely a small red flower that rode upright like a canoe. Never was a stretch of water free from this color. Then the mirror-reflecting quality of this transparent water made a double picture to the charmed gaze—the inverted and magnified bank of exotic and gorgeous growth and the gold and green of palms, *mapes*, bamboos, and other trees against the blue sky and white clouds on the pall of rainy gray.

It was much, of course, to cast flies over a little river where none had ever been cast before. The nato proved that. Yet how soon they grew suspicious and cunning! When we pricked one it was time to cast somewhere else; and after raising and landing several, we learned the wisdom of resting that pool.

All anglers are lovers of nature, and artists in their hearts. Color is a passion with them. I once knew an ignorant fellow who treasured gaudy trout flies not alone for the effectiveness of their lure. Music of running water, of wild birds, the wind in the trees, the sense of utter solitude—these are things dear to every fisherman.

In Tahiti birds are rare, but the song of the sea on the coral reefs makes up for that lack. As for the rest, and infinitely more, the pearl of the Pacific possesses them in a degree which cannot be written of rationally. The appalling beauty and isolation of Tahiti are things that should not be experienced long by a white man.

Peter told us a funny angling story that he brought from Russell, New Zealand.

A Scotchman read my book, *Angler's El Dorado*, and decided he must go fishing in New Zealand waters. To this end he bought an expensive Hardy tackle, split cane, steel-center rod, fine reel, etc., and took ship for Auckland. In due time he arrived at Russell and started out fishing with the boatmen he had engaged. While drifting off Cape Brett the Scotchman had a strike. The fish started off and began going faster and faster. Meanwhile the boatman was engaged in putting the man's harness on and hooking it to the rod. The fish by this time was going with the speed of an airplane. In short order he ran all the six hundred yards of line off the reel and came solid against the end. It jerked the angler out of his seat and hard against the gunwale, banging his face on the wood. Then, *snap!* went the line.

The Scotchman sat up, most bewildered. "Thank God that's over!" he cried.

"It was a great black marlin, sir," declared the boatman, excitedly.

"Zane Grey might have thought that was a fish! . . . *I* know it was an earthquake!"

CHAPTER EIGHT

DAYS on end, waiting, running, hoping! Weary the barren waves, weary the rod, weary the line and its heavy bait! Then came news that the channel between Moorea and Tahiti was once more alive with birds and bait, and bonito were selling in the market at a franc each. Swordfish were following the canoes.

That news came on a Saturday. Early Sunday morning we were off from camp and ran round the point in less than two hours. There was a lee between the islands and up to the northward, in a line from Papeete to the north point of Moorea we found birds and bonito scattered all over.

Once more we went to fishing with all the old eagerness and patience. Captain Mitchell raised a fine marlin that took the bait and then let it go. I had to report a full day, but no sight of swordfish. We ran in to Papeete and stayed there all night. Next morning we were out early along with the market fishermen in their little boats. The sea was dark and rippling, under a cool light breeze, and everywhere we turned there would be a squalling flock of birds over bonito boiling the water. After a while the sea grew fairly rough, which is fine for marlin-fishing. Sometimes my bait skimmed the waves and at others it dove a foot or two. And at one of the latter times a purple form flashed up and, snatching the bait, took to the surface and was off like a rocket. I did my best to hook the fish. He ran, leaping straight for Cappy's boat, and if he had not seen it and sheered off, surely would have cut the line. We had not been able to get after him so quickly as was needful, and when he leaped opposite Cappy's boat he had out four hundred yards of line, with a great bag in it. I felt the strain go slack and knew he was gone. Afterward Cappy told us that the strain on the line was so strong it whirled the fish in a somersault. Then the hook tore out.

I raised another marlin that afternoon and sighted a third. Cappy reported a blank day.

Our native boatmen collected interesting data that evening. One canoe had to quit fishing because of the marlin that followed it. Another claimed to have seen three swordfish among the bonito. I took much of this with a grain of salt. Finally Charley and Peter met two canoeists who asserted positively that two marlin followed their canoe for miles. One was of ordinary size, but the other was as long and thick as the trunk of a flamboyant tree on the main street of Papeete, where the information was given. Peter said he believed the man. Lastly, Mr. Wainright, an Englishman of our acquaintance, vowed that a fifteen-foot swordfish attacked his launch and forced him to run in a hurry.

All the instances that I can recall in California and New Zealand where a marlin hit the boat were, I am positive, just accidents in the mad flurry of a fish in its efforts to escape. But in these South Pacific waters fish are larger, swifter, and very much more aggressive and ferocious than elsewhere, and we have heard too many tales of attacks, and the natives are too genuinely afraid of swordfish, to doubt any longer.

The third morning we started out before sunrise, assuredly a beautiful one to leave the shore of Papeete. Both islands were magical in the soft pearl light of dawn. Before we were an hour out we spotted birds. They were halfway across the channel and covered an area two miles square. It took us an hour to catch four bait, a singular fact, when Cappy's natives pulled in bonito as fast as they could fling their shells back. But it is that way sometimes.

I settled back comfortably to watch my bait, when out of the blue burst a thick muddy-colored brute of a shark and nailed that fine bait before I could move. We had to whip him and get him in to save the leader. Soon, with another bait overboard, I felt that I could sit back and enjoy the wonderful scene. I have fished in a number of places I liked better than these Tahitian waters, but perhaps not one so beautiful. Scarcely had I settled back again when another shark cut my bait in two. This was productive of language. Peter put our third bonito on and dropped it over, then uncoiled a kink in the leader. A big shark sheered out from under the boat and took that one. "Bloody murder!" yelled Peter, hanging on to the leader. "The sea's full of sharks!" This shark got our third bait. Then the fourth and last went over. Somehow I had a feeling something would happen to it. I was right.

We trolled to and fro, and finally came near enough to Cappy to signal him. He turned and we gradually drew close. When my boat stopped and my bait sank I was about to shout to Cappy and ask for some fresh bonito. But the words froze on my lips.

A long, dark purple shape, quick as light, loomed out of the depths and took my bait.

Jimmy yelled: "*Mauu!*"

He was standing up, he had sharp eyes I had learned to trust, and we had already met with three sharks—facts which caused me to go against my own judgment. So I put on the drag and pulled. The bait came away from the fish. That alone was enough to prove there was no shark. You can never pull a bait away from a shark.

I saw my bonito shine. I saw the long, dim, dark shape come again.

Suddenly Jimmy yelled: "*Beeg swordfish!*" and I released my drag just as the marlin took my bait. He went away and down, slowly and easily. When I came up on him I knew there was no doubt about his being well hooked. But that did not wake him up. He swam around, going deeper, though not with any haste.

We were a happy crew. Bob, who had been sitting on top, raved about the size of the fish. "Oh, I couldn't open my mouth. I knew it was no shark. . . . Biggest swordfish I ever saw!"

This was a thrilling exclamation. Still I had not had a good look at the marlin and was not to be misled. Jimmy held up two fingers: "Two feesh!"

Whereupon we signalled Captain again to approach. When he was within hailing distance, I yelled, "Another marlin!"

But I hardly needed to have taken the trouble. Nobody on Cappy's boat heard me. I saw Areireia leap for the teaser on his side and knew what was up.

"Look sharp, Bob," I called.

Giant Tahitian Striped Marlin, 1040 Pounds

Water Color of the Island—Tahiti

They had no time on the other boat. Captain had a magnificent strike and a moment later a 400-pound swordfish was in the air, curved in a circle. He swung the bait round his head and slung it far, hook and all.

Meanwhile my fish was behaving well, slow and deep. All but John ran forward, yelling like mad. I could not see, so I shouted to John, "What's up?"

"Another big swordfish!" yelled John. "Cappy's got another. . . . Um! *There!*—Gee, what a jumper! . . . By jinks! He got away, too."

The natives with Peter and Bob trooped aft, their eyes shining.

"Cappy lost another! By gad! we want to look out."

I was attending to my own fish, that began to telegraph me things up the line.

"Ocean's full of marlin—big ones!" boomed Cappy, through his megaphone.

My own state was one of unconscious bliss. I did not think. I only felt. It certainly was lovely out there. No game like fishing! How blue the sky, wonderful the water, gorgeous the islands!

My marlin took a slow run, and came up about a hundred yards away to thresh on the surface and stick out his head. "Aw, small!" I ejaculated, regretfully, entirely forgetting that you can never tell the size of a swordfish from his head.

That changed the tenor of the situation. I had only another fish on, which I must get, of course, but I did not have any heart-bursting suspense. He went down and stayed down. Peter said: "I'm curious about this fish. Acts like a silver marlin. He might put it in high soon."

Which kindly hint I did not absorb. My fish began to move out astern, still deep down, and he took a couple of hundred yards of line. Here I should have turned the boat. But I did not. My state was too pleasant to permit of stern details of angling.

Presently he began to go pretty fast, yet still I vacillated. What did I care, with all that 500 yards of line? I was already counting on hanging that marlin up on the main street of Papeete—the first time for such an event in the history of that thoroughfare. But I did tell John to back the boat. He should have done it full speed astern; still, the blame was mine.

Then this infernal marlin leaped, to show me a long, thick, deep body, a huge tail. He was one of the largest of the regular striped marlin species. I was so surprised I could not think. Next he did what Peter had hinted—he put it in high and the line melted off my reel. Quick as a flash I reached to release the wheel of the drag. How tight it stuck! But I got it turned back half, which I thought surely was enough. Faster! And he sent aloft a great white splash, out of which he leaped high and far—and to freedom. Even with only a light drag that four hundred yards of line behind his speed and weight was too much—it broke. I knew it. I felt the release—a jar that jerked me forward, and my rod upward. For a moment I sat there staring. I could not realize the catastrophe. It was too sudden, too cruel, too maddening.

"He's gone," I said. Later Bob claimed I was very quiet and cool. No words could describe what I was inside. I got up and let Peter wind in the line. It had broken about the middle of the double. I took the end, tied it to the arm of the chair, and winding it round my gloved hands I pulled with all my might. I could not break it. So I could only speculate on the enormous strain that it had taken before breaking.

Everybody looked pretty sick. I asked Peter how big the marlin was. "Fine fish, sir. Bigger than the one we lost at Bora-Bora."

Jimmy said, "Three hundred kilos."

Six hundred pounds was coming close. But my guess was 700.

That happened about the middle of the morning, and we had fifty miles of water to troll, back to Flower Point. I did not see how I could fish it, or ever again. My state changed absolutely from utter happiness to sheer despair. Nothing but time could alleviate it.

We headed round the island. I sat up on deck for three hours before I could begin to feel myself again. We ran through more live bait, and off Guild's got among canoes again. One of the natives yelled to Cappy and pointed. There were marlin behind his canoe, one small, the other big. Of course the smaller got the bait, and the larger disappeared before we could cover the water. Then we hung around to watch Cappy fight and whip this fish—breaking our hoodoo.

CHAPTER NINE

TIME is probably more generous and healing to an angler than to any other individual. The wind, the sun, the open, the colors and smells, the loneliness of the sea or the solitude of the stream, work some kind of magic. In a few days my disappointment was only a memory—another incident of angling history.

On the 15th of May—which was the seventh day of clear, hot, sunny weather—I stayed in camp to do some neglected writing, and let Cappy run out alone off the east end, where we had not scouted for several weeks. He returned to report a rather choppy sea, but he had raised two marlin, one of which was a good-sized fish that came for his bait three times to refuse it, no doubt because it was stale. Tuna, a small species, were numerous, and there were some bonito showing.

"Same old story," averred the Captain. "If I'd had a fresh bait I'd have hooked that bird. A lunker, too. All of 500 pounds."

Just what had transpired in my mind I was not conscious of then. It all came to me afterward, and it was that this game was long, and some day one of us *might* capture a giant Tahitian marlin. We would go on trying.

That night the dry spell broke. The rain roared on the pandanuis roof, most welcome and dreamy of sounds. Morning disclosed dark, massed, broken clouds, red-edged and purple-centered, with curtains of rain falling over the mountains. This weather was something like March come back again for a day!

I took down a couple of new feather gigs—silver-headed with blue eyes—just for good luck. They worked. We caught five fine bonito in the lagoon, right off the point where my cottage stands.

Jimmy held up five fingers: "Five bonito. Good!" he ejaculated, which voiced all our sentiments.

Cappy had gone up the lagoon toward the second pass, and we tried to catch him, to give him a fresh bait. As usual, however, Cappy's natives were running the wheels off his launch, and we could not catch him. The second pass looked sort of white and rough to me. Cappy went out, however, through a smooth channel. Presently we saw a swell gather and rise, to close the channel and mount to a great, curling white-crested wave which broke all the way across. Charley, who had the wheel, grinned up at me: "No good!" We turned inshore and made for the third pass, some miles on, and got through that wide one without risk. Afterward Cappy told me Areireia knew exactly when to run through the second pass.

We headed out. A few black noddies skimmed the dark sea, and a few scattered bonito broke the surface. As usual—when we had them—we put out a big bonito on my big tackle and an ordinary one on the other. As my medium tackle holds one thousand yards of thirty-nine-thread line it will seem interesting to anglers to speak of it as medium. The big outfit held fifteen hundred yards of line—one thousand of thirty-nine thread and five hundred yards of forty-two for backing; and this story will prove I needed it.

Off the east end there was a brightness of white and blue, where the clouds broke, and in the west there were trade-wind clouds of gold and pearl, but for the most part a gray canopy overspread mountain and sea. All along the saw-toothed front of this range inshore the peaks were obscured and the canyons filled with down-drooping veils of rain.

What a relief from late days of sun and wind and wave! This was the kind of sea I loved to fish. The boat ran easily over a dark, low, lumpy swell. The air was cool, and as I did not have on any shirt, the fine mist felt pleasant to my skin. John was at the wheel. Bob sat up on top with Jimmy and Charley, learning to talk Tahitian. The teasers and heavy baits made a splashing, swishy sound that could be heard above the boil and gurgle of water from the propellers. We followed some low-skimming boobies for a while, and then headed for Captain M.'s boat, several miles farther out. A rain squall was obscuring the white tumbling reef and slowly moving toward us. Peter sat at my right, holding the line which had the larger bonito. He had both feet up on the gunwale. I noticed that the line on this reel was white and dry. I sat in the left chair, precisely as Peter, except that I had on two pairs of gloves with thumb-stalls in them. I have cut, burned, and skinned my hands too often on a hard strike to go without gloves. They are a nuisance to wear all day, when the rest of you, almost, is getting pleasantly caressed by sun and wind, but they are absolutely necessary to an angler who knows what he is doing.

Peter and I were discussing plans for our New Zealand trip next winter—boats, camp equipment, and what not. And although our gaze seldom strayed from the baits, the idea of raising a fish was the farthest from our minds. We were just fishing, putting in the few remaining hours of this Tahitian trip, and already given over to the hopes and anticipations of the New Zealand one. That is the comfortable way to make a trip endurable—to pass from the hard reality of the present to the ideal romance of the future.

Suddenly I heard a sounding, vicious thump of water. Peter's feet went up in the air.

"*Ge-zus!*" he bawled.

His reel screeched. Quick as thought I leaned over to press my gloved hand on the whizzing spool of line. Just in time to save the reel from overrunning!

Out where Peter's bait had been showed a whirling, closing hole in the boiling white-green water. I saw a wide purple mass shooting away so close under the surface as to make the water look shallow. Peter fell out of the chair at the same instant I leaped up to straddle his rod. I had the situation in hand. My mind worked swiftly. It was an incredibly wonderful strike. The other boys piled back to the cockpit to help Peter get my other bait and the teasers in.

Before this was even started the fish ran out two hundred yards of line, then turning to the right he tore off another hundred. All in a very few seconds! Then a white splash, high as a tree, shot up, out of which leaped the most magnificent of all the leaping fish I had ever seen.

"GIANT MARLIN!" screamed Peter. What had happened to me I did not know, but I was cold, keen, hard, tingling, motivated to think and do the right thing. This glorious fish made a leap of thirty feet at least, low and swift, which gave me time to gauge his enormous size and his species. Here at last on the end of my line was the great Tahitian swordfish! He looked monstrous. He was pale, shiny gray in color, with broad stripes of purple. When he hit the water he sent up a splash like the flying surf on the reef.

By the time he was down I had the drag on and was winding the reel. Out he blazed again, faster, higher, longer, whirling the bonito round his head.

"Hook didn't catch!" yelled Peter, wildly. "It's on this side. He'll throw it."

I had instinctively come up mightily on the rod, winding with all speed, and I had felt the tremendous solid pull. The hook had caught before that, however, and the big bag in the line, coupled with his momentum, had set it.

"No, Peter! He's fast," I replied. Still I kept working like a windmill in a cyclone to get up the slack. The monster had circled in these two leaps. Again he burst out, a plunging leap which took him under a wall of rippling white spray. Next instant such a terrific jerk as I had never sustained nearly unseated me. He was away on his run.

"Take the wheel, Peter," I ordered, and released the drag. "Water! Somebody pour water on this reel! . . . *Quick!*"

The white line melted, smoked, burned off the reel. I smelled the scorching. It burned through my gloves. John was swift to plunge a bucket overboard and douse reel, rod, and me with water. That, too, saved us.

"After him, Pete!" I called, piercingly. The engines roared and the launch danced around to leap in the direction of the tight line.

"Full speed!" I added.

"Aye, sir," yelled Peter, who had been a sailor before he became a whaler and a fisherman.

Then we had our race. It was thrilling in the extreme, and though brief it was far too long for me. Five hundred yards from us—over a third of a mile—he came up to pound and beat the water into a maelstrom.

"Slow up!" I sang out. We were bagging the line. Then I turned on the wheel-drag and began to pump and reel as never before in all my life. How precious that big spool—that big reel handle! They fairly ate up the line. We got back two hundred yards of the 500 out before he was off again. This time, quick as I was, it took all my strength to release the drag, for when a weight is pulling hard it releases with extreme difficulty. No more risk like that!

He beat us in another race, shorter, at the end of which, when he showed like a plunging elephant, he had out four hundred and fifty yards of line.

"Too much—Peter!" I panted. "We must—get him closer—Go to it!"

So we ran down upon him. I worked as before, desperately, holding on my nerve, and when I got three hundred yards back again on the reel, I was completely winded, and the hot sweat poured off my naked arms and breast.

"He's sounding. . . . Get my shirt. . . . Harness!"

Warily I let go with one hand and then with the other, as John and Jimmy helped me on with my shirt and then with the leather harness. With that hooked on to my reel and the great strain transferred to my shoulders, I felt that I might not be torn asunder.

"All set. Let's go," I said, grimly. But he had gone down, which gave me a chance to get back my breath. Not long, however, did he remain down. I felt and saw the line rising.

"Keep him on the starboard quarter, Peter. Run up on him now. . . . Bob, your chance for pictures!"

I was quick to grasp that the swordfish kept coming to our left, and repeatedly on that run I had Peter swerve in the same direction, in order to keep the line out on the quarter. Once we were almost in danger. But I saw it. I got back all but one hundred yards of line. Close enough! He kept edging in ahead of us, and once we had to turn halfway to keep the stern toward him. But he quickly shot ahead again. He was fast, angry, heavy. How his tail pounded the leader! The short powerful strokes vibrated all over me.

"Port—port, Peter!" I yelled, and even then, so quick was the swordfish, I missed seeing two leaps directly in front of the boat as he curved ahead of us. But the uproar from Bob and the others was enough for me. As the launch sheered around, however, I saw the third of that series of leaps—and if anything could have loosed my chained emotion on the instant that unbelievably swift and savage plunge would have done so. But I was clamped. No more dreaming! No more bliss! I was there to think and act. And I did not even thrill.

By the same tactics the swordfish sped off a hundred yards of line and by the same we recovered them and drew close to see him leap again, only two hundred feet off our starboard, a little ahead, and of all the magnificent fish I have ever seen he excelled. His power to leap was beyond credence. Captain M.'s big fish, that broke off two years before, did not move like this one. True, he was larger. Nevertheless, this swordfish was so huge that when he came out in dazzling swift flight, my crew went simply mad. This was the first time my natives had been flabbergasted. They were as excited, as carried away, as Bob and John. Peter, however, stuck at the wheel as if he was after a wounded whale which might any instant turn upon him. I did not need to warn Peter not to let that fish hit us. If he had he would have made splinters out of that launch. Many an anxious glance did I cast toward Cappy's boat, two or three miles distant. Why did he not come? The peril was too great for us to be alone at the mercy of that beautiful brute, if he charged us either by accident or by design. But Captain could not locate us, owing to the misty atmosphere, and missed seeing this grand fish in action.

How sensitive I was to the strain on the line! A slight slackening directed all my faculties to ascertain the cause. The light on the moment was bad, and I had to peer closely to see the line. He had not slowed up, but he was curving back and to the left again—the cunning strategist!

"*Port*, Peter—PORT!" I commanded.

We sheered, but not enough. With the wheel hard over, one engine full speed ahead, the other in reverse, we wheeled like a top. But not swift enough for that Tahitian swordfish.

The line went under the bow.

"Reverse!" I called, sharply.

We pounded on the waves, slowly caught hold, slowed, started back. Then I ordered the clutches thrown out. It was a terrible moment and took all my will not to yield to sudden blank panic.

When my line ceased to pay out I felt that it had been caught on the keel. And as I was only human, I surrendered for an instant to agony. But no! That line was new, strong. The swordfish was slowing. I could yet avert catastrophe.

"Quick, Pete! Feels as if the line is caught," I cried, unhooking my harness from the reel.

Peter complied with my order. "Yes, by cripes! It's caught. Overboard, Jimmy! Jump in! Loose the line!"

The big Tahitian in a flash was out of his shirt and bending to dive.

"No!—Hold on, Jimmy!" I yelled. Only a moment before I had seen sharks milling about. "Grab him, John!"

They held Jimmy back, and a second later I plunged my rod over the side into the water, so suddenly that the weight of it and reel nearly carried me overboard.

"Hold me—or it's all—day!" I panted, and I thought that if my swordfish had fouled on keel or propellers I did not care if I did fall in.

"Let go my line, Peter," I said, making ready to extend the rod to the limit of my arms.

"I can feel him moving, sir," shouted Peter, excitedly. "By jingo! He's coming! . . . It's free! It wasn't caught!"

That was such intense relief I could not recover my balance. They had to haul me back into the boat. I shook all over as one with the palsy, so violently that Peter had to help me get the rod in the rod-socket of the chair. An instant later came the strong electrifying pull on the line, the scream of the reel. Never such sweet music! He was away from the boat—on a tight line! The revulsion of feeling was so great that it propelled me instantaneously back into my former state of hard, cold, calculating and critical judgment, and iron determination.

"Close shave, sir," said Peter, cheerily. "It was like when a whale turns on me, after I've struck him. . . . We're all clear, sir, and after him again."

The gray pall of rain bore down on us. I was hot and wet with sweat, and asked for a raincoat to keep me from being chilled. Enveloped in this, I went on with my absorbing toil. Blisters began to smart on my hands, especially one on the inside of the third finger of my right hand, certainly a queer place to raise one. But it bothered me, hampered me. Bob put on his rubber coat and, protecting his camera more than himself, sat out on the bow, waiting.

My swordfish, with short, swift runs took us five miles farther out, and then welcome to see, brought us back, all this while without leaping, though he broke water on the surface a number of times. He never sounded after that first dive. The bane of an angler is a sounding fish, and here in Tahitian waters, where there is no bottom, it spells catastrophe. The marlin slowed up and took to milling, a sure sign of a rattled fish. Then he rose again, and it happened to be when the rain had ceased. He made one high, frantic jump about two hundred yards ahead of us, and then threshed on the surface, sending the bloody spray high. All on board were quick to see that sign of weakening, of tragedy—blood.

Peter turned to say, coolly, "He's our meat, sir."

I did not allow any such idea to catch my consciousness. Peter's words, like those of Bob and John, and the happy jargon of the Tahitians, had no effect upon me whatever.

It rained half an hour longer, during which we repeated several phases of the fight, except slower on the part of the marlin. In all he leaped fifteen times clear of the water. I did not attempt to keep track of his threshings.

After the rain passed I had them remove the rubber coat, which hampered me, and settled to a slower fight. About this time the natives again sighted sharks coming around the boat. I did not like this. Uncanny devils! They were the worst of these marvelous fishing waters. But Peter said: "They don't know what it's all about. They'll go away."

They did go away long enough to relieve me of dread, then they trooped back, lean, yellow-backed, white-finned wolves.

"We ought to have a rifle," I said. "Sharks won't stay to be shot at, whether hit or not."

It developed that my swordfish had leaped too often and run too swiftly to make an extremely long fight. I had expected a perceptible weakening and recognized it. So did Peter, who smiled gladly. Then I taxed myself to the utmost and spared nothing. In another hour, which seemed only a few minutes, I had him whipped and coming. I could lead him. The slow strokes of his tail took no more line. Then he quit wagging.

"Clear for action, Pete. Give John the wheel. . . . I see the end of the double line. . . . There!"

I heaved and wound. With the end of the double line over my reel I screwed the drag up tight. The finish was in sight. Suddenly I felt tugs and jerks at my fish.

"*Sharks!*" I yelled, hauling away for dear life.

Everybody leaned over the gunwale. I saw a wide shining mass, greenish silver, crossed by purple bars. It moved. It weaved. But I could drag it easily.

"*Mauu! Mauu!*" shrilled the natives.

"Heave!" shouted Peter, as he peered down.

In a few more hauls I brought the swivel of the leader out of the water.

"By God! They're on him!" roared Peter, hauling on the leader. "Get the lance, boat-hook, gaffs—anything. Fight them off! . . ."

Suddenly Peter let go the leader and jerking the big gaff from Jimmy he lunged out. There was a single enormous roar of water and a sheeted splash. I saw a blue tail so wide I thought I was crazy. It threw a six-foot yellow shark into the air!

"Rope him, Charley," yelled Peter. "Rest of you fight the tigers off."

I unhooked the harness and stood up to lean over the gunwale. A swordfish rolled on the surface, extending from forward of the cockpit to two yards or more beyond the end. His barred body was as large as that of an ox. And to it sharks were clinging, tearing, out on the small part near the tail. Charley looped the great tail and that was a signal for the men to get into action.

One big shark had a hold just below the anal fin. How cruel, brutish, ferocious! Peter made a powerful stab at him. The big lance-head went clear through his neck. He gulped and sank. Peter stabbed another underneath, and still another. Jimmy was tearing at sharks with the long-handled gaff, and when he hooked one he was nearly hauled overboard. Charley threshed with his rope; John did valiant work with the boathook, and Bob frightened me by his daring fury as he leaned far over to hack with the cleaver.

We keep these huge cleavers on board to use in case we are

attacked by an octopus, which is not a far-fetched fear at all. It might happen. Bob is lean and long and powerful. Also he was angry. Whack! He slashed a shark that let go and appeared to slip up into the air.

"On the nose, Bob. Split his nose! That's the weak spot on a shark," yelled Peter.

Next shot Bob cut deep into the round stub nose of this big black shark—the only one of that color I saw—and it had the effect of dynamite. More sharks appeared under Bob, and I was scared so stiff I could not move.

"Take that! . . . And that!" sang out Bob, in a kind of fierce ecstasy. "You will try to eat our swordfish!—Dirty, stinking pups! . . . Aha! On your beak, huh! Zambesi! . . . Wow, Pete, that sure is the place!"

"Look out, Bob! For God's sake—look out!" I begged, frantically, after I saw a shark almost reach Bob's arm.

Peter swore at him. But there was no keeping Bob off those cannibals. Blood and water flew all over us. The smell of sharks in any case was not pleasant, and with them spouting blood, and my giant swordfish rolling in blood, the stench that arose was sickening. They appeared to come from all directions, especially from under the boat. Finally I had to get into the thick of it, and at that armed only with a gaff handle minus the gaff. I did hit one a stunning welt over the nose, making him let go. If we had all had lances like the one Peter was using so effectively we would have made short work of them. One jab from Peter either killed or disabled a shark. The crippled ones swam about belly up or lopsided, and stuck up their heads as if to get air. Of all the bloody messes I ever saw that was the worst.

"Makes me remember—the war!" panted Peter, grimly.

And it was Peter who whipped the flock of ravenous sharks off. *Chuck!* went the heavy lance, and that was the end of another. My heart apparently had ceased to function. To capture that glorious fish only to see it devoured before my eyes!

"Run ahead, Johnny, out of this bloody slaughter-hole, so we can see," called Peter.

John ran forward a few rods into clear water. A few sharks

WATER COLOR OF THE SHIP

followed, one of them to his death. The others grew wary, and swam around and around.

"We got 'em licked! Say, I had the wind up me," said Peter. "Who ever saw the like of that? The bloody devils!"

Bob took the lance from Peter, and stuck the most venturesome of the remaining sharks. It appeared then that we had the situation in hand again. My swordfish was there still, his beautiful body bitten here and there, his tail almost severed, but not irreparably lacerated. All around the boat wounded sharks were lolling with fins out, sticking ugly heads up, to gulp and dive.

There came a let-down then and we exchanged the natural elation we felt. The next thing was to see what was to be done with the monster, now we had him. I vowed we could do nothing but tow him to camp. But Peter made the attempt to lift him on the boat. All six of us, hauling on the ropes, could not get his back half out of the water. So we tied him fast and started campward.

Halfway in we espied Cappy's boat. He headed for us, no doubt attracted by all the flags the boys had strung up. There was one, a red and blue flag that I had never flown. Jimmy tied this on his bamboo pole and tied that high on the mast. Cappy bore quickly down on us and ran alongside, he and all of his crew vastly excited.

"What is it? Lamming big broadbill?" he yelled.

My fish did resemble a broadbill in his long black beak, his widespread flukes, his purple color, shading so dark now that the broad bars showed indistinctly. Besides, he lay belly up.

"No, Cappy. He's a giant Tahitian striped marlin, one of the kind we've tried so hard to catch," I replied, happily.

"By gad! So he is. What a monster! . . . I'm glad, old man. My word, I'm glad! I didn't tell you, but I was discouraged. Now we're sitting on top of the world again."

"Rather," replied Peter, for me. "We've got him, Captain, and he's some fish. But the damn sharks nearly beat us."

"So I see. They are bad. I saw a number. . . . Well, I had a four hundred pound swordie throw my hook at me, and I've raised two more, besides a sailfish. Fish out here again. . . . Have you got any fresh bonito?"

We threw our bait into his boat and headed for camp again.

Cappy waved, a fine happy smile on his tanned face, and called: "He's a wolloper, old man. I'm sure glad."

"I owe it to you, Cap," I called after him.

We ran for the nearest pass, necessarily fairly slow, with all that weight on our stern. The boat listed half a foot and tried to run in a circle. It was about one o'clock and the sky began to clear. Bob raved about what pictures he would take.

"Oh, boy, what a fish! If only Romer had been with us! I saw him hit the bait and I nearly fell off the deck. I couldn't yell. . . . Wasn't it a wonderful fight? Everything just right. I was scared when he tried to go under the boat."

"So was I, Bob," I replied, remembering that crucial moment.

"I wasn't," said Peter. "The other day when we had the boat out at Papeete I shaved all the rough places off her keel. So I felt safe. What puts the wind up me is the way these Tahitian swordfish can jump. Fast? My word! This fellow beat any small marlin I ever saw in my life."

I agreed with Peter and we discussed this startling and amazing power of the giant marlin. I put forward the conviction that the sole reason for their incredible speed and ferocity was that the struggle to survive was magnified in these crystal-clear waters around Tahiti. We talked over every phase of the fight, and that which pleased me most was the old whaler's tribute:

"You were there, sir. That cool and quick! On the strike that dry line scared me stiff. But afterward I had no doubt of the result."

We were all wringing wet, and some of us as bloody as wet. I removed my soaked clothes and gave myself a brisk rub. I could not stand erect and my hands hurt—pangs I endured gratefully.

We arrived at the dock about three o'clock, to find all our camp folk and a hundred natives assembled to greet us. Up and down had sped the news of the flags waving.

I went ashore and waited impatiently to see the marlin hauled out on the sand. It took a dozen men, all wading, to drag him in. And when they at last got him under the tripod, I approached, knowing I was to have a shock and prepared for it.

But at that he surprised me in several ways. His color had grown darker and the bars showed only palely. Still they were there and helped to identify him as one of the striped species. He was bigger than I had ever hoped for. And his body was long and round. This roundness appeared to be an extraordinary feature for a marlin spearfish. His bill was three feet long, not slender and rapier-like, as in the ordinary marlin, or short and bludgeon-like, as in the black marlin. It was about the same size all the way from tip to where it swelled into his snout, and slightly flattened on top—a superb and remarkable weapon. The fact that the great striped spearfish Captain Mitchell lost in 1928 had a long, curved bill, like a rhinoceros, did not deter me from pronouncing this of the same species. Right there I named this species, Giant Tahitian Striped Marlin. Singularly, he had a small head, only a foot or more from where his beak broadened to his eye, which, however, was as large as that of a broadbill swordfish. There were two gill openings on each side, a feature I never observed before in any swordfish, the one toward the mouth being considerably smaller than the regular gill opening. From there his head sheered up to his hump-back, out of which stood an enormous dorsal fin. He had a straight under maxillary. The pectoral fins were large, wide, like wings, and dark in color. The fin-like appendages under and back of his lower jaw were only about six inches long and quite slender. In other spearfish these are long, and in sailfish sometimes exceed two feet and more. His body, for eight feet was as symmetrical and round as that of a good big stallion. According to my deduction it was a male fish. He carried this roundness back to his anal fin, and there further accuracy was impossible because the sharks had eaten away most of the flesh from these fins to his tail. On one side, too, they had torn out enough meat to fill a bushel basket. His tail was the most splendid of all the fish tails I have ever observed. It was a perfect bent bow, slender, curved, dark purple in color, finely ribbed, and expressive of the tremendous speed and strength the fish had exhibited.

This tail had a spread of five feet two inches. His length was fourteen feet two inches. His girth was six feet nine inches. And his weight as he was 1,040 pounds.

Every drop of blood had been drained from his body, and this with at least 200 pounds of flesh the sharks took would have fetched his true and natural weight to 1,250 pounds. But I thought it best to have the record stand at the actual weight, without allowance for what he had lost. Nevertheless, despite my satisfaction and elation, as I looked up at his appalling shape, I could not help but remember the giant marlin Captain had lost in 1928, which we estimated at twenty-two or twenty-three feet, or the twenty-foot one I had raised at Tautira, or the twenty-eight-foot one the natives had seen repeatedly alongside their canoes. And I thought of the prodigious leaps and astounding fleetness of this one I had caught. "My heaven!" I breathed. "What would a bigger one do?"

CHAPTER TEN

CAPTAIN M. returned before sunset to share my joy and to express again his complete gladness in my good fortune. He meant it, too, and I had to reply, ruefully: "I believe you, Cap, and it makes me feel small. For when, the day off the Cavellis in New Zealand, I ran down on you to see your 976-pound black marlin I was so sick with envy and despair that I nearly jumped in to drown myself."

"Well, old man, I'm happy because this means so much to you, because you've tried so hard and stuck it out when most fishermen would have quit—because you deserve it. Now, by Jove! we can go ahead with your plans."

He related a singular observation of that day. A 400-pound marlin had rammed his bonito bait clear through and then had refused it.

Captain's native boatmen, all pure-blood Tahitians, were profoundly excited over my great marlin. They were delighted as well, though it was plain, and quite natural, that they would rather have had their angler and their boat catch the swordfish.

The photographing of the fish was in the nature of a celebration, in which more than a hundred natives participated. My native boatmen, Eetuarii (Jimmy) and Punua (Charley) were in a seventh heaven of exaltation. Jimmy lorded it over all of them. Indeed, I felt again that he had the blood of chiefs in him. He stalked about in a stately manner, his head high, his eyes flashing, and his mouth closed. I suspect Jimmy's vanity had a great deal to do with this last. For with his front teeth missing he was not calculated to induce the native lasses to leave home for him. So instead of laughing uproariously and shouting in his deep bass, he kept silent. And not the least of my pleasure in that event was to watch him.

Later our two native boat crews got into an argument over the swordfish. We could understand very little of the rapid interchange of jargon, but the violent gesticulations were clear enough. Charley here undertook to propound facts about the great marlin, and when these were scornfully repudiated by Peto, Arearea and Amaru, he valiantly stood his ground. When Charley argued that the marlin leaped ten meters and more Arearea took violent exception to this. They had it hot and heavy, until Jimmy came out to roar at them, and step out a distance of at least forty feet, as the length of jumps. Also Jimmy stood very tall and lifted his long arm higher to indicate the height of the leaps. He convinced them, too, but I had a suspicion that it was more on account of Jimmy's commanding personality than real belief.

Next they got into a fight over the respective merits of the *Tahiti* (my boat) and its angler and crew, and of the *Moorea* (Cappy's boat) and its angler and crew. I never saw a Navajo council or argument that could compare with this one. These Polynesians were natural-born orators. Cappy and I were unable to discern which of us came out on top, but we had a hearty laugh over it.

Owing to the mutilated condition of the swordfish, it was unfortunately impossible to preserve the skin. But I kept the spear, the tail, and the perforated gill-cover, which, when exhibited in Papeete, caused a sensation. The French officials never had understood our fishing. Indeed, the present governor had engaged the chief of Vairao to spy upon us, to see what we were doing, and ascertain if possible whether or not the United States wanted to take Tahiti for a naval base. After this, however, we were evidently better understood. The idea of white men visiting Tahiti for something beside French liquors, the native women, or to paint the tropical scenery, had been exceedingly hard to assimilate. For my part I did not blame them for making such a mistake. Our friends among both French and Americans, however, were delighted with my good fortune. We felt what a pity that Ham-Fish and Carrie-

Finn were not there to see my catch. I received a wireless message from them: "What a cute fish! Tickled pink! Ham and Carrie."

Also one from my wife. "What ho, Ulysses! You've hooked a better fish at home, which *might* get away. Penelope."

Father Emmanual Rougier, head of the museum at Papeete, persuaded me to let him have a motion-picture film to show at the Paris Exhibition in 1931.

The most delighted of the French colony, however, was Madam Francine Brault, who had insisted upon numerous occasions that I could not have good luck fishing unless I carried three fifty-centime coins in my pocket. These she finally sent me, and sure enough, the day they came I caught my wonderful swordfish. Needless to say, in the future whenever I go in quest of a great game fish I shall have those three talismans of good fortune with me.

We still had Monday, Tuesday, and Wednesday to fish; but I felt that this 1930 adventure at Tahiti was closed. Still I followed Cappy all over the east-end water. The weather remained perfect, the birds and bonito were, if anything, more numerous. On Monday my boat had a double-header—two swordfish rushing the baits at once—out of which I hooked a husky small marlin that cut didos all over the sea. When landed, he turned out to be one of the bronze striped spearfish, short, thick, stocky, all muscle. I guessed his weight at 130—and he actually weighed 175 pounds. These Tahitian swordfish are extremely heavy and we always underestimate them.

On the way in that evening Cappy passed us, spreading wide his hands to signify a blank day. He was indeed having about as hard and unprofitable a season as mine of 1929, when I fished eighty-three days without a fish—assuredly the most remarkable record I ever attained.

On this day I had trolled for eight hours steady—and dragging a ten-pound bait by your hand for that period is harder than digging for coal—and I was standing up behind Peter and Bob, who held down the chairs and on to the lines. They were laughing and talking, as usual. The natives were up front, smoking. John was at the wheel, sending us along at a good fast clip. The sea was darkly purple behind us; ahead it was gold and opal and pearl, to match the beginning of a glorious Tahitian sunset. The mountains appeared to be an exquisite emerald velvet, except the peaks, which were draped in effulgent clouds.

I was trying to absorb all this beauty and sweetness and wildness when a cracking thump of violently agitated waters galvanized me out of such a revel in dreaming sensation. Even before Bob yelled like a maniac I saw a circling hole close up behind his bait, then a swift and angry eddying of white seething water, and then a huge, wide, pale purple shadow, blazing, fleeing, vanishing. It left an impression of prodigious power.

"That was a thundering whale!" ejaculated Bob.

"It was, so help me Jehoshophat!" replied Peter. "Look sharp. He may come back."

"No!" I said, as soon as I could speak. "He missed. Like a lion, he won't come again. . . . I saw him go."

"What was it?"

"Another of those striped giants," I rejoined, soberly. Indeed, the incident had a queer effect on all of us. So close! We trolled around for half an hour, then headed campward again, just as the sun set. I was not disappointed or sorry. I was just sort of staggered. It had almost happened again. Perhaps if we had not been trolling so fast —— But conjectures were vain.

All during the hours of the two following days, wonderful to be on the sea, though yielding no sign of our game, I felt growing on me the profound nature of these Tahitian fishing waters. It would be difficult to make clear my sense of their repulsion, mystery, peril, fascination, and incredible possibilities. After three long and arduous trials I had just begun to know how to fish them. A prodigious urge to come back, to seek and find and conquer, gripped me more powerfully than ever. Yet the mere thought was torturing. To bear again the toil and heat, the long wait and the sameness, when other new and unknown waters were calling—this seemed an insupportable idea. Palmerston Island, the Paumotus, New Caledonia, and on to New Guinea, and the Cocos Islands of the Indian Ocean, on and on to the St. Brandos group, Isles of Death, lost in the midst of that great waste of waters, on to Madagascar —— What madness possessed me to thrill and yearn over these far-flung spots of the globe, unknown to fishermen; when in more accessible Tahitian and Marquesan waters roamed fish monsters no scientist or naturalist or angler had yet dreamed of? But that is the way I am made! The ideal was to gain them all, a natural, excusable, and almost futile ambition. There was a great prize-fighter once whose heart broke because, of all men in the world, only one lived whom he could not whip. Fishing is like that, except that you can substitute for one man a number of big fish.

So during these last few days I feared the dream of these longings had become reality and that I would undertake the impossible. Once having committed myself and given myself over to anticipation, there flocked to mind a thousand thrilling supports to the enterprise, many of which, happily, were not selfish. But to record them here, when this story is what Jimmy called "*Fee-nish*," would only detract from an absorbing introduction to the next. Wherefore I close, thrilled by Cappy's un-English ejaculation of sheer bliss, and Bob's boyish *whoopee!* seeing in mind R. C.'s expressive face and upflung hands, wondering what Romer's reaction would be, and lastly how my younger son, Loren, would take the news that he was to go next time.

THE END